PRAGMATIC PSYCHOTHERAPY

PRAGMATIC
PSYCHOTHERAPY

RICHARD DRISCOLL, Ph.D.

Bearden Professional Associates
Knoxville, Tennessee
and
Linguistic Research Institute
Boulder, Colorado

 VAN NOSTRAND REINHOLD COMPANY
NEW YORK   CINCINNATI   TORONTO   LONDON   MELBOURNE

92850

Manufactured in the United States of America

Published by Van Nostrand Reinhold Company Inc.
135 West 50th Street,
New York, N.Y. 10020

Van Nostrand Reinhold Company Limited
Molly Millars Lane
Wokingham, Berkshire RG11 2PY, England

Van Nostrand Reinhold
480 Latrobe Street
Melbourne, Victoria 3000, Australia

Macmillan of Canada
Division of Gage Publishing Limited
164 Commander Boulevard
Agincourt, Ontario M1S 3C7, Canada

15 14 13 12 11 10 9 8 7 6 5 4 3 2 1

Library of Congress Cataloging in Publication Data

Driscoll, Richard.
  Pragmatic psychotherapy.

  Bibliography: p.
  Includes index.
  1. Psychotherapy. I. Title. [DNLM: 1. Psycho-
therapy. WM 420 D781p]
RC480.D74 1983   616.89′14   83-10422
ISBN 0-442-21983-0

Preface

The increasing popularity of eclecticism underscores the need for an adequate framework for organizing and integrating various approaches to psychotherapy. This book suggests, outlines, and illustrates a comprehensive framework, and shows that it can be used to advantage in an eclectic approach to psychotherapy.

The approach is presented in three sections. An introductory chapter covers initial considerations. Section I outlines the common language concepts that we use to structure observation and description, and shows how these concepts can be employed to integrate the concepts and terminologies from various theoretical systems. Section II outlines procedural guidelines for effective interventions and draws parallels to techniques advocated by other therapeutic orientations. In Section III, these concepts and guidelines are brought together in applications to the key issues in self-critical tendencies. You might read these sections in order, as the King of Hearts instructed the White Rabbit: "Begin at the beginning, and go on till you come to the end; then stop." But each section is written to stand on its own, so that you are quite free to begin where your interests take you, without penalty. Those interested primarily in clinical applications might begin with the second section or with the third, then take the remaining sections in backward order, and finish with the introduction.

This book is admittedly ambitious. Its objectives are to present a system of concepts and guidelines for psychotherapy; to show that the system can be used to integrate various familiar therapeutic approaches; and, further, to portray sufficiently how the system is used so as to provide a training manual for those who wish to consider practicing as common language pragmatists. The overall objective is to articulate a general system for the practice of eclectic psychotherapy.

The focus throughout the book is on considerations for organizing and improving psychotherapy practice. Concepts and guidelines are liberally illustrated to give a sense of their use in actual practice. The illustrations used are composite illustrations: they involve issues seen frequently with many clients, and tactical interventions which have been used repeatedly to good effect and which convey the sense of the actual clinical sessions. The intention is to present enough of this approach to enable trainees to use some of its main elements, and to enable experienced clinicians to organize their own eclectic practice more comfortably.

Many of the concepts and guidelines presented here should be familiar already. The concepts are those of everyday, ordinary language made explicit, and the guidelines pull together the good sense that runs through numerous existing approaches to psychotherapy. Common language pragmatism is a specific way of selecting and organizing familiar elements, and so in that sense is itself a particular approach to eclectic psychotherapy. The eclectic system outlined here has two major features: (1) use of a system of common language concepts to structure observation and description of behavioral phenomena; and (2) emphasis on the pragmatic or "in order to" aspect of human behavior, both in the analysis of clinical issues and in the organization of therapeutic interventions.

The current approach spans disciplines, and should speak to counselors and psychotherapists from the range of disciplines including (alphabetically) clinical and counseling psychologists, clinical social workers, marriage and family therapists, pastoral counselors, psychiatrists, and related mental health professionals. This approach is for those who deal on a personal level with human psychological problems.

The emphasis here is on a specific system and on the ways in which it can be used as an integrative framework for eclectic practice: there is no attempt to give an extensive presentation or review of the main current approaches to psychotherapy. Aspects of other approaches are mentioned in order to show how they are integrated into the present framework. Such comments are sufficient to show the connections for those already familiar with the particular approaches, but brief enough so that those who are unfamiliar can readily skip through them without interrupting the flow of the reading. Those aspects of other approaches which are mentioned are not picayune points but central features which should be understood by individuals familiar with these approaches. Because they are well known (and in the interests of making reading easier), these aspects of other approaches are not referenced unless they are relatively new. For those interested in primary references I suggest the following: for psychotherapy systems, Corsini's (1979) *Current Psychotherapies;* for theoretical foundations, Hall & Lindzey's (1970) *Theories of Personality;* and for research, Garfield and Bergin's (1978) *Handbook of Psychotherapy and Behavior Change.*

One last note on style: the pronoun "he" is commonly understood in everyday language as a masculine pronoun *or* as an inclusively generic pronoun indicating an individual of either sex, with its meaning usually clear from the context, while "she" is always feminine. The peculiarities of these semantic conventions open the way to ambiguities in some contexts and to questions of sexist bias in others. Generic pronouns do not belong in ambiguous contexts. But when the reference is clear, generic "he" and "his" pronouns are used here for convenience in preference to the alternative "he or she" and "his or her" constructions which can be somewhat awkward in whatever variations. I trust in the intelligence and goodwill of my readers to identify these generic pronouns as such and to understand that no sexist implications are intended.

Acknowledgments. I express my appreciation to those who have contributed to the manuscript, especially to Peter Ossorio, for his many years as a teacher, clinical supervisor and consultant, and friend; to Ray Bergner, Gail Boatman, Bill Calhoun, Keith Davis, Nancy Davis, Don Ferguson, James Holmes, Gary Klukken, Paula McMorran, and Mary Shideler for their helpful comments; and finally, to those who have invited me to share intimately in the problems and joys of their lives and who have worked together with me in constructing the therapeutic solutions that comprise the thrust of this book.

Three sections have been revised and adapted from earlier versions of this material. "If It Works, Don't Fix It" is revised from the *Psychotherapy Bulletin,* 1980, *14*(3), 52–55. "Outline of Guidelines for Pragmatic Psychotherapy" appeared in K.E. Davis (Ed.), *Advances in Descriptive Psychology* (Vol. 1), Greenwich, Conn.: JAI Press, 1981, pp. 273–276. The material on self-criticism also appeared in the same issue of *Advances,* pp. 321–355; and in *Psychology Today,* 1982, *16*(7) 45–49. The material from JAI Press is used by permission.

R.D.

Contents

PRAGMATIC PSYCHOTHERAPY

1
Considerations for a Comprehensive Eclecticism

This introductory chapter notes the strengths and weaknesses of current eclecticism, and introduces common language pragmatism as a comprehensive framework for eclectic practice.

ECLECTICISM

An eclectic is one who attempts to understand and to draw upon a variety of approaches. Uncommitted to any single primary theoretical orientation, eclectics prefer instead to sort and choose from among many orientations, and to use their own intuition and judgment in figuring out what is worthwhile, and what should be applied where, when, and with which sorts of clients.

Eclectic psychotherapy has itself become a major approach to counseling and psychotherapy, and recent surveys have found the numbers who identify themselves as eclectics to be substantially higher than the number of adherents to any single theory orientation. A survey by Smith (1982) found that 41% of clinical and counseling psychologists identified themselves as eclectics, compared to 11% who considered themselves psychoanalytic; 10%, cognitive behavioral; 9%, person-centered; and 7%, behavioral; the remaining 22% were scattered among the other categories. A survey by Garfield and Kurtz (1976) showed that 55% of clinical psychologists saw themselves as eclectic, and an earlier survey by Kelly (1961) placed the estimate at that time at 40%.

Even among those who do identify with a specific theoretical orientation, there is a tendency nonetheless to use aspects of alternative orientations. One might find analytically oriented therapists who suggest brief isolation for children's temper tantrums, and behavior therapists who are sensitive to a client's conflicting attitudes and feelings (cf. Wachtel, 1977). Many authors popularly identified with particular theoretical schools are freeing themselves from the associated ideologies and reaching out for commonalities with other forms of psychotherapy (cf. Goldfried, 1980). It would be unusual indeed to find any experienced practitioner in any orientation who has learned nothing at all from competing orientations, and in that sense some element of eclecticism is involved in all present approaches to psychotherapy. Eclecticism in some form might be expected to continue as a major influence in the foreseeable future.

Available and in current use are a variety of insights and techniques, many of which are associated in most of our minds with one or another of the different schools of psychotherapy. Some of these apply and are effective in some situations; others apply and are effective in other sorts of situations. *The appropriateness of any particular insight or intervention is due not to the school of psychotherapy with which it is associated, but to its fittingness to the particular problems of the case at hand.* An ability to use insights and techniques from a variety of schools increases flexibility, and enables us to better tailor observations and interventions to the problems of the particular clients. A working knowledge of the contributions from various psychotherapy orientations may therefore yield real advantages, especially with complex and difficult cases. The formidable advantage of eclecticism is that it frees us to choose appropriate insights and techniques from various schools, and so expands the breadth and flexibility of our practice.

Eclectic practice is limited in one important way, however, for it lacks an explicit framework within which to understand, organize, and utilize its various elements. The eclectic relies instead on intuitive understandings and judgment for figuring out when and where to apply specific aspects of one or another of the various orientations. Practice in the absence of an explicit integrating viewpoint can too easily become unorganized and fragmented. Eclecticism in its current form is perhaps not so much a single, coherent orientation as a loose collection of insights and techniques: it is each practitioner's understanding of what is valuable and of which are the best ways to proceed.

Eclecticism is an approach with considerable strengths, in that one may draw from the best of a number of approaches, and also with apparent and disconcerting weaknesses, in that one finds oneself without any single integrating viewpoint to organize the practice. Practicing as an eclectic is something like riding a tiger, for you have available more power than you know how to properly manage, and at the same time you have good reason not to let go. We stand to benefit considerably from an articulated system to organize and manage the various insights and techniques.

It is not so surprising that eclecticism emerged prior to any articulated integrative framework, for eclecticism as a major orientation was never anticipated by the prevailing scientific traditions. Eclecticism emerged not out of any articulated philosophical or theoretical system, but rather out of practical necessity as practicing therapists again and again faced the challenges of finding workable solutions to pressing clinical problems.

The shift to eclecticism has occurred gradually through many small and sometimes unnoticed changes, so that the extensiveness of the shift from single theories to an eclectic viewpoint might easily be underestimated. Eclecticism involves alterations of many tenets of the familiar theoretical traditions and is in essence an alternative to those traditions. One of the key tenets of the theoretical traditions is that a single general theory would provide a comprehensive framework for understanding and dealing with human behavior (cf. Koch, 1963). The popularity of eclecticism indicates that many no longer expect a complete outlook from any single theoretical system. Eclectics look elsewhere, to something else, to integrate the various theories and also to integrate their therapeutic practice. Something other than an articulated theory is used to integrate things, and it is the nature of this oftentimes elusive "something else" which is the major concern of this book.

COMMON LANGUAGE PRAGMATISM

Our approach here is to make use of what eclectics are already doing, and to organize and build upon that to form an explicit integrative eclectic system. McWilliams (1981) notes that:

> A comprehensive eclecticism . . . [requires] a superordinate framework within which specific elements (theories, techniques, etc.) can be subsumed and their relation to other positions determined. This

framework must . . . [be complementary] with the eclectic position, and the new system's utility ultimately rests on the qualities of these superordinate components of the network. (p. 301)

Experienced therapists function in an intuitive and commonsense manner, and are often unable to state any theoretical formulations as a basis of what they are doing. Yet why should they be expected to offer theories as justifications? Psychotherapy interventions emerge from everyday understandings and social competencies which have been augmented and improved upon by training and practical experience. Those theoretical formulations which are used are thus blended into existing understandings and competencies: but they do not overturn or replace such competencies, nor do they serve as a beginning or foundation for such competencies. We seek here to understand and clarify these everyday understandings and social competencies, and to build upon them.

The comprehensive system presented here is constructed from four complementary and essentially compatible traditions: ordinary language conventions—specifically, the insights and analytic methods of the ordinary language philosophers; "Descriptive Psychology" as formulated by Peter Ossorio and associates; "common-sense" psychology as outlined by Fritz Heider; and "pragmatic" considerations as outlined by the early American pragmatists.

The methods of ordinary language analysis have successfully resolved or at least clarified a great many seemingly intractable problems in philosophy, and we apply here the power of these methods to clarify the often confusing issues between competing theoretical systems. A book by Pitkin (1972) provides an excellent and easily readable introduction to Wittgenstein and the language analytic methods. Ossorio's Descriptive Psychology is systematic and comprehensive, and has clarified many of the common language concepts used here. Its basics can be found in Ossorio (1978) and Davis (1981); the clinical applications used here are presented in a seminar transcript (Ossorio, 1976). Heider's common-sense psychology is read in social psychology but is not well known in the clinical and counseling areas; the main reference is Heider (1958). Pragmatism, as presented by notables such as William James, John Dewey, and Charles Pierce, was popular at the turn of the century but was passed over and ignored in psychology's subsequent turn toward broad general theories. We attempt here to revive and profit from some of the good sense of the pragmatic philosophy.

Our approach to understanding things is a common language or descriptive approach: *common language,* in that we utilize ordinary language concepts to provide a common basis for communication; *descriptive,* in that we emphasize adequate observation and description of the particulars at hand, rather than broad generalizations. We use the system of concepts to observe and describe, to critique the adequacy of our descriptions, and thus to attempt to understand the range of concerns in our fields.

The obvious objective of psychotherapy is not merely to understand, but to benefit troubled persons. The emphasis is thus on *influence,* and on the concepts, understanding, procedures, and competencies used to generate therapeutic changes. The term *pragmatic psychotherapy* is chosen for our approach because it refers to the use of language in social influence and because it includes as a bonus a nice array of additional appropriate meanings. Pragmatic, according to Webster's, also means active; it means emphasizing practical considerations rather than ideology [or theory]; it means seeing the significance of an idea in its practical consequences; it means dealing with things in a manner which shows their interconnections; and it means prescribing the means to the attainment of happiness. Each of these is a feature of our pragmatic approach.

The pragmatic eclecticism presented here has two salient features: (1) *the use of a system of common language concepts to structure observation and understanding of behavioral phenomena;* and (2) *an emphasis on the pragmatic or "in order to" aspect of human actions, both in clinical analysis and in the organization of therapeutic interventions.* Many features of this approach are not new. What is new about the approach is the way in which already familiar elements are placed together and shown to be adequate and effective for the tasks at hand. The emphasis is on clarifying the already existing good sense in psychotherapy, and on applying it in appropriate and sometimes innovative ways to the problems of psychotherapy.

The approach encourages the inclusion of everyday observations and experiences, and so nourishes and expands upon our already existing understanding and social competencies. It also serves to integrate various theoretical propositions, which may be categorized by and in some instances straightforwardly translated into our common language, and various therapeutic techniques, which are organized by our guidelines. The range of therapeutic insights and interventions is thus understood and organized here in the same system, regardless of which theoretical schools claim these therapeutic elements as their own.

Schools of psychotherapy are identified by characteristic observations—insights, understandings, and theories—and by characteristic interventions—techniques and procedures to generate changes. Eclectic therapists use the insights and information and also the techniques and procedures from the various competing schools. A comprehensive framework must be able to manage both the range of insights and the range of techniques from the existing schools of psychotherapy.

Language is intricately involved both in understanding things and in social influence. It is involved in understanding in that it is on the basis of familiar concepts and terms that we see, identify, and communicate about what is going on. It is involved in influence and change processes, for it is mainly through the use of words that we communicate with and affect others in our face-to-face social interactions. Language analysis traditionally distinguishes between syntactics, semantics, and pragmatics (cf. Morris, 1955): *syntactics* refers to the grammar, *semantics* to the meaning of words, and *pragmatics* to the use of words to do things. Semantics and pragmatics are emphasized here: semantics in that we clarify the meaning of key concepts and words used to understand and communicate about things, and pragmatics in that the primary focus is on language as a means of human influence. By beginning in language analysis, we gain a novel access to the wide array of psychotherapy insights and techniques.

CONCEPTS, OBSERVATION, AND UNDERSTANDING

One who attempts to understand and integrate the various schools is struck first by the vast and awesome array of specialized concepts and terminologies. Each theoretical system has generated its own special concepts and terms, and the related therapy approaches are easily identified by their use of such terms. The frequent use of the term "reinforcers," for instance, identifies one as behaviorally oriented, just as the use of the term "secondary gains" identifies one as psychoanalytically oriented, or the use of the term "strokes" identifies one as an adherent of transactional analysis.

One encounters formidable problems in attempting to integrate the concepts and terminologies from the various theories. Such concepts may be complementary in some ways and incompatible in other ways. Try to consider the concepts of primary and secondary reinforcers, overt and covert reinforcers, primary and secondary gains, alpha and beta needs, tension reduction, maintenance of internal homeostasis, maintenance of family homeostasis, payoffs, strokes, actualization, self-actualization, and the completion of gestalts. Each of these is an important element in one or more of the familiar theories. Each is considered to be a fundamental element in human motivation, but beyond that their relationships to each other become extremely complicated and often ambiguous and confusing.

Conceptual and linguistic confusion contributes to theoretical confusion. How does one begin to make sense of and splice together formulations from the various theoretical systems? Formulations from different theories may be contradictory propositions; they may be essentially similar propositions which merely *appear* incompatible because they are phrased in incompatible terminologies; they may be complementary propositions, covering related aspects of an area; and of course they may be unrelated, focusing on separate issues and not really comparable at all.

Specialized concepts and terminologies impede communication across theoretical encampments, for they cause confusion and frustration as those in opposing theoretical orientations fail to understand and accept the meaning of one another's basic concepts. The problem is so pervasive that it reminds one of the tower of Babel in the Old Testament: the tribes gathered together to construct a great tower to the heavens, but because of the sin of arrogance they were condemned to speak different languages; communication was impeded, and the tower could not be constructed. A common basis of communication is required in any cooperative enterprise, and the absence of a shared language system has surely impeded our ability to integrate the various propositions in the behavioral sciences.

On the basis of what views were so many special concepts formulated? Social sciences theorists (e.g., Skinner, 1938) have tended to ignore or minimize the value of ordinary language, seeing it as ambiguous, imprecise, mundane, and unscientific: theoretical concepts and terminologies were introduced to overcome the apparent limitations of ordinary language. The process was based in part on a paradigm of science suggested by the natural sciences and in part on the tendency of any field to generate its own "in-group" language conventions. Investigators in the physical or natural sciences had generated new terms to describe newly discovered fundamentals such as atoms and molecules; subatomic electrons, protons, and neutrons; and so on. Social sciences theorists sought similar advances, it appears, through similar patterns of theoretical concepts and terms which were expected to deal with the newly construed "real fundamentals" of human behavior. But the patterns used in one field are not easily translated into another field, and misguided attempts to do so can make quite a mess. New concepts and terms were appropriate in the physical sciences, in that the fundamentals being investigated were indeed new, and no ordinary language conventions were available to refer to them. The social sciences stand in contrast, for they deal with behaviors, persons, relationships, and so on which are familiar to all and are covered already in ordinary language conventions. New theory-based concepts and language conventions are unnecessary in the social sciences, and do not produce the same integrative solutions as those in the natural sciences.

Social groups use customized language conventions to make those in the group seem special and to exclude others. Several fields have generated their own special languages: in medicine, the patient does not bleed, but rather he "hemorrhages"; in law, one does not sell a house, but rather "the party of the first part has sold and hereby does sell for now and for all time to the party of the second part. . ."; and so on. An interest in appearing special may have been operating to promote special languages in social sciences theorizing.

To the lay public, one who uses special terminologies may seem more knowledgeable than one who speaks in everyday language. Atkinson and Carskaddon (1975) showed that interviewers were rated as more knowledgeable about psychology when they used psychological jargon than when they spoke in concrete and easily understood layman's language. The sad conclusion here is that as psychologists we may be rated more knowledgeable when we use specialized languages which make us less understandable.

Since language difficulties are so much an aspect of the current problem, it is reasonable to seek a solution in a conceptual or language system which may be used across the various positions and orientations. Such a system must be readily understandable, and comprehensive and neutral enough to be used through the range of subject matter within our field.

One obvious solution is to make use of our already existing ordinary language system. Ordinary language is our shared language, for in addition to being social scientists we are all persons, and we all understand and are competent in the everyday language of our general human communities. A commitment to ordinary language would provide a common and already available basis for communication, and would free us from problems of so many theory-based languages.

Our everyday language is a system with considerable strengths and extensive complexities, variations, subtleties, and nuances. Ordinary language is already rich in its coverage of human actions, persons, relationships, social organizations, and so on. It has served mankind through the ages and is used to convey that which is important to individuals, to communities, and to existing ways of life. Also, it has undergone continual adaptation and change, to maintain pace with a changing and sometimes expanding range of man's individual and social concerns.

Even an average individual has years of experience and practice, acquiring in those years a sophisticated competence in the use of the language. The extensiveness of ordinary language competencies goes too easily unnoticed, however. One need not analyze a language in order to use it appropriately, although it is only through careful analysis that the strengths and complexities are fully appreciated. A failure to recognize these strengths has been a key factor in the tradition of inventing new language systems.

The use of an ordinary language system does carry with it some problems, although they are not so extensive or so intractable as some have assumed them to be. Ambiguities do exist of course in ordinary language conventions, and these should be taken seriously. An individual word may have an entire family of related and overlapping meanings; therefore, an intended meaning is not always communicated as clearly and rigorously as one might wish. But one need not become frustrated or suspicious of the entire language because of such ambiguities and inconsistencies. Our approach is to seek to understand and to resolve these ambiguities. We analyze the important concepts and terms to make them systematic and explicit, so that we may use the language in a clear and unambiguous manner. We attempt to choose words which are descriptively appropriate to particular applications and to make the meaning as explicit as our usage requires. A principle of linguistic responsibility is involved which requires that ordinary language meanings be respected. What is advocated here as a shared or common language is thus a *version* of ordinary language, in which the major concepts have been analyzed and are now specified and secured, and are suitable for general usage in an integrative approach to our subject matter.

In this same vein, Shontz (1965) notes that

> there are difficulties . . . with respect to the use of words. It is essential that key terms be applied consistently and that they have explicit meanings which do not deviate markedly from generally accepted definitions. . . . the need is not to devise original expressions or to attach broader implications to existing terms; it is, rather, to delimit and restrict the interpretation of words already in common use. (p. 20)

The objective here is to gain the benefits both of our ordinary language and of a technical and scientific language system. It is the basis in ordinary language which makes our common language system easily understandable and thus suitable as a shared or common basis of communication. It is the clarification of key concepts which makes the system rigorous enough for use in scientific undertakings, and allows comparison and integration with alternative formulations. Our approach as social scientists is to understand and accept our language and to improve on it where necessary, so that it may be used to better advantage in our practical undertakings.

The common language system so formulated is expected to be easily understandable and, at the same time, comprehensive and neutral enough to serve adequately through the interests and complexities of the behavioral sciences. Its adequacy cannot be argued at the outset but must be shown point by point through application and continuing evaluation. What should be apparent at the beginning is that there is considerable need for an integrative system, that current theoretical systems have yet to agree on an adequate solution, and that an explicit version of ordinary language offers a promising possibility. Our common language concepts are presented in Section I, and are further elaborated through their applications in clinical analysis and treatment.

Two Principles for Observation

While the system of concepts structures our observations, it does not in itself say what is so in any given instance. We must find that out for ourselves through observations of the particulars of the case at hand, followed by some critique and evaluation of the adequacy of the observations. Two axioms make explicit our approach to finding out about our worlds (Ossorio, 1981).

Empiricism: The first, the empiricist principle, is simply: *We know about the real world through observation (and thought).* It shows the logical connection between knowing about things and observation, and places observation as the most fundamental source of knowing. The empiricist principle is at the basis of any scientific enterprise, although note that here it is observation rather than measurement which is taken to be essential. This point is important, for conventions in the social sciences have too often stressed measurement rather than straightforward observation, and in so doing have unnecessarily restricted the field of inquiry. One should be free to choose measurement or direct observation on the basis of which is more appropriate to the concerns at hand. Straightforward observation is the more important to the psychotherapist, in two ways. As therapists we are interested in the meaning or significance of things, which must be observed directly—the meaning of spoken or written statements, for instance, is not measurable but is seen only through direct observation. And in addition, practical considerations in our sessions force us to observe what goes on and to act immediately on our observations, so that it would be impossibly cumbersome to introduce and apply instruments of measurement for each observation. A requirement of measurement would be unnecessarily and unfairly restrictive, and the standard of straightforward observation serves us well in everyday clinical practice.

Common Sense: Observation has its problems, for not all observers are going to agree on the subtleties of complex phenomena. Straightforward observation is unfortunately as fallible as it is indispensable. So it is especially important to be able to critique our observations and to assess and evaluate their adequacy. The second principle here guides such critiques in that it provides a standard for justification of observations and for negotiation over differences of opinions; it is stated simply as: *We take things to be as they seem unless we have reason enough to believe otherwise.* This principle is an observational axiom in that it is the manner in which we already do and must operate in our everyday activities. We see things on the basis of how they seem to us, and we act on those observations unless we have reason to question or reevaluate. This is an obvious practical necessity in that it is impossible to operate otherwise: we could hardly observe things to be as they do not seem to us to be, for what would be the basis then of our perceptions?

It is the use of this principle as a standard in criticism and evaluation which is especially important here as a cornerstone for a commonsense approach. Things may or may not be as they appear, and the significance of the principle is that it gives an initial credibility to the way things appear to us and places the burden of proof on any challenges to those appearances. The rationale is as follows: when we wish to support and justify our observations, we must do so by appealing to logic and to further observations; if we were then required to support and justify each of those further observations, we would be trapped with wheels spinning in the unending repetition of an infinite regress, and nothing would ever be resolved. Skepticism carried to an extreme is not a quest for truth but rather a rejection of the practical commonsense requirements for negotiating and agreeing on what is and is not so. We must avoid the "never sure of anything" position of naive skepticism and the "how can we ever know anything really?" epistemology of the logical positivists. We should be required to justify observations which appear puzzling, but we cannot be required to justify all observations; those which appear correct must be accepted on face value unless there is sufficient reason to question and reevaluate them.

When we do suggest an alternative to appearances, we must accept the burden of proof of drawing on further observation so that—in the light of that further observation—it is our alternative, rather than the original view, which comes to appear correct. The principle is thus a logical requirement for the negotiation and resolution of conflicting viewpoints. Where we introduce alternatives to common sense, we should be required as a minimum to mention the ordinarily accepted views, show in what sense they are wrong, and show how the new formulations are an actual improvement upon prevailing views. This standard requires an innovator to take into account and appeal to the good sense of his audience, rather than ignoring everyday understandings and presenting innovations as if they were to remake anew the structure of our entire world views. Appeals to appearances and to common sense are taken here as a requirement for the successful resolution of competing viewpoints.

The importance of appeals to our existing good sense is stated clearly by several writers. Alfred North Whitehead (1929) notes that

> science is rooted in . . . the whole apparatus of common sense thought. You may polish up common sense, you may contradict it in detail, you may surprise it. But ultimately your whole task is to satisfy it. (p. 110)

In a similar vein, physicist J. Robert Oppenheimer (1956) notes that

> all sciences arise as refinements, corrections, and adaptations of common sense. (p. 128)

These statements are meant as generalizations of how good science is done; they can also be taken as prescriptions for how we should attempt to do it.

Familiar theories include some propositions which appeal to our common sense, and others which either ignore or, in some important manner, contrast with and even contradict our everyday views and opinions. The inclusion of assertions which are contrary to common sense contributes to the apparent originality of the theories. Hall and Lindzey (1970) note the issue as a prescription in their popular text on personality theories:

> The successful theorist must develop a dispassionate willingness to do radical violence to common assumptions concerning behavior. (p. 597)

Commonsense understandings are acquired not through mere speculation and assumption but through years of observation and experience; the reference to them as "assumptions" concerning behavior is to note that they are sometimes inaccurate. On the justification of such violations, Hall and Lindzey prescribe that

> The . . . personality theorist [should be] *freed from obligation to justify theoretical formulations that depart from normative or customary views of behavior.* (p. 597)

Considerable separation has been tolerated and even expected between the construction of a theory and its validation: the theorist was to be free from obligation to justify his propositions in order to encourage speculation and originality, with the expectation that continuing empirical research would later validate some of those propositions and invalidate others. Those original propositions which are sufficiently confirmed by evidence and argument become themselves in time the prevailing commonsense opinions in the field.

It is important to note that formulations typically *qualify* as theories to the extent that they appear to be alternatives to everyday understandings, and not when they merely build upon and utilize everyday understandings. Any statement of common sense is just that—common sense—and is not generally given the prestige and status accorded to original psychological theorizing. Formulations which ignore or violate everyday understandings are more easily included as essentials in theoretical systems. Heider (1958) notes:

> An assertion of a tendency contrary to the obvious . . . is felt to be a paradox, and often . . . imports a sense of great psychological profundity. (p. 181)

Were I to say that some of the things persons do are on purpose, and other things are by accident or mistake, or are otherwise unintentional, then this is what most of us would figure anyway: it appears ordinary and mundane, and would hardly qualify as theoretical in the usual sense of the word. Were one to argue that there are no accidents, as Freud did, then that is in clear violation of our everyday experience and understanding. It strikes one as startling and exciting, and appears to have a depth or significance which goes far beyond ordinary good sense. One might be sympathetic with the formulation and use it, as Freud did, as a cornerstone for a general system of intrapsychic determinism. Or one might be unsympathetic, considering it unmanageably ambiguous—if there were no accidents, should we no longer bother with seat belts?—or just plain wrong. Whether sympathetic, unsympathetic, or merely confused, we should all be in agreement on one point: the statement is highly theoretical, in the sense that it is speculative, violates our everyday common sense, and is as yet unsupported by sufficient argument and evidence to become itself the prevailing opinion in our field.

The requirements for therapeutic practice contrast somewhat with those for original scientific inquiry. In a system for therapeutic practice, the emphasis should be on propositions which are more stable and reliable rather than on those which are so speculative, and this is especially so for a system suggested as an integrative system. In our pragmatic approach, we draw from common sense and from those aspects of theories which seem sufficiently confirmed that they have become themselves the prevailing opinions. We attempt to avoid those aspects of theories which are as yet speculative and do not command wide agreement among other professionals. Our approach shall be to clarify common sense, to analyze and perhaps alter it in some of its particulars, and to apply it in new and more constructive ways to clinical problems. There is no intention here to do it radical violence.

Ours is a "back to basics" approach, in which easily understood foundations are clarified and are used to better understand and organize the various alternative viewpoints.

LANGUAGE AS INFLUENCE

Everyday language functions not merely in understanding things but in social relations as a means of influencing others. The uses and effects of language as social influence were emphasized by the American pragmatists and by the ordinary language analytic philosophers. They are emphasized in communications approaches (cf. Haley, 1963) and are considered in varying degrees in most other approaches to psychotherapy. Social influence issues may be easily overlooked nonetheless, and some emphasis and reminders are thus in order. "Words are also deeds," notes Wittgenstein (1968, par. 546) in a most important and fundamental analytic principle. Words are also deeds, in that by saying something one thereby acts to *do* something—to change or influence someone or to accomplish something. Several illustrations should be helpful.

"You say the stupidest things," says Pam to a schoolmate, Julie, in the course of an argument. The statement here is a counterattack, and an attempt to undermine and thus to gain advantage in an ongoing argument. It is an obvious attempt, however, and Julie sees it for what it is, treats it as such, and continues with a counterargument of her own.

Try another version, however, which is more subtle and therefore more lethal. "Some of your friends were talking about you," says Pam, "and they were laughing about some of the stupid things that you say." Such a statement has an immediate impact, for it impels Julie to wonder which friends were talking about her and what else they were saying; and it evokes in her suspiciousness and rage at those yet unnamed schoolmates who have been talking about her so freely. Julie's attention here is on assessing the information, and on rearranging her attitudes and feelings toward those so-called friends. Pam's statement may or may not have been entirely truthful, and may have been lifted entirely out of context. It is the focus on the information itself and on its truthfulness, however, which causes Julie to miss the significance of the remark. The significance of the statement is that it devastates its victim: it is a grand slam in the subtlest and most underhanded of traditions.

In focusing narrowly on the information offered, Julie thereby misses the significance of the statement, and she leaves herself in no position at all to deal appropriately with it. It is essential in so many communications not merely to see the information offered, but also to see the significance of the action—the influence intended and actually attained through the communication.

Consider a similar illustration in a recurring emotional outburst. "I've had it," screams an exasperated mother. "If anyone says one more thing to me, I'm going to have a nervous breakdown." The information in the statement is that she is fragile and that any further pressure is sure to cause calamity. The significance of the statement is that the mother effectively stonewalls any further intrusions, silences the opposition, and gains temporary freedom from family pressures. Is the mother really as fragile as she informs her family she is? That question cannot be answered from the minimal information so far, although we should see that she is not entirely powerless: it is clear that she has in her possession an explosive strategy of influence and that she does not refrain from using it. In understanding this woman, one should consider not merely the truth of the information she offers, but also the statement as an action and the influence she exerts through the action.

Sometimes the information is merely a means to sidetrack someone. Suppose Howie, a youngster, is watching television, and his mother tells him to turn off the TV and get himself ready for bed. Howie responds, "You never let me do anything." Mother accepts the challenge and answers, "You get to do a lot of things." Howie continues, "Yea, but never anything that is fun." Thus the squabble goes on, and the deed is done. Howie has sidetracked mother in her attempt to get him to bed. He has not convinced her of anything he was saying, and yet she has the losing position, for he stays up and she fails to exercise authority over him. The accuracy or truthfulness is somewhat immaterial here and has little bearing at all on the significance of the statement. The significance of the comment is that he foils her attempt to get him to bed.

One may say something *in order to* share interesting or important information, but one does not say something *merely* because it is true. One does not say something about the weather merely because it is true, any more than one mentions that he has on clean underwear merely because it is true that he does have on clean underwear. A person mentions something in order to accomplish something he wants or has reason to accomplish; a person does not mention things he has no reason to mention. One mentions the weather in order to share information, to be cordial, or to avoid talking about anything of real significance. Or one may mention the weather for some other reason, but always and necessarily as a means of doing something, and not merely because the statement is true.

The principle which applies to statements in general applies similarly to statements which are expressions of emotions. A statement expressing an emotion is made not merely because it accurately expresses the emotion, but also in order to do something which one wants or has reasons to do. As an illustration let us take an "I love you" statement which Julie expresses to her sweetheart Jim on a cool evening in a Z car overlooking the lake. She says "I love you" not merely because she feels love, but in order to communicate something she wants or has reason to communicate. Perhaps she is affectionate and turned on to him, and says "I love you" to excite him, and to invite and encourage him to further intimacies. Perhaps, on the other hand, she is refusing his advances, is concerned that he is insecure and angry, and says "I love you" to reassure him that she really does love him. In the same vein, perhaps she is herself insecure of his affections, and she says "I love you" in order to obligate him to return her love and thus to bind him to her. There are other possibilities as well.

Saying "I love you" is a means to a variety of ends, and there is ample room therefore for miscommunication. Perhaps she says "I love you" in order to reassure and intrigue him, but he takes it wrong: he has been obligated and manipulated by these same words many times before and so does not see the genuine affection she intends but feels trapped by the words and looks for a way out of the relationship. It could also as easily be the other way around: perhaps she has little genuine sensitivity to his welfare, but is insecure and says "I love you" in order to obligate him; in his naiveté and inexperience, he takes this as genuine affection and feels obligated to return the commitment she appears to be making. There is a considerable range of what one might communicate or miscommunicate through expressions of love.

We understand our everyday concept of love more fully as we see and understand the range of ways in which it is used. One would have a limited understanding of the language of love should he fail to realize that words of love are spoken sometimes to entice, invite, or reassure, and sometimes to commit, obligate, or manipulate.

By saying things, we construct aspects of our social worlds. Consider making a promise. If Julie promises to get away early to be with her sweetheart, then by doing that she is making a commitment to him. The promise is not merely a representation of a feeling or a plan to be with him that existed prior to the promise; rather, it is a social commitment which comes into existence as she makes it. Making a promise is not the simple representation of something which existed previously, but the creation of something which exists only as and when it is given.

The same is so for assigning responsibility. If you tell your youngster that he is going to be responsible from now on for getting himself ready in the mornings, then you are not merely representing something that already exists. Rather, you are trying to get him to take responsibility and get himself ready, and you are giving notice that he shall be held responsible for the outcome. Issues such as responsibility, when dealt with as abstract entities, can be quite vague and elusive. When we look at who is holding whom responsible and for what sorts of things, then the issues are more easily understood. The assignment of responsibility is a matter of social interaction.

Language is thus seen to function not merely in order to share understanding and information, but also and in many ways to influence. The content or information in a statement is ordinarily apparent. As psychotherapists, we need to be aware perhaps most importantly of the significance of the statement—of the influence the client seeks and the influence actually attained through the statements that are made. The social influence aspect of language is critical in understanding our clients' statements.

Consider the following two sentences from a session between a sensitive female therapist and a practiced victim of personal inadequacies. The client has been continuing on and on about how he is unattractive and worthless, has no friends, and is the sort of person nobody wants as a friend. The therapist comments: "You feel nobody could possibly want to be your friend. I understand that you must feel quite alone." The client appears wronged and lashes back: "What would you know about any of this? You have your husband, your friends, your job. You don't understand what I'm going through, and I don't think you can understand!"

The therapist's comments were true enough in their particulars, and were made in order to clarify the client's position and to show that she does understand what he is going through. The comments were reasonably empathic, and in most situations would be appropriate and constructive. The client's response is therefore puzzling, and we must look for further information to make sense of it. Perhaps he was wary of close involvements, seeing only the pain and anguish they entail, and perhaps he was especially wary of this woman, who was warm and sympathetic but also attractive, more successful than he, and socially quite unattainable. Thus, he might have made the comments in order to stay on guard against her or to undermine her confidence in herself, demean her, and so put himself one up in his relationship with her. Should she miss the significance of what he is doing, she might question her own adequacy as a therapist and indeed lose confidence in herself. Should he by his comments successfully undermine her confidence, then she would lose as a therapist and he would lose as a client as well, since a stable collaborative relationship is essential for therapeutic effectiveness. Seeing what he is doing by what he says provides a basis for a more appropriate therapeutic response. Awareness of the pragmatic or "in order to" aspect of what is said is essential to understanding our clients.

Our comments must be more than merely true in order to be therapeutic. Avoiding untruths is perhaps a minimum standard, for comments which are false or confusing promote misunderstandings and mistrust. But being truthful is no guarantee that we will be effective. In the case just mentioned, the therapist's comments were quite true, but could lead nonetheless to deterioration of the relationship and to therapeutic failure. Therapeutic comments must address the issues at hand in a manner the client can understand, accept, and respond to constructively. It is effectiveness, rather than merely truth, which must be emphasized in the construction of therapeutic interventions.

Therepeutic statements are thus made not merely because they are so, but rather in order to influence a client toward changes which will be beneficial to him. The concept of psychotherapy as a process of social influence is a rather obvious one and is supported by writers of varied orientations (e.g., Frank, 1961; Pepinsky and Patton, 1971; Strong, 1968, 1978). Some practitioners view psychotherapy as a process of constructing the conditions facilitative to individual insight and growth, and so might object to the word "influence," but the apparent controversy is more a matter of semantic quibbling than of substantive differences. We influence others by constructing the conditions which promote understanding and change, for how else would it be done? Other issues are matters of genuine contention, but the element of therapeutic influence is a basic in our shared concept of psychotherapy.

The client's responses to our interventions may be what we want or, as in the previous exchange, they may be contrary to what we want. Saying something is for better or for worse a means of doing something, and as therapists we cannot escape this pragmatic or social influence aspect of language. Nor, incidentally, can we escape it by remaining silent, for that too can have an effect on those to whom we are refusing to speak. We use the "in order to" or influence aspect of statements as an organizing basis for our interventions.

Understanding and Influence

The complementary issues of understanding and influence appear again and again in a variety of familiar areas. In linguistics, "semantics" refers to the meaning of words and "pragmatics" to the impact. In clinical analysis, the "content" is the information in the statements, and "process" refers to the ways people are affecting each other through what they are saying. In psychotherapy, we make use of insights into what is going on and techniques to make changes: psychotherapy, like any social activity, involves both observation and action. Statements as representation are judged by their truth and completeness; statements as influence are judged by their impact or significance and by their usefulness.

The distinction between the understanding and the influence aspects of statements is critical, and shall serve us well in various ways throughout this presentation. As psychotherapists, we observe and we act: the common language concepts delineate the *seeables,* and the guidelines organize the *doables* of therapeutic interventions.

SECTION I
COMMON LANGUAGE CONCEPTS

2
Human Behavior

We are interested in what persons do or might do; here, "doing" is meant in the broadest sense of seeing, experiencing, attempting, and/or achieving something. It is essential to be able to observe, describe, and communicate about various occurrences of behavior, and to do so we need a shared set of concepts of behavior which can be easily understood and used by all. This chapter outlines our common language concepts of behavior.

In presenting a concept, it is best to begin with a complete and most understandable version and from there to branch out to other less complete versions. A most complete and understandable version is termed a "paradigm" case or model case (cf. Wilson, 1963), and the less complete versions are then derivative or deficient versions. A complete and most understandable automobile, for instance, is one which runs, for although not all autos run, it is through experiences with those which do run that one understands autos as vehicles of transportation. Autos which do not run are incomplete or deficient automobiles, and are seen as automobiles at all only because they are similar enough to the fully functioning versions. In outlining the concept of behavior, we begin therefore with a complete and most understandable formulation, and use that to understand other less complete forms of behavior.

PURPOSIVE ACTION

Behavior as formulated here in its complete and most understandable sense is termed purposive action, and this section explicates the concept of purposive action. Concepts are best understood not in the abstract but through illustration and analysis, and that is the approach which is followed here.

Consider an incident which, for the benefit of "Doonesbury" fans, takes place on a typical day in Joanie Caucus's child care center. The participants are two youngsters, Howard and Jennie, and of course Joanie, who assigns herself the responsibility of somehow understanding and managing the ensuing commotion.

In the incident in question, Howie speeds around a corner, lunges forward, and slams into Jennie, sending her sprawling onto the floor, shaken and crying. Joanie intervenes to soothe hurt feelings, to clarify the incident, to administer justice, and to make it less likely that this sort of thing will happen again.

In attempting to understand the incident, one would probably begin with a factor which remains intentionally ambiguous in the description so far: Did Howie do it on purpose, or was it an accident? This is an obvious first question and an important one, for if Joanie is to intervene effectively she must base her response on an accurate understanding of Howie's action. If it was indeed an accident, she might caution him to be more careful, to walk around corners rather than run. She might tell Jennie it was an accident, have Howie apologize, and expect the incident to be forgotten. If, on the other hand, the incident occurred on purpose, it is a more serious matter and stronger measures are called for. Joanie might try to find out Howie's reasons for what he did and attempt to convince him that what he did was wrong. She might warn him against doing it again, or punish him, so that he sees he cannot get away with such acts. Also, since Joanie Caucus supports independence for women, she might encourage Jennie to hold her own, join the fracas, and make a tackle or two herself.

Such might be Joanie's responses. Other adults might respond somewhat differently, although most or all of us would be similar in this important way: all would draw some conclusion about whether the collision was an accident and would treat Howie somewhat differently according to whether the collision was seen as purposive or as accidental.

The distinction between purposive actions and accidents or other inadvertent occurrences is important. It is embedded throughout human relationships, in our social interactions, in our everyday understanding of human action, in our language, in the "forms of life" we lead. Shift for a moment from Howie's minor incident to an actual crime, and consider the difference between manslaughter and murder. Manslaughter, of course, is unintentional or accidental killing, whereas murder is the purposive killing of another human being. The perpetrator's aims are important not only to understanding the action itself, but also obviously to selecting an appropriate response to the action.

Given the significance of the issue, an obvious question to ask is, How does one know if an action is purposive? This is an appropriate question, but one which should be set aside for a moment in order to explore something more fundamental: If it is a purposive action, what is that? What is involved in a purposive action which is missing in an accident, a mistake, or some other *un*intended occurrence? What exactly is the difference? If Howie's collision with Jennie is purposive, what is necessarily involved which might be missing if it were an accident? Included in the answer are three factors, which are parameters or aspects of the concept of purposive actions.

1. If Howie's collision is purposive, then he *wants* to hit Jennie; he has some reason to hit her; he is motivated to hit her. For an action to be purposive, one must be motivated to do it. If he does not want to hit her but does so inadvertently, then the collision is not purposive because the necessary motivation is missing.

2. If Howie's collision is purposive, then he *knows* that Jennie is there in front of him; he sees her; he is aware of her presence. In order for an act to be purposive, one must have the necessary understanding of the situation to perform the act. If Howie speeds around the corner, is not looking and does not see Jennie, then his collision is not purposive because the necessary awareness is missing.

3. If Howie's collision is purposive, then he *knows how* to hit Jennie in the way in which he does hit her. To continue our illustration, recall that Howie lunges forward into Jennie in what may also be described as a diving or tackling motion. But Howie is a young child and physical coordination is involved in a tackle. A toddler, for instance, concentrates mainly on staying on his feet and does not have the competence to make a tackle. If Howie does not know how to tackle, but falls and lunges forward, then the act is not purposive because the necessary competence is missing.

Thus, if Howie's collision with Jennie is purposive, each of three factors is involved: Howie *wants* or has reason to hit her, he *knows* she is there, and he exercises a competence or *know-how* which he does

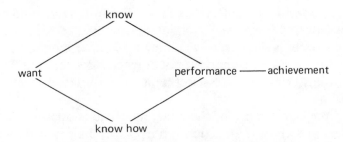

Figure 1.   The five parameters of purposive action.

possess. If one or more of these factors is missing, then the action is accidental, inadvertent, or otherwise unintentional. A purposive action includes these three factors, as well as two additional ones which have already been mentioned in the original description: as he lunges forward, Howie *performs* the physical movements appropriate to hitting Jennie, and in actually colliding with her he *achieves* the desired outcome.

Thus, in a purposive action one wants a particular outcome, has the knowledge relevant to the attempt, performs the appropriate motions, and achieves what one wants, not through accident or coincidence but through the exercise of one's competence. The schematic in Figure 1 was introduced by Ossorio (1966) to show the intrinsic relatedness of these five parameters.

If Howie's collision is a purposive action, it may be schematized as shown in Figure 2. Purposive action thus involves motivation, cogni-

Figure 2.   A collision as a purposive action.

tion, competence, movements, and effects, as schematized in Figure 3. Note the range of ordinary language terms in each category.

The schematic used here was introduced by Ossorio, but the con-

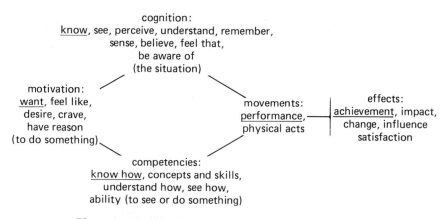

Figure 3. Ordinary language aspects of purposive action.

cept of action it portrays is that commonly used in human affairs. In schematizing the concept, we clarify and explicate something which persons use implicitly in their everyday observations of human action. In this sense the schematic of behavior is similar to a diagram of a sentence, for it portrays the qualities that those sorts of things must and actually do have.

Note here that cognition (seeing and knowing) is included as an integral element in our complete and most understandable formulation of behavior. Behavior is not a matter of going through life blindly with your eyes closed stumbling into things, but rather a matter of acting on what you see and take to be the case. The present formulation contrasts, of course, with that of the classical behaviorists, who banished cognition from their own version of "behavior," thereby bequeathing to later neo- and cognitive behaviorists the unaesthetic problems of reintroducing cognition and of jerry-rigging it back into a system which was constructed specifically to eliminate it. Our formulation avoids the problem of reintroducing cognition by never seeking to eliminate it in the first place.

A purposive action, as the term is specified here, is an act in order to attain the outcome, in contrast with accidents, mistakes, and other inadvertent acts: it does *not* imply that the person must be conscious of and able to state his aims. In some purposive actions the person is not consciously aware of his aims and objectives, and in others the person is conscious of and able to articulate what he is trying to do. The term "purposive" in ordinary language is used generally as it is used here to indicate simple "in order to" action, but it is used sometimes in the broader sense to indicate actions in which one is consciously aware of his aims. Our use of the term here clarifies and systematizes the simpler meaning and specifically excludes the latter reference to conscious awareness. By thus specifying and limiting the usage, we avoid problems of multiple meanings so that key terms may be used in an unambiguous way suitable to a formal or scientific language.

Purposive action is our concept of behavior in a complete and most understandable sense. As such, it serves to anchor the concept of behavior and to make understandable other, less complete forms of behaviors such as accidents, mistakes, attempts, failures, and so on. Such forms of behavior are similar to completed purposive actions, but with something altered or missing. An *accident,* as we have seen, is an act causing an outcome in which one is not trying to cause that outcome. An *attempt* or *try,* on the other hand, is an act done in order to attain an outcome. An unsuccessful attempt or *failure* is an act in order to attain an outcome, in which the outcome is not attained. A *mistake,* similarly, is an attempt in which the necessary understanding is missing so that the appropriate outcome is not attained.

Since cognition is included as a parameter of behavior, the range of mental, perceptual, and cognitive events can be understood in a similar manner as incomplete variations on the more complete concept of behavior. To *see* (observe, read, listen, hear, experience, be conscious of) is to do something which does not affect the situation proper but affects only what one knows about the situation. Similarly, to *think* (contemplate, puzzle, plan, speculate, conclude, etc.) is to do something which has no overt performance and does not affect the situation proper but affects instead what one knows about the situation. Behavior in its most complete and understandable sense involves seeing, wanting, moving, and having an effect; these mental events then are forms of behavior in which the overt movements and external effects are missing.

The formulation of purposive action is also a template for understanding those actions which involve something more than simple purposive actions. *Conscious* actions are purposive actions in which the person is aware of and able to state his aims and objectives (cf. Plotkin, 1981); *planned* or *premeditated* actions are purposive actions that are planned ahead of time. Conscious actions thus are purposive actions with an additional cognitive element—consciousness of one's purposes—and planned actions are purposive actions with a prior element—a motivation and plan to do it identifiably prior to the act. Purposive actions contrast with accidents; conscious actions contrast with unconscious purposive actions; and planned actions contrast with actions which are spontaneous or impulsive.

Incomplete and dysfunctional actions have component parameters similar to those of complete purposive actions, but with something altered or missing. Actions which are incomplete and dysfunctional can be outlined using the same schematic, as illustrated in Figure 4.

Figure 4. Aspects of incomplete or dysfunctional actions.

Incomplete and dysfunctional actions are characterized by motivations which are in conflict with each other, by insufficient understanding or actual misunderstandings of the situation, by insufficient competencies and actual misunderstandings of how to get things done, by performances which are ineffective or inappropriate to the situation, and by mistakes, failures, unintended losses and other secondary consequences, frustrations, and dissatisfactions.

The outline of the concept of purposive action helps make sense of these less complete or more difficult to understand forms of behavior, since they are all similar to purposive actions but with something altered or missing. The concepts are thus particularly important in organizing clinical issues, for the behavior of troubled persons is frequently incomplete and dysfunctional, involving as it often does conflicting motives, misunderstanding, limited competencies, and unconventional approaches to unobvious ends. An understanding of the importance of each of these factors is included in our assessment and psychotherapy intervention approach. Some of the interventions aim at cognition, some at motivations, some at competencies, and others at outcomes, based on which of these aspects of the action are particularly problematic.

The schematic also enables us to see better the correspondence between common language concepts and aspects of various familiar theories. Several of the major concepts from popular theories are categorized in Figure 5 by their places in the concept of purposive action.

Figure 5.   Theory-based concepts as aspects of purposive action.

An array of concepts can thus readily be classified together on the basis of their position in our schematic of behavior:

(1) *Motivation:* Ordinary language contains a broad range of motivational concepts, and we consider motivations not by postulating that some are more primary than others but by attempting to observe and describe whatever particular motives are actually involved in specific behaviors. Many major theories, in contrast, postulate single motivational factors which are considered primary and fundamental causes of motivations; other motivations are then considered to evolve from, and be secondary to, the primary ones. The principle of "homeostasis"—tension reduction and the maintenance of physiological equilibrium—is postulated as a primary motivation in psychoanalytic and in early behavioristic orientations: it involves tension reduction through sex and aggression in analytic formulations, and drive and tension reduction through the satisfaction of

physiological requirements such as food in behavioral formulations. The principle slightly altered reappears again as the maintenance of family homeostasis in several family systems theories. "Actualization" or "growth," which contrasts with homeostatic stability, has been postulated as primary in several humanistic formulations. Overcoming inferiority by striving for superiority is suggested in Adlerian formulations, and identity is fundamental in Glasser's reality approach. The attainment of "strokes," or social recognition, is a primary motivation in transactional analysis. Anticipating coming events is the primary motivation in Kelly's personal construct theory. And so on, for there are of course any number of motivations which might easily be postulated as primary and fundamental, and used to explain or reinterpret the entire range of other observable motivations.

(2) *Cognition:* "Internal mediating events" and later "coverants"—Homme's (1965) contraction for "covert operants"—are terms used in the behavioral and cognitive behavioral schools to indicate what one thinks or takes to be the case. "Projections," "rationalizations," "transferences," and so on from the analytic school—theoretical underlying causal processes aside—are all basically misunderstandings of things. "Phenomenological fields" and "life space" from phenomenologists and humanists are what one sees and takes to be so. Construct theory talks about what a person "construes" to be so. Such apparently diverse concepts belong together here as ways of talking about what persons experience, understand, or misunderstand about their situations.

(3) *Competency (know-how):* "Constructs" in personal construct theory are the distinctions one knows how to use to observe and structure his world, and so correspond to our everyday concept of "concepts." "Behavioral repertoires" from operant conditioning are what one knows how to do; these correspond to our everyday concept of skills.

(4) *Performance:* The movements parameter of behavior might be specified by measurements of the actual physical movements, although taking measurements would be awkward and is seldom done. The movements in some behaviors are easily observable, while those in others are generally unobservable, for example, the inner mouth and vocal cord movements in conversation which are usually unobservable in everyday contexts. Some actions, such as "waiting" or

"ignoring someone," are conducted not by any specific set of movements but more commonly by the absence of some other possible performances.

(5) *Achievements:* "Reinforcers" officially are "stimulus events which maintain or increase the frequencies of the preceding behaviors." However, as the term is commonly used, reinforcers are also the good things that one achieves through one's actions. "Primary reinforcers" are usually physiological necessities, and "secondary reinforcers" are usually social or symbolic gains such as attention or money. "Positive reinforcers" are actual gains, and "negative reinforcers" are the resolution of aversive situations. "Overt reinforcers" are observable achievements, whereas "covert" or "self-reinforcers" translate into ordinary language as satisfactions. "Primary gains" from the analytic school are the alleviation of tensions (through sex and aggression), and "secondary gains" are social benefits such as attention. "Payoffs" from transactional analysis are the social benefits of manipulative actions. Social recognition and superiority are emphasized by Adlerians. "Validation" in personal construct theory is the confirmation of one's expectations. These concepts belong together here in that they are ways of stating the outcomes and satisfactions achieved through one's actions.

Behavior: There are also special terms used for human action. The term "operants" is used by behaviorists for those actions which affect the situation (and sometimes for those which do not). "Games" in transactional analysis are actions which are inauthentic and manipulative—involving concealed motivations leading to surprising social payoffs. "Transactions" in transactional analysis are actions which cause a response from another person.

Our common language concepts can be used in this manner to categorize a wide array of concepts and terminologies from the various theoretical orientations. The categorizations serve as a guide in attempts to evaluate and integrate these concepts, for one might compare and contrast concepts which belong in the same category but should not do so with concepts which belong in separate categories. The categorizations also guide one in evaluating and integrating the insights and information encoded in the various theoretical formulations, since such information can be transferred into our common language concepts, and thereby integrated with other available information and better utilized in our practical endeavors.

Let us return now to Howie's collision with Jennie and to a question left on the back burner: How does one know if the act was purposive? Recall the semantic clarification introduced earlier: the term "purposive" is used here to indicate actions done in order to accomplish something and to contrast with accidents, mistakes, and other unintended acts; as used here, it does *not* indicate that the individual is necessarily conscious of the purpose of his actions. Thus if Howie did act purposely, he is not necessarily aware that he meant to do it or, aware that he meant to do it but anticipating unpleasant consequences, he may nonetheless argue that it was an accident, in which case he is of no help with the problem anyway. Howie may or may not provide an accurate assessment, and while his comments should be considered, they are not to be taken as a final authoritative say in the matter.

So how does another observer make the assessment? How does Joanie, for instance, determine whether the act was purposive or accidental? Any answer here must take into account the particulars of the specific situation, for no single general solution should be expected to apply across situations. Joanie sees that it is purposive (or accidental) as she understands enough of the particulars of the situation and arrives at an appropriate conclusion.

If Joanie saw, for instance, that Howie was looking the other way, then he did not see Jennie and the requisite cognition is missing, so she should rule it an accident. On the other hand, if she observed that he was looking at Jennie, then obviously he did see her. And if he altered his course to hit her, then his performance gives him away, and she should surely judge the collision purposive. If she saw that the situation offered Howie clear opportunity to see and to avoid Jennie, and knew already that Howie is often angry at Jenny and harasses her continually, then Joanie should rule his action purposive. Note here that Joanie uses observations of the situation and of Howie's individual characteristics to judge the purposiveness. Such situational and individual factors will be explored more fully in Chapter 3. If Joanie does not have enough firm information, she may have suspicions but she should avoid forming final conclusions. And of course Joanie, like anyone else, can sometimes misperceive what happens and arrive at incorrect conclusions.

Obviously some people are better observers, some are poorer, and some errors in observation do occur. Joanie, like anyone else, makes observations on the basis of her abilities to do so, and there are of course limits to such abilities. But we need not call into question the concept of purposive action on the basis of some inevitable errors. Anyone who seeks certainty as a basis for empirical observation is not facing the necessary practical considerations. Infallibility in the everyday world is an impossible ideal, and it is only from an ivory tower that one may be guided by a doctrine of immaculate perception. A more reasonable course is to acknowledge the limitations and seek to improve our practical abilities as observers of human actions. The present analysis, clarifications, and illustrations of common language concepts are directed to this aim.

SIGNIFICANCE

If Howie's collision is purposive, an additional issue is involved: What is he doing by doing that? What are the reasons for the action, what are the further purposes, what are the additional aims and outcomes of the action? The meaning or *significance* of the action is formally included here as a final parameter of behavior.

Recall that in the original description of the incident, Howie collides with Jennie, causes her to fall down and cry, and gets Joanie Caucus involved with him. The same issues of purpose which were involved in the collision are involved again in understanding these further consequences of the action. Given that Howie hurt Jennie, was that on purpose, or was it an inadvertent consequence—something he did not expect and would rather not have had happen?

Include now some additional information. Joanie, in her attempts to build confidence and professional identities, has been spending extra time with the girls. Howie interprets this to mean that Ms. Caucus favors the girls: he feels neglected, and also envious and angry at the girls for getting the attention and at Ms. Caucus for ignoring him. Howie's collision with Jennie may have been to even the score, to get back at her for being the favorite: the significance of the action would be that it hurts Jennie and scores one for Howie. Howie may have done it in order to frustrate and upset Joanie, and thus to even the score there as well: so the significance of the action would be that it upsets Joanie. Howie may have done it to involve Joanie, to gain from her the attention he feels he is missing: the significance of the action would be that it gets Joanie's attention.

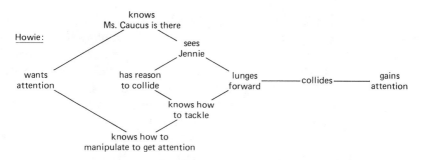

Figure 6.   The significance aspect of an action.

Let us take one of these possibilities to continue the illustration: Howie collides with Jennie in order to gain attention from Ms. Caucus. Where Howie gains attention from Joanie and does so purposely, then that too may be schematized as a purposive action, as shown in Figure 6. Note that one aspect of the action, colliding with Jennie, nests within the second aspect of the action, getting attention from Ms. Caucus. Colliding with Jennie is the way or *means* by which it is done, and gaining attention from Ms. Caucus is the *significance* of the action.

In any purposive action we must ask what the reasons for doing it are, and what the aims and objectives are. Is Howie lonely and doing it for attention, or angry and doing it in order to get even? Some judgment is called for. Specifying the reasons and purpose will be seen to be important in a variety of clinical issues.

Reasons

Purposive action is done in order to accomplish something and thus for some reason or reasons. *Reasons* are considerations for actions: they are states of affairs one sees or might see from which it makes sense to act in particular ways. Reasons involve both cognition and motivation, for they are understandings of things which matter enough to involve motivations to address them. One who sees himself as neglected has reason to seek attention or companionship; one who sees himself as mistreated or persecuted has reason to seek redress. The observations one makes concerning those things that matter to him give him reasons to act in particular ways.

The concept is further specified by two simple axioms from Ossorio

(1981). There is a clear linkage between reasons and behavior, as noted in the first: *If a person has a reason to do something, he will do it, unless he has a stronger reason not to.* Reasons are seen therefore in the occurrence of behavior, for a person does something when he sees sufficient reasons for doing it. And reasons are also seen in the absence of expected behavior, for one does not do something if he sees no reason to do it or if he has a better reason not to. Having reasons to do something does not imply that one is necessarily conscious of and able to articulate those reasons, any more than acting purposively implies one is conscious of and able to articulate his objectives. A person's reasons are reflected most clearly in his behaviors: actions, as the adage goes, speak louder than words. One might have reasons for, and at the same time reasons against doing something; that corresponds, of course, to the ambivalences and psychological conflicts so strongly stressed in psychoanalytic and other related writings on psychopathology.

Reasons combine together, as noted in a second axiom: *If a person has a second reason for doing something, then he has a stronger reason than if he had only one of those reasons.* Combinations of reasons are involved in many actions, so it is not a matter of one *or* another of the possible reasons but of whatever combinations of reasons the person actually has. By understanding a combination of several operative reasons, we may gain a better analysis of particular clinical behaviors than we would by committing ourselves to only one of those reasons. The psychoanalytic concept of "multiple determination" parallels this commonsense view that several reasons for and against may weigh in the choice of a particular action.

Language

The pragmatic or social influence aspects of language introduced earlier can be easily understood in the light of the behavioral concepts outlined here. Saying something is a form of human action and is seen to involve the same elements involved in other sorts of actions. One says something not merely because it is so or because one thinks, feels, or sincerely believes that it is so. One says things as a way to do something. As with other actions, the objectives do not always correspond to the effects, and one must look at both objectives and effects to understand the action aspect of a statement. The words one uses in saying something are the *means* by which it is done, and the impact (sought and actually attained) is the *significance* of the action.

Activities and Social Practices

Much of what is done involves not merely single acts but patterns or intelligible sequences of actions, engaged in by one or more persons. These sequences are termed activities or social practices, and include the wide range of whatever is done by one or more individuals. One action is followed by further actions by the same person or by other persons; this is schematized in Figure 7 as was done with single actions.

Figure 7.   Activities as sequences of purposive actions.

The issues of significance seen in single acts are important similarly in lengthy activities. One may engage in an activity as a means to further aims or for the satisfactions of the activity itself, with nothing further in mind. One may play soccer as a means of avoiding schoolwork, to practice for an upcoming state championship, or for the enjoyment of the game and with no further aims in mind.

Those activities which ordinarily involve inherent meaning and satisfaction are termed social practices. Raising children, for instance, is a familiar social practice in that ordinarily one's children matter and one raises them in order that they be raised well, rather than out of further or ulterior considerations.

Several "in order to" steps may be required to get to the final significance of an activity. A parent may require a child to do his schoolwork in order to encourage him to learn the material, in order to help him attain a good education, in order to provide him with what he needs to do well in life. But such sequences of explanation are necessarily finite, for explanation must end somewhere. We arrive sooner or later at something which is being done for its own sake— for the meaning and satisfaction of the practice itself, and not for some further objectives. We arrive at a social practice which is being done for the intrinsic meaningfulness of the practice and not as an instrumental means to something further.

Full participation in a social practice includes doing the activity, and also understanding the meaning and satisfaction of the practice. But everyone who engages in a social practice does not do so necessarily because of its inherent meaningfulness. One may do so for further aims, and some persons are unable to appreciate the meanings and satisfactions of available social practices. Every parent who raises children, for instance, does not necessarily appreciate the intrinsic meaning of doing that, and there are some parents who raise their children in order to minimize the energy expended, to avoid social embarrassments, to satisfy the child welfare worker, or whatever. Here as elsewhere the significance must be considered to really understand the occurring behaviors.

CLINICAL ILLUSTRATION

The distinction between purposive and inadvertent acts so essential in everyday relationships is similarly essential in competent clinical practice. In some cases the issue is obvious: if Howie were to have recurring collisions and you were to consult with Joanie on these incidents, you would surely assess whether or not the collisions were purposive and use your conclusion as a basis for your interventions. Is the kid aggressive, or does he need glasses? Although unmentioned in familiar theories, the distinction is so obvious and essential that you could hardly imagine a competent clinical consultant going in and simply ignoring it. We are sensitive to the issue not because of training in particular theories, but rather because of our preexisting everyday concepts and social competencies.

In some cases, issues of purpose are subtle and perplexing, and require the full measure of our observational abilities and clinical judgment. One should not use the effects of an action as a single or generally reliable indicator of the objectives, and the failure to distinguish between purposes and outcomes is one major source of observational error. Consider a woman client who goes from one unsatisfactory relationship to another, continually seeking a man with whom she might share intimacy and commitment. She becomes involved with a fellow who seems to be a promising candidate—he has enough of the apparent qualifications—and after initial warmth and intimacies, she finds herself annoyed and hostile toward him, suspicious of his motives, and unwilling to allow the relationship to progress further. Eventually, should she continue, she will sour the relationship and eliminate the possibilities it contains. In destroying the relationship she in effect is destroying what seems to be a chance for happiness and fulfillment, and such an action can easily be interpreted as self-destructive.

However, if a therapist focused only on the obvious outcome, he or she would be missing the essential features which make the action understandable and amenable to successful intervention. He might make the interpretation, "You are being self-destructive," which is a mediocre to poor interpretation since it is already obvious and confronts the client with her failure while offering no assistance. He might ask, "Why are you being so self-destructive?" which is an absolutely awful intervention since it asks for an answer the client is probably unable to produce and implies that the client necessarily has reasons for being self-destructive. He might ask, "Why do you want to make yourself unhappy?" which is again awful in that it implies directly that the woman actually wants and seeks the unfortunate outcome of her actions.

Suppose additional information reveals that the woman is actually afraid of the consequences of intimate involvement: she fears that a man who comes to know her deeply would see through her facade and find out that she is shallow; that the man could not be really committed, as he might appear to be, but would only be using her to his advantage; or that for any number of other reasons, she would be rejected and badly hurt by the relationship. Thus, she undermines the relationship in order to protect herself from the humiliation and pain which she sees as the inevitable consequence of continuing the intimacy, and perhaps also to show the man that he cannot get away with misusing her as it seems he would. The reasons for her actions are seen here to be understandable ones. The woman is acting not in order to be self-destructive, but rather in order to protect herself from what she sees as the destructive consequences of the relationship. The main *outcome* or effect of the actions may be self-destructive, but the aim, objective, or *purpose* is self-preservation.

Understanding the woman's reasons opens possibilities for constructive intervention, for example: "You fear that if he sees you for who you really are he will not accept you, and you are protecting yourself by rejecting him before he tires of you and rejects you. There are some advantages to that and some obvious problems as well. Let's sort through them and see what we can figure out.''

The importance of the aim or purpose continues as a theme throughout the present exposition, and a standard for assessment of purposes should be maintained: an action must be seen as an attempt to achieve something which one might understandably value and want to achieve. In this case, self-preservation and avoidance of rejection are easily understandable and thus are possible explanations of the action. Self-destruction is not in itself understandable as a final reason or value, and thus was passed over in favor of a more sensible explanation. While observers may differ sometimes on what is and is not intrinsically understandable, the standard should be maintained across observers: the significance of an action properly assessed must be something that the person understandably wants or has reason to attain, and not merely something which occurs as an unsatisfactory consequence of the action.

SUMMARY

This completes the outline of our common language concepts of behavior. The concept of purposive action has been essential in organizing the outline, for the range of recognizable human behaviors can be easily understood as purposive actions, as incomplete or dysfunctional forms of such actions, as purposive actions with additional elements, or as combinations and sequences of purposive actions. The various aspects of purposive action are the parameters of behavior, since they are the ways in which any behavior can be identified and distinguished from other behaviors.

These common language concepts cover the broad range of what is considered human behavior and show the necessary interconnections between the various aspects of behavior. They include the range of what is considered behavior in everyday conversation and serve also to organize the behavioral concepts from various theoretical systems. The breadth of these concepts is extremely important: since any behavior might be observed, described, identified, and discussed by using them, it is unnecessary to go outside these concepts to communicate about the particulars of any behavior.

3
Explanations of Human Behavior

Why does a person do what he does? Why does he see things, and feel and act as he does, rather than in some other way? Why does he participate in particular activities and social practices rather than in others? How do we explain a person's experiences and actions?

One order of answers has already been given implicitly in the concept of behavior as purposive action. A person acts as he does because he sees reason to do so and in order to get something he wants: thus he sees things certain ways, wants things, has a sense of how to try for them, and so on. In our everyday explanations we may mention one or more of any of these factors. Thus we might say a youngster is acting obnoxiously because he feels neglected, or because he knows how to manipulate, and in order to get attention or to get even. We might say a young woman is being cold and aloof toward her fiancé because she sees him as untrustworthy, and in order to protect herself from a hurtful involvement, to retaliate for what she misperceives as neglect on his part, or in order to feel superior to him. Such information serves as explanation, for it offers us a better understanding of previously puzzling aspects of the actions. In this manner, aspects of an action which had not been considered are used to explain other aspects of the action which were puzzling.

Aspects of the behavior itself comprise the first order of explanation, and there are two additional, although thoroughly complementary, orders of explanatory factors: situations and individual characteristics are considered together here as the second order of factors; the means by which those situations and individual characteristics were acquired are the third. These categories of factors are referred to as *orders* of explanation—they are logically ordered in that the first describes the behavior itself; the second, the immediate factors contributing to the behavior; and the third, prior factors which contributed to those immediate contributing factors.

Thus, the three orders of explanations are:

1. Additional aspects of the action itself which help one to understand other aspects of the action that appear puzzling
2. Some combination of situations and/or individual characteristics which explain why someone does something
3. The means by which such situations and/or individual characteristics were acquired

Together these should cover the range of what are used as everyday psychological explanations and the range also of behavioral and social sciences explanations. Second and third order explanations are outlined here in turn.

SITUATIONS AND INDIVIDUAL CHARACTERISTICS

To explain an action, one may look next at one or the other of two complementary factors: the person's situation or distinctive individual characteristics. The concept of *situations* here includes all those aspects of the real world which pertain or might pertain to the person's actions: it includes one's circumstances, relationships, status or social position in those relationships, the actions of others, supports, pressures, opportunities, and so on. The concept of distinctive *individual characteristics* here includes the range of intellectual and personality characteristics which distinguish the tendencies of one individual from the tendencies of others in similar situations. Individual characteristics include one's inclinations and abilities to see and act.

Consider as an illustration a man who is extremely jealous of his wife. He is suspicious that she is having affairs, obsessed, emotionally tormented, and angry. He questions her when she is late or when she is not where she said she would be, and he accuses her continually of being unfaithful. How does one explain the patterns? One looks to this husband's situation and circumstances, or to his individual characteristics, in order to understand his suspicions, jealousies, obsessions, and accusations.

Is this husband a particularly jealous individual? Is he characteristically suspicious, jealous, obsessive, and accusatory? Is this an aspect of his personality? Is jealousy one of his distinctive individual characteristics? Perhaps, although perhaps not—the information so far is insufficient, and one needs to look further.

Suppose that the wife frequently comes in late or stays out all night, gives the bewildered husband little account of her whereabouts, takes calls from unidentified persons, refuses to answer his questions, and complains that he is a suspicious fool and should take care of his own business instead of hers. Here the situation itself provides sufficient account of the jealousy. The wife's actions are suspicious, and that gives the husband grounds for suspicion and good reason to question her and to seek answers. The husband's behavior here gives little important information about his inclinations toward jealousy, other than that he acts in usual and expectable ways in these particularly difficult circumstances. Indeed in such circumstances, if he were not suspicious then that in itself would call for some special explanation.

Suppose on the other hand that there are little or no grounds for suspicion because the wife's actions are reasonable ones which can easily be accounted for in ways that do not indicate unfaithfulness or deceit. Yet the husband treats every minor misdemeanor as proof of major wrongdoing, interrogates rashly and without plausible evidence, and discredits or ignores the answers he is given. Here, the jealousy must be accounted for by the individual characteristics of the husband. Suspiciousness, jealousy, and antagonism are individual personality characteristics of this man. It is because they are unusual or excessive, and not merely expectable from the circumstances, that the suspiciousness and accusation reveal distinctive individual personality characteristics. Individual characteristics are seen not straightforwardly from patterns of actions but are estimated from patterns in the light of the existing circumstances, relationships, and so on.

Separating situational and personality contributions is essential in assessment and intervention. The jealous husband would have problems were his wife cheating on him and he would have problems were it strictly his imagination—but he would not have the *same* problems. Appropriate therapeutic intervention addresses the pertinent contributing factors.

A person's behavioral patterns are understandable here from his situation and his individual characteristics; thus, the following behavior explanation formula:

$$B = f(S \text{ and } IC), \text{ or}$$
*B*ehavior is a function of *S*ituations and *I*ndividual *C*haracteristics.

An expansion of this formula in Figure 8 shows the range of concepts included in each category. The first column in Figure 8 is behavior in the broadest sense; this includes overt actions, as well as the observations and experience which accompany those actions. Taken together, sequences and patterns of actions along with the attendant experiences and satisfactions comprise the various *ways of life* that one might lead. It is thus single acts and, further, the form, quality, and way of life one leads which are understandable from one's situations and individual characteristics.

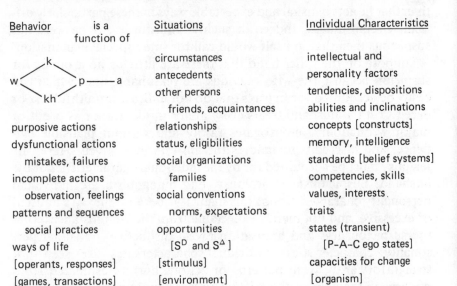

Behavior is a function of	Situations	Individual Characteristics
(diagram: w, k, kh, p, a)	circumstances	intellectual and
	antecedents	personality factors
	other persons	tendencies, dispositions
	friends, acquaintances	abilities and inclinations
purposive actions	relationships	concepts [constructs]
dysfunctional actions	status, eligibilities	memory, intelligence
mistakes, failures	social organizations	standards [belief systems]
incomplete actions	families	competencies, skills
observation, feelings	social conventions	values, interests
patterns and sequences	norms, expectations	traits
social practices	opportunities	states (transient)
ways of life	$[S^D \text{ and } S^\Delta]$	[P-A-C ego states]
[operants, responses]	[stimulus]	capacities for change
[games, transactions]	[environment]	[organism]

Figure 8.   Facets of behaviors, situations, and individual characteristics.

In the previous illustration, the husband sees his wife's actions as suspicious, feels hurt and angry, thinks obsessively about her conduct, and acts to accuse her of infidelity. It is the entire behavioral sequence of observation, emotion and motivation, action and outcome which is understandable from situational and individual factors. What he sees is understandable from his wife's actions and from what he is capable of seeing; what he feels is understandable from what he sees and from his standards and attitudes toward such things; what he does is understandable from his observations, from his feelings and motivations, and from the available opportunities.

Situations

A person's situation is everything in the real world which pertains, or which might or should pertain, to that person's actions. The term "circumstances" is closely synonymous with situation. A wide range of concepts is used to identify various facets of situations.

Your situation might include anything which exists or occurs around you. It includes physical objects and also, and perhaps most important, other persons and the actions of other persons. Other persons, on the basis of their relationships to you, are identified as your friends, adversaries, intimates, acquaintances, lover(s), family (spouse, parents, children), and so on. On the basis of such relationships, you have complementary status and social position, so that you are identified and treated as a friend, adversary, intimate, and so on in particular relationships. Networks of such relationships comprise groupings such as families, communities, and other forms of social organizations. Social groups have norms and expectations of what persons are to do. Situations involve pressures, injunctions, supports, and opportunities to do some things and not others. All these are situational characteristics in that they are aspects of the world which pertain to a person's behavior.

Note that a person's status in a situation is included here as an aspect of that situation, and not as an individual personality characteristic. One may identify with his status, and some status seems to follow you around from situation to situation. But in the final analysis, it is the social situation which confers status and which can take it away. Status concepts are ways of talking about aspects of social relationships. For instance, to be in a school situation in which you have many friends is to have the status 'popular" in that school. The status "popular" is clearly conferred by those friendships and is not easily transferable to a rival school in which cliques have already formed.

Several concepts from familiar theories refer to aspects of situations. The term "stimuli" from the experimental and behavioristic literature officially signifies the physically measurable aspects of a situation, but the term as commonly used refers to unmeasurable aspects as well. The term "environment" introduced from biology may refer similarly to any aspect of a situation. Object relations uses the term "object" to refer to another person.

"Antecedents" in behavioral formulations are events which evoke an action. General adversities are termed "unconditioned aversive stimuli" in behaviorism and "activating events" in the rational-emotive ABC formulation. "Discriminative stimuli (S^D and S^Δ)" in operant conditioning signify whether an opportunity exists: S^D translates to ordinary language as "opportunity" or "indicator of an opportunity," and S^Δ means "no opportunity." Various concepts and terms from familiar theoretical formulations are thus identifiable as facets of situations.

Individual Characteristics

Individual characteristics are distinctive inclinations and abilities to see, to evaluate, and to act in particular ways; these include the range of intellectual and personality characteristics. Individual characteristics concepts refer to inclinations and abilities, and are *not* implicit or overt references to physiological structures and processes.

One's *concepts* are the distinctions one uses to observe and structure his world. "Constructs" from personal construct theory refer to the individual's concepts. An individual retains information and misinformation which he can recall and apply; intelligence is the ability to figure things out.

One's *standards* and related beliefs are value-laden distinctions, and correspond to the ways one sees and evaluates things on a good-bad dimension. Persons have standards of right and wrong, and beliefs that some things are right and good while other things are wrong and awful. The evaluations one makes serve as the most reliable indication of his standards and beliefs.

Similar concepts are included in several orientations. "Belief systems" in Ellis's rational-emotive formulation are used to evaluate adversities: someone with "rational beliefs" evaluates adversities as tolerable and manageable; someone with "irrational beliefs" sees them as intolerable and catastrophic. "Personal injunctions" in transactional analysis are beliefs that particular actions are not permitted and should not be done. Self-concept problems in client-centered formulations usually involve harsh personal standards by which one evaluates oneself as wrong and bad. In behaviorism, "conditioned aversive stimuli" are conditions which a particular individual sees as threatening and stressful: direct references to standards and beliefs are omitted, but the issues are covered nonetheless by these supposedly more objective equivalents. From separate orientations, these concepts cover similar tendencies to evaluate things as intolerable, not permissible, unacceptable, aversive, or otherwise unpleasant and wrong.

Traits are tendencies to act in particular ways across situations. "Probabilities" and "frequencies" refer to the same things for the behaviorist: where we would ordinarily say a child tends to be disruptive or simply *is* disruptive, a behaviorist covers the same ground by saying that he emits a high frequency of disruptive behaviors. Tendencies to involve oneself in particular patterns are termed "scripts" in transactional analysis.

Values and *interests* are what matters. These are one's priorities—what one would be motivated to accomplish, everything else being equal. Among its many meanings, the term "reinforcer" in behaviorism refers to that which an individual values and is interested in striving to achieve.

Competencies include one's concepts, memory, and intelligence, which are cognitive abilities, and also *skills,* which are performance abilities. "Behavioral repertoires" in behaviorism correspond to skills—what one is competent to do. These factors appear directly as the "know-how" aspect of behavior.

States are fluctuations in individual tendencies: in a particular state, a person tends to respond somewhat differently from the ways in which he would respond if not in that state. While angry or exhausted, one has tendencies that one does not have when calm or rested. States might involve emotions (angry, afraid), moods (excited), attitudes (intrigued), or energy level (alert, exhausted). The "hours of food deprivation" parameter in operant conditioning indicates a state of hunger in which the animal is motivated to strive for food. "Parent, adult, and child (P–A–C)" ego states in transactional analysis indicate fluctuating tendencies to act in ways loosely similar to parents, adults, and children. The critical parent state indicates a critical attitude, the nurturing parent state, a supportive attitude; the adult state, thoughtfulness; the free child state is a playful mood, and the adapted child state is a compliant or rebellious stance toward authority. Transactional analysis is wedded to categorizing actions by their origins in one or another of these ego states.

In this manner, concepts from various theories are easily organized and blended into our ordinary language concepts of individual characteristics.

Behavior = f(Situations and Individual Characteristics)

Behavior is understood from situations and individual characteristics; thus, the behavioral explanation formula $B = f(S \text{ and } IC)$. The three factors are conceptually related, in that any two of them can be used to estimate the third—as in geometry when two angles of a triangle are given, the third can be calculated. Each factor is logically understandable from the other two: behavior from situations and individual characteristics; individual characteristics from behavior, with allowances made for the contribution of the situations; and situations themselves from the persons' reaction, with allowances made for their distinctive individual characteristics.

The complementary categories of situations and individual characteristics include all present psychological factors which contribute to behavior, for the rule here is that anything that does contribute must be placed in one or the other of these two categories. The formula is thus tautological, and it is this obvious and nonfalsifiable quality which makes it suitable as a conceptual tool to structure empirical observations.

Specific behaviors, situations, and individual characteristics go together in ways that should make sense. In our everyday perceptions, we rely on configurations of these three factors to see what is going on. Observations of any two of the factors provide a cross-check for our observation or estimate of the third because, if they do not go together properly, then an error has been made in one or more of the observations. We may use estimates of any two of the factors to evaluate and improve our estimates of the third. The logical relatedness of these factors is especially important in clinical practice, where we must make observations and estimates based on sometimes less than adequate information. We can cross-check our observations against other observations and see if things add up properly.

The use of situations and individual characteristics to understand behavior is a commonsense idea, and is adapted into several familiar formulations. In Lewin's field theory, behavior is a function of the person and the environment. In S–O–R behavior theory, the *S*timulus acts through the *O*rganism to elicit a *R*esponse. In Ellis's rational-emotive ABC formulation, *A*ctivating events are interpreted by *B*elief systems to yield emotional *C*onsequences. S–O–R behaviorism weights the situation, which acts through the individual to yield behavior, while the rational-emotive formulation weights the beliefs of the individual, which interpret the situation. Each formula has its own unique qualities, but the everyday concept of behavior as understandable from situational and individual characteristics runs through all of them.

The familiar orientations can be classified and rated on their management of each of these three factors. Analytic orientations tend to overlook situational contributions, while family systems formulations in contrast are strong on relationship and social position factors but tend to ignore individual personality characteristics. The reputation which behaviorists have for ignoring individual personality factors is unwarranted, since individual differences factors are camouflaged but included nonetheless in the behaviorists' own unique concepts and terms.

Persons

Persons are extremely complex beings, and a rich variety of concepts is available to characterize what may be interesting and important about particular persons. The concepts used in ordinary language and also in psychological and social sciences to characterize persons can be seen to fall easily into the three categories of behavioral, social-situational, and individual personality characteristics outlined here. Persons engage in patterns of actions, and are identified and characterized by what they see and do in their lives and, thus, by their behavioral characteristics. Persons live and act in networks of social relationships, and are characterized by their noteworthy status or positions in these social relationships and, thus, by their situational characteristics. Persons also have distinctive individual inclinations and abilities, and are characterized by their noteworthy intellectual and personality characteristics.

For instance, we could describe Joanie Caucus as one who spends her days settling squabbles (behaviors), as one who has a job as a day-care mother (status and social position), and as one who values teaching children to treat each other fairly (individual characteristics). Each of these says something about Joanie and identifies her as who she is. Similarly, we could describe the jealous husband as one who interrogates his wife continually (behaviors), as the husband of a long-suffering but quite faithful woman (status and marital situation), and as one who has a suspicious bent (individual characteristics).

Through descriptions from one or more of these three categories, we identify and communicate what is noteworthy about particular persons. Persons are also identified by their physical appearances; therefore, physical characteristics are included as a fourth attribute of persons.

ACQUISITION OF PERSONAL CHARACTERISTICS

Our third order of explanation involves the ways by which present situations and individual characteristics were acquired. How did the circumstances and relationships in which the person is involved come about, and how did he acquire the particular individual characteristics that he has? How, in other words, did he get to be where he is, and how did he get to be who he is? We look to past occurrences to answer these questions.

Social Transitions

Major changes in one's circumstances, relationships, and status are commonly referred to as *transitions*. Such transitions include any form of social inclusion, promotion, accreditation, and gain, or social exclusion, demotion, degradation, and loss. Familiar examples of social transitions are leaving home, graduating, finding a job or losing one, making friends or enemies, gaining recognition or losing favor, breaking up with a sweetheart, getting married, becoming a parent, retiring, and so on. Such changes may be instigated by one's own actions, but they also involve the attitudes and actions of other persons.

If the wife were indeed unfaithful, as the husband so strongly suspects, then we might ask how he became involved in that sort of marriage. Perhaps as a youngster he was introverted and inexperienced. A young girl wanted to get away from home and grabbed on to him with all the affection one might have for a "get out of jail free" card. He, in his insecurity and naiveté, missed the obvious expediency and had barely adjusted to marriage by the time she had her sights set on greener pastures. (To hear his mother, it would seem that all mothers' sons are lost to marriage in just this manner. Consider this nonetheless as merely one of many possibilities.)

On the other hand, perhaps they were well suited for each other in their early relationship, but he was committed to his work and insensitive to her concerns and feelings, and would not involve himself in the intimacies which should be expected in a marriage. He ignored or misunderstood her attempts to talk about the problem, and out of loneliness and boredom, she turned to another man. Thus he finds himself very much on the outside.

Perhaps he was committed to a liberal ideology that opposes the restrictiveness and lack of freedom of marriage. He argued his wife into it, and together they embarked on an open marriage in which each of them would be allowed to have intimacies with others outside of the marriage. It sounded free and exciting in principle, but now that it is really happening things are frighteningly out of control. The husband has feelings that he had not expected and finds the situation intolerable.

Any number of other explanations are also possible, of course, for there are countless ways one gets involved in particular situations: the actual explanations must be based on observation and analysis of the case at hand. These explanations are essentially social histories which should take into account the sequences of behavioral, situational, and individual factors by which the situation came about. The explanation of how this man got involved with an unfaithful wife might say something about the choices he makes, about his incompatibilities with this particular woman, or perhaps about the problems of choosing a mate early in life and on the basis of necessarily limited information. An explanation of how current relationships were acquired might be used to better understand the natures of the persons involved. Problem situations are the offspring of limited vision and maladaptive inclinations, of the inconsiderateness or ill will of others, and also of unfortunate and sometimes unavoidable happenstance.

Some orientations suggest more general explanations. Analytic and related orientations focus on the needs being fulfilled through messy relationships, implying that the person has unconscious motivations to be involved in such problems. Transactional analysis emphasizes "scripts," which are plans for one's life, and holds that messy situations occur because one follows a script to bring them about. Social transitions are dealt with at considerable length in sociology and anthropology, and to lesser extent, in social psychology and in relationship and family approaches to psychotherapy.

Learning and Maturation

Individual characteristics are acquired through *learning* and through a broad wastebasket category which includes maturation and "other than learning" factors.

Were the wife faithful but the husband characteristically jealous, then we might ask how he acquired that individual personality characteristic. Perhaps in a first marriage he was secure and settled but his wife was not, and she played the field continually for the duration of their marriage. Unable to forgive or forget, he became embittered toward women and hardened himself against ever caring enough to be vulnerable. So he carries his hurt and rage over to his present wife and now looks for betrayal.

On the other hand, perhaps as a youngster his mother showered him with attention and special considerations but was cold and embittered toward his father, so that he came to see affection from a woman as something given to a child but not to a man. These views render him unable as a man to accept love and nurturance from a woman, for a woman's love makes him feel small and dependent. In the marriage, he has expected his wife to be weaker and to look up to him, which has not always been possible since she is herself a competent and successful person and he, because of human limitations, is not always a hero. He has thus been unable to accept the love and reassurance which she gives, and unable also to gain reassurance through his ideal of masculine superiority. He has become easily annoyed at his wife, feeling she does not respect and love him, and his annoyance has made matters worse, for the marriage suffers by comparison to his wife's outside friendships. In this manner he has become increasingly insecure, suspicious, and jealous, trapped not by his wife but by his own misconceptions.

Perhaps he became infatuated with his secretary, and has felt guilty about it and troubled that his wife might find out. If his wife were also interested in somebody else, then that would be equitable and would allay his guilt; he fantasizes that she might be interested, and finds himself both intrigued and aroused by the thought, but also insecure and angry that she would do such a thing. The imaginings come to seem too real; he becomes unreasonably suspicious of his wife and accuses her of wanting other men.

There are any number of ways one can become overly suspicious and jealous, just as there are any number of ways one can acquire any of a range of other distinctive individual characteristics. If someone has a given personality characteristic, he has acquired it in one of the ways in which it can be acquired, but not necessarily in the same way it might have been acquired by someone else. We are cautioned, therefore, against expecting any single generalization or theory to provide a reliable account of how individual characteristics are acquired. We must observe and investigate, for adequate understanding is based on adequate observation of the particular case at hand.

In clinical practice the issue is not so much how the person acquired a particular characteristic, but rather how he can alter or rearrange troublesome tendencies and acquire more constructive ones. The means by which present characteristics were acquired may be of some importance nonetheless, for they may give some leads to the means by which current changes may be made and more beneficial characteristics acquired. Learning occurs through what one sees and does, and is thus an outcome of one's behaviors. One learns new inclinations and abilities through observations and practice. The category of learning includes insight and conditioning, training and socialization, learning through observation and learning by participation, study (intended learning) and unplanned everyday learning, and so on.

Some generalizations of how learning occurs are included in most major theories of behavior, personality, psychopathology and psychotherapy. Behavioral orientations emphasize "conditioning," which refers (as in ordinary language) to learning that occurs through continuing and often wearisome repetitions. In operant conditioning, "reinforcement"—the achievement of something one wants—is a quite obvious way of learning which acts get you what you want. "Extinction"—the failure to gain what you want—is a way of learning which acts are ineffective. The term "modeling" refers to teaching by example.

Several formulations see adversities as the means by which one learns troublesome tendencies. In behavioral orientations, fears of things are learned from repeated pairings of those things with other things which are themselves naturally frightening. Being subject to "parental injunctions" in transactional analysis leads youngsters to acquire their own restrictive personal injunctions, from which they construct scripts. In client-centered formulations, the "conditions of worth" by which one is judged lead youngsters to judge aspects of themselves as wrong and unacceptable, to deny those aspects, and by so doing to invite further problems.

Several orientations—notably analytic, dynamic, and object-relations—suggest that the early years are of more importance in acquiring personality characteristics, while others, most notably behavioral orientations, emphasize that learning continues to change individual characteristics throughout life. An excellent review of the research by Kagan et al. (1978) suggests that the importance of infancy and early childhood has been overestimated, and that later childhood and adolescent experiences are more important in personality development. Some suggest that the young adult years may be the most important. In any case, we do not have to focus on any single age but should keep our eyes open to influences which occur at whatever ages.

Processes other than Learning. Individual characteristics are acquired by processes other than learning, notably by maturation, by changes generally explained physiologically, and also by transient state changes. Maturation includes increases in intellectual abilities and personal maturity as one grows up, sexual maturation, and so on. Those changes attributable directly to physiological factors include changes in temperament from poor nutrition, senility, or other types of brain impairment, and any of the range of changes caused by the actions of various psychotropic medications. Examples of state changes include becoming confused from too little sleep or becoming immobilized by fear. While some of these changes are explained by physiological factors, it is the changes themselves, and not the physiological explanations, which belong in our present categorization of psychological explanations.

The various explanations here are obviously quite diverse, for the only real requirement for placing intellectual and personality changes in this "other than learning" wastebasket is that they cannot be attributed to learning.

THE STRUCTURE OF PSYCHOLOGICAL EXPLANATION

Three orders of explanation have been surveyed:

1. Further description of the action itself, including motivations, understandings, competencies, aims, and so on;
2. Descriptions of the situation and individual characteristics which contributed to the action; and
3. Descriptions of the ways in which the situation and individual characteristics were acquired.

The categorization scheme is outlined in Figure 9. Behavior is thus explained by situations and individual characteristics, which in turn are explained by how they were acquired. The outline includes present factors (behavior, situations, and individual characteristics) and past factors (social transitions, and learning and maturation). The outline is not itself an explanation for behavior, but rather a way of organizing the various sorts of explanations. The scheme has been constructed to cover the entire range of what qualifies as psychological explanation. Answers to the question, Why did he do that? are given through descriptions of factors in one or more of these categories.

Plausible explanations from each category can be collected together in a single illustration. Suppose a young woman said "No!," and we wish to explain why. It is a simple enough behavior, involving as it does only one word, and only one syllable at that. But no behavior is necessarily that simple, and this one should do for an illustration. Look first to the behavior itself: Perhaps she said no because she misunderstood the man's intentions, in order to get out of a commitment, or in order to pay him back in spades for making her so insecure. Look next to the situation or individual characteristics which make the

Figure 9.   Explanations of behavior.

behavior understandable: she said no to his invitation because he called so late in the week or because he had been showing interest in another girl; and she said no because she is used to having her own way all the time and has a spiteful streak when someone crosses her. Look finally to the way the situation and individual characteristics were acquired: she was in this mess with him because she had been cold and aloof, and had taken him for granted; and she is tempermental because she was ignored while growing up, but she could get what she wanted by throwing a scene and was never taught to compromise. We get a good explanation here of the whys of the woman's behavior.

The scheme categorizes everyday psychological explanations as well as behavioral and social sciences explanations. Several key concepts from familiar theoretical formulations have been shown to fit easily into our common language categories, and other concepts could be shown to fit in much the same manner. Some of these concepts are roughly equivalent to ordinary language concepts and can be easily translated into ordinary language. Other concepts are not directly translatable, but can be better understood and organized by the common language system. The categorization system is argued to be complete not because every conceivable explanation has been shown to fit, but rather on the basis of logical considerations. All psychological explanations of behavior fit logically into one or more of these broad categories.

These are explanations of behavior, and some qualify also as *causes*. In everyday conversation, people speak about what causes you to feel or act the way you do, or the cause of your problems, but causes and causal language must be understood as shorthand. Every behavioral event is understandable from several contributing factors, and each of those factors is understandable in turn from numerous other contributing factors. Thus, things are understandable from configurations and sequences of contributing factors. But not all such contributing factors can be noted, and mentioning one or two of them usually provides enough information to suit one's purposes. What people refer to as "causes" then are contributing factors which have particular relevance to their purposes. See "cause" as shorthand for "noteworthy contributing factor."

The various psychological theories deal with particular aspects from one or more of these explanatory categories and frequently broaden them into purportedly general explanations of human behavior. These theories can be compared and contrasted on the basis of which aspects they focus on and which they ignore.

There are domains of explanation outside the strictly psychological explanations outlined here, including physiological explanations and, in obvious contrast, theological and mystical explanations. Physiological explanations, such as androgens, endorphins, lithium levels, or left- or right-hemisphere brain functions, are descriptions of physiological entities and processes. Theological explanations, such as God's will or God's plan, a guardian angel or spirit guide, or God-given free will, are portrayals of a higher order or meaning of life or of agents in another realm. Physiological explanations enjoy a widespread respectability, while theological and mystical explanations are often considered speculative and unconfirmable. The strictly psychological concepts outlined here do not compete with physiological or other explanations of human actions, but are expected to complement and coordinate with them.

This system of concepts has a breadth and completeness which qualifies it as a single system through which we might try to understand the range of concerns in the behavioral and social sciences. It thus meets the initial requirements for a comprehensive eclectic framework. We might need further observations and better analysis to explain something, and we might need more effective interventions. What we do not need is to try to abandon the structure of our familiar, ordinary language concepts.

4

Psychopathology and Psychotherapy

Our concepts of human action provide the framework for our concepts of psychopathology and psychotherapy.

PSYCHOPATHOLOGY

What is it that is wrong with persons, that is treated through psychotherapy? Everyone has some grasp of the concept of psychological problems—or psychopathology—although it may be difficult to articulate. The various names for such problems include maladjustment, problems in living, instability or emotional instability, mental disorder and—in its more serious form—mental illness or insanity. Theories of psychopathology focus variously on underlying pathogens, on mental or emotional states, on overt behaviors, on families, or on larger social organizations. Analytic and dynamic orientations see the pathology not in overt actions but in underlying inner conflicts which are viewed as causes of the manifest symptoms. Behavioral orientations see pathology in the observable behaviors themselves. Family systems orientations see the pathology not in the individual or in his behavior, but in family relationships which are viewed as the cause of individual symptoms. These are all related to each other in that they are theories of the same thing—psychopathology. An explicit concept of psychopathology is necessary in order to clarify the essential relatedness of these viewpoints.

Disorders are best understood via their relation to proper functioning, and so too with mental disorders. A range of social practices or ways of life is generally available to persons: full participation in a way of life includes the activities and the meaning and satisfaction as well. A healthy person is one who is able to participate and find meaning in available social practices; an unhealthy person, by contrast, is one who is impeded in his ability to do so. Thus, the concept of mental disorder: *psychopathology is a significant restriction in one's ability to participate fully in available social practices* (cf. Ossorio, 1983).

The concept of restriction in abilities is seen as well with physiological or medical illnesses. One might easily imagine two persons having the same strain of virus, with one person feeling ill and restricted to bed rest, and the second person feeling well and continuing normal daily activities; the effects of a virus are not the same for different people and under different conditions. In the first case the virus is a pathogen—a disease—while in the second case it is merely an innocuous foreign agent. In physiology as in psychology, a condition *qualifies* as a form of pathology to the extent that it impedes healthy functioning. In psychology we are mainly concerned not with physiological conditions but with behavioral, social, and personality factors which impede healthy participation.

Consider excessive alcohol consumption as a common dysfunctional behavior pattern. One might easily imagine two persons who drink the same amount but who are affected differently by it. One of them misses work and is about to get fired, has little personal involvement with his wife, family, or former friends, and lies to himself and others to cover the extent of his drinking. The second man, in contrast, manages his job well, is personable and conscientious, enjoys family and friends, and jokes good naturedly about the excessiveness of his drinking. The first person, all would agree, is an alcoholic, and has disabling mental or emotional problems. The second man, in contrast, should not be considered to have serious mental or emotional problems, in that he is able to participate in his version of what appears to be a meaningful and enjoyable way of life. It is thus the limitations imposed by alcohol, rather than the amount one consumes, which qualify alcohol consumption as a common form of psychopathology.

Similarly, unresolved insecurities and resentments toward one's mother and father may impede one's abilities to manage present relationships with persons in authority, and so qualify as causes of present psychological problems. Similar resentments which do not impede present relationships are of less importance and would not qualify as psychopathology. The same principle applies in family relationships. Dysfunctional families may undermine and confuse, and bring forth the worst in individual family members. To the extent that they so impede healthy participation, families too are rightly seen as causes of psychopathology.

Any factors which restrict participation might qualify as causes of psychopathology. Causes thus might be situational or personality factors, or the experiences and actions which are understandable from, and in turn generate, such problem factors. The past conditions by which such factors were acquired might also be included as causes. The various theories of psychopathology stake out positions on which such factors are most important.

Psychological and emotional problems are understood from situational and individual characteristics in the same way that anything one does is so understood. Situational and individual factors are primary means of understanding and categorizing adjustment problems, and of understanding and organizing intervention techniques which address such problems. These factors are therefore included in our concept of psychopathology. Situations are included because particular situations introduce stresses which overtax existing capabilities and so cause psychological problems. Individual characteristics are included because troubled individuals are often especially weak in their abilities to manage a wide range of situations.

Matches or mismatches between situations and individual characteristics are also important. Individuals have their own unique needs and inclinations which make them well suited to some situations and not to others. One individual may thrive on structure and be confused and miserable without it; another may thrive on independence and be stifled by structure; and the very same two individuals who were so filled with love and optimism living together as singles may be trapped and miserable together as marrieds. We need to weigh both factors, and the matches or mismatches between the factors. Problems arise from stressful situations which overtax otherwise adequate abilities, from general inabilities to manage much of anything at all, and from unfortunate mismatches between one's circumstances and one's individual inclinations or abilities.

Experiences and actions, social relationships, and personality characteristics generally interweave in any adequate case analysis, and should be seen as complementary rather than as competing explanations of psychopathology. It is not experiences versus actions, or social relationships versus personality which is "the cause" of psychopathology. Rather, it is configurations and patterns of these factors which cause psychopathology: We understand the problems as we weigh the contributions of such factors and see the necessary interconnectedness among them.

Present and past contributing factors must be clearly separated. Present contributing factors may be explained by factors in the immediate past, and those explained by factors further in the past, and so on in endless sequence: each present contributing factor has a continuing chain of past factors which contributed to bring it about. Behavior is understood from situations and individual characteristics, and these in turn from the means by which they came about, and these in turn from the means by which they came about, and so on. Present relationships, personality characteristics, and consequent experiences and actions are the immediate causes of psychological problems; past occurrences were the causes then of these present causes.

A person's participation is seen as restricted by comparison to some appropriate, healthy, or even exceptional alternatives. We see inabilities by comparing what the person actually does with what one might do instead which would be more adaptive. In clinical assessment, it is important to understand what might be appropriate or healthy ways of managing existing situations and to see the occurring patterns as indications of an inability to respond in any of those healthy ways.

Awareness of an individual's inabilities also makes existing unconstructive patterns more understandable. When a situation calls for a person to do something he is unable to do, then he will do something he can do. Inappropriate and problematic actions are necessarily indications of an inability to act in a more adaptive and fulfilling manner.

Consider a woman who is taken advantage of, and mistreated by, family and friends, and who by her passivity allows the mistreatment to continue. Such a person might in turn lose confidence in herself and feel she is a worthless nobody, or she might find self-righteous satisfaction in being morally better than those who mistreat her and thus maintain a secret sense of superiority. She might become resentful, undermine and manipulate others to get her way, and so further spoil her social relationships; or she might have explosive outbursts of anger and become afraid that she is losing control of herself. She might hold others responsible for her life and so avoid taking responsibility herself. She might withdraw from close relationships to avoid the anguish they entail. Such patterns are all understandable manifestations of the mistreatment this woman is unable to stand up against. They are all related here, in that they are all manifestations of the same restricted ability to make the necessary stands and so redress the mistreatment. An assessment of this case might include any of the existing behavioral, social, and personality factors. One should surely mention what this woman is unable to do which, if she could do, would solve the existing problems. Most fundamentally, she is unable to make stands, and anything which addresses that inability would improve the surrounding manifestations of the problem.

Thus, good clinical analysis looks at what one is doing which contributes to the problems, and at the situational and individual characteristics which make what one is doing understandable. It also looks at what the person might be doing instead which would alleviate the problems, at the situational and individual changes which would enable him to do that, and at the ways in which we might bring those changes about. The objective of therapy then is to bridge the gap to enable the person to do that which would solve the problems.

The same factors which are manifestations of the problem may also be additional contributing factors which further augment the problem. If the mistreatment causes the woman to feel she is a worthless nobody or to construct a secret superiority to those who mistreat her, then these contribute in turn in her continuing passivity and must be addressed in an attempt to promote assertiveness. She becomes assertive as she gains some confidence in herself, sees that she has the right to make stands, and chooses the challenges of confrontations over the familiar safety of resenting those who take advantage of her. When her assertive stands are successful, her rights become established, her social relationships improve, and her confidence in herself increases, thus further altering the original pattern. In turn, these more constructive alternatives make it easier to relinquish the resentments and other satisfactions of the passive victim position and to continue asserting herself.

Mental, emotional and behavioral, and social and personality factors are thus seen as causes, as consequent manifestations, and from there as further causes of restricted abilities to participate. It is through the identification and alleviation of factors which are causes that one alleviates major restrictions in abilities to participate.

Social practices involve sequences and patterns of actions, and an inability to do any of the necessary particulars may thus restrict participation in the entire practice. On a specific level, psychopathology is a restriction in one's ability to engage in those actions necessary to available social practices. Major restrictions in functioning may be due to circumscribed failures and limitations, and in such cases alleviating seemingly minor inabilities may have major constructive benefits to a person's overall well-being. In other cases the problems are broader and more embedded. In the case just described, an inability to be appropriately assertive severely impedes the woman's participation in more satisfying forms of social relationships. Better social relationships and better ways of life become available through the alleviation of such critical inabilities.

The concept of psychopathology involves *significant* restrictions in abilities. We all have limitations, of course, for everyone has some areas in which he or she is less than adequate and more limited than many others. These various psychological limitations do not thereby qualify as psychopathology, however, in so far as their impact remains manageable. It is only when personal limitations result in a major inability to participate that the condition qualifies as psychopathology.

Clinical cases involve complex and often unique configurations of mental and behavioral, social, and personality patterns. Traditional diagnostic taxonomies are generally considered to be crude and overinclusive categorizations, and more important, to be oftentimes irrelevant as a basis for psychotherapeutic interventions. Our alternative here is the use of individual case formulations which attempt to grasp the essentials of a particular case so as to provide a basis for therapeutic treatment. The emphasis here is not on any particular theory of psychopathology, but rather on the concepts, principles, and construction of individual case formulations.

PSYCHOTHERAPY

A definition of psychotherapy follows directly from our concept of psychopathology as restrictions in abilities: *Psychotherapy is an attempt to alleviate restrictions in one's abilities to participate in meaningful and satisfying ways of life.* The cornerstone of the definition is in the objectives and purpose. One might also mention that psychotherapy involves a relationship between therapist and client, that the client mentions problems and the therapist gives interpretations and suggestions, and so on. Our concept is anchored here by its objectives and purpose, and the various particulars follow as the means to that purpose.

Psychotherapy is an *attempt* to alleviate restrictions, for we intervene in order to accomplish the aims and objectives but there is no guarantee each time that any intervention will be successful. The practice must be anchored by its aims and objectives because, since particular techniques and procedures are not always effective, they are unsuitable therefore as defining attributes.

Psychotherapy is conceived of broadly enough here to include any psychological interventions which are conducted to gain therapeutic changes. It includes methods traditionally considered verbal approaches and those considered behavioral approaches. The requirement is that interventions are done in order to redress limitations in abilities to participate.

The concepts of behavior, situations, and individual characteristics so important in understanding psychopathology are likewise important in its treatment. One who seeks therapy generally does so because he is living a life in which he is dissatisfied and because he is unable on his own to alter it for the better. As ways of life are generated from situations and individual characteristics, so too are changes in ways of life brought about through changes in these factors. Major changes are attained usually through combinations and sequences of changes in behaviors, circumstances, and personality characteristics. Entering psychotherapy, for instance, is itself a change in one's circumstances, for it introduces a new and important relationship, gives one a place or status within that relationship, and subjects one to the various influences of the therapeutic endeavor. The process of psychotherapy changes one's individual characteristics, for one acquires new ways of seeing things and acting which are carried into other areas of his life. Changes in one's actions, in turn, generate further changes in his relationships as others come to see him in new ways and treat him differently. These changes, in turn, improve one's confidence and lead to further changes in one's own attitudes and inclinations, and so the process continues.

A program of assertiveness training to alter passivity might convince the client that he does have rights; challenge the attitudes which contribute to passivity, including his tendency to blame others whenever things go wrong; show how assertive responses can solve his problems; introduce and illustrate appropriate responses, and have the client practice them; and provide social support for his efforts in order to improve his confidence. The immediate objective is to increase his inclinations and abilities to act assertively. The client may be extremely apprehensive during his initial assertive responses, but by acting assertively, he may establish his rights, and improve his status and position in social relationships. In turn, improvements in relationships should improve confidence and outlook, and provide a friendlier atmosphere in which to live. Here, changes in individual characteristics, actions, and social relationships go hand in hand.

Some interventions work by changing attitudes and abilities so that the client more easily adapts to existing circumstances. Others work by changing directly the circumstances the individual faces: an obnoxious youngster might be treated through consultation with his parents to teach them to be stricter and more consistent, so that the youngster faces fewer opportunities to profit by misbehavior and better benefits for cooperation.

In marital and family sessions, there are opportunities to directly affect the attitudes of each individual and the relationships other family members have toward that individual. The opportunity to generate complementary changes in both personality characteristics and relationships is one of the major benefits of marital and family sessions.

Several familiar orientations might be loosely characterized by their attempts to change primarily one or the other of these complementary factors. Those focusing on managing situations and relationships include behavior modification and family systems orientations; those emphasizing individual personality changes include psychoanalytic, psychodynamic, object relations, client-centered, and Gestalt approaches. As eclectics we observe and weigh both situational and personality aspects of client problems, and are free to draw upon insights and techniques from any of the various orientations as we see fit.

The focus here is on changing present factors, and the role of the past should be mentioned. The past is connected logically to situations and individual characteristics since these were acquired through past experiences. However, the constraints the past places on present options are too easily overestimated. Clients sometimes ask: "Since the way I am is caused by my past, and I cannot alter my past, then how can I expect to change?" Note that the question leaves out the important intermediate concept of individual characteristics and goes directly from past learning to current behavior. A good answer involves reintroducing individual characteristics; for example, we might say: "What you have learned from the past are ways of seeing and reacting to things, which are essentially habits. The habits exist not in your past but in your present, and can be changed. Change the habits, and the spell of your past is broken."

Only present contributing factors are subject to change, and therapeutic improvements occur through changes in factors which are in the present entirely and not in the past. We can change someone's memories of past experiences and we can change the significance he gives to those experiences, but the past itself is completed and immutable, and it cannot be changed. The logic of this point need not be taken as a prejudice against talking about the past. We might investigate the past in order to make better sense of existing problems and to help the client restructure his (present) understanding of himself and of his relationships. Investigation of the past is thus a means to understand or try to change present viewpoints, but it is not a logical requirement for therapeutic changes and should not be seen as a necessary objective in and of itself.

Procedural Guidelines

Some aspects of therapeutic interventions are specific to each individual client, and other aspects are more generally important in any therapeutic situation. The specific ways we phrase things are usually adapted to the individual client and to the particulars of the problems, as are the ways we sequence the interventions. But everything need not be figured anew each moment with each individual case. The nature of psychotherapy is such that there are identifiable principles and objectives which are generally important across sessions, and with a wide variety of clients, as the means to attain therapeutic outcomes. These more general aspects of psychotherapy are presented in the following chapters as guidelines for therapeutic practice.

The guidelines are themselves objectives which are steps toward the overall objective of alleviating restricted abilities. As intermediate objectives, they bridge the gap between the overall objectives of therapy and the particular play-by-play interventions by which such objectives are accomplished (cf. Holmes, 1970). Particular statements are made in order to accomplish these guideline objectives, which in turn are in order to accomplish the more general overall objectives. The guidelines are prescriptive in that they are suggestions to act to attain particular outcomes and to avoid others. The guidelines are the doables and "do not-ables" of therapeutic practice.

Various familiar techniques can be seen as attempts to attain one or more of the guideline objectives, and a variety of apparently unsimilar techniques may be classified together because they are used to attain the same or similar changes. The guidelines serve in this way to organize the use of familiar techniques from separate orientations. The guidelines serve also to help generate and understand new and creative interventions, for they specify the general objectives and give leeway for us to tailor the ways we accomplish those objectives.

Each of the guidelines presented is a synthesis of the practical good sense that runs through one or more, and in some cases a majority, of the various approaches to psychotherapy. Some of the guidelines are easily seen as summary statements of the principles and objectives suggested in a great many of the familiar psychotherapy orientations. Others involve principles actually suggested in only a few orientations and implicitly accepted, ignored, or in some cases even contradicted by other orientations. Orientations might agree on the major objective but suggest their own specific techniques to implement it.

The guidelines serve to draw together and organize procedural considerations of effective eclectic practice, and each is expected to make good sense to a majority of experienced eclectics. The standard for inclusion is not that all the principles are accepted already by everybody, for that would be too limiting, but rather that when properly considered, each should be judged by most eclectics to be important to therapeutic practice.

The approach to psychotherapy suggested by these guidelines is a synthesis of various familiar elements and not necessarily original or unusual in many of its particular features. What is innovative about the approach is the means by which the techniques and procedures are selected, integrated, and shown to make sense together as coordinated elements in a coherent therapeutic practice.

Included in each of the guidelines is the rationale and some suggestions and illustrations of how one can implement the guideline. The aim is to outline guidelines for an integrated eclectic approach and to make them familiar enough to enable one to use them in actual practice. The guidelines are organized into five main categories but are not steps or phases of psychotherapy: each is to be applied across a course of standard therapeutic sessions. The following chapters outline some 25 guidelines for pragmatic practice.

SECTION II
PROCEDURAL GUIDELINES

5
The Therapeutic Relationship

The guidelines presented in this chapter are considerations for maintaining an appropriate therapeutic relationship. They include maintaining appropriate attitudes and feelings toward our clients, encouraging our clients to see us as allies and as credible, and sharing responsibility for therapeutic improvement.

1. Be on the client's side.
2. Maintain an alliance.
3. Maintain credibility.
4. Communicate an understanding of the client's position.
5. Share responsibility for improvement.

1. BE ON THE CLIENT'S SIDE

Motivations of counselor, psychotherapist

Psychotherapy is conducted for the benefit of the clients, rather than for the benefit of the therapist, the mental health agency, society, or other parties. The best interests of the client are primary and should be given priority, with few exceptions, over other considerations.

Before proceeding with issues of therapeutic interventions, the motivations involved in those interventions will be dealt with briefly. Motivational issues include our feelings, concerns, attitudes, and such toward our clients and also our commitments to our own standards of good therapy. "Be on the client's side" is a reminder of the importance of maintaining motivations to act in the best interest of the client, and of avoiding or resolving feelings and attitudes contrary to this purpose.

The motivations which therapists should have are easily stated in principle and not always so easily maintained in practice. As psychotherapists we should have feelings and attitudes of acceptance, confidence, comfortableness, compassion, concern, fair play, interest, involvement, practical optimism, respect, stability, and warmth toward our clients; we should avoid, or examine and resolve, feelings and attitudes of aloofness, anger, arrogance, boredom, condemnation, egotism, frustration, guilt, insecurity, and pity toward our clients.

The importance of the positive feelings over the negative ones should be apparent, for interventions made from the positive ones are generally better than alternative interventions made from the negative ones. When our energies are bound up with our own personal issues of anger, frustration, and insecurity, we are not free to give our attention fully to our clients. The importance of positive feelings is emphasized in client-centered, Adlerian, and reality therapy orientations, and is mentioned by other orientations as well. Client-centered therapy prescribes that we should have warmth and "unconditional positive regard" for our clients: the "unconditional" means that we should not turn foul and criticize and condemn. Psychoanalytic and psychodynamic training stresses the resolution of "countertransference" reactions, which are our generally negative or inappropriate attitudes and feelings held to be reactions to our patients' misinterpretations of us. The term "countertransference" translates into everyday language as "taking it too personally." In short, client-centered exhorts us to love our clients, and psychodynamic interprets our tendencies to hate them. These two are the flip sides of the same issue.

Although many of the more active orientations such as behavioral orientations do not emphasize the therapist's attitudes, it would be wrong to conclude that the attitudes of these practitioners are therefore more problematic. Sloane et al. (1975) found that the level of warmth and respect behavior therapists have toward their clients is as high as that of client-centered or other therapists who focus more on their relationship to their clients. My own impression, similarly, is that the more active therapists seem to be at least as warm and respectful as the less active ones. Why is it that orientations which do not emphasize their own attitudes and feelings do as well here as those who do focus on these issues?

Troublesome reactions such as anger, frustration, and insecurity are most often generated in therapists by the failures of our clients to progress in combination with insinuation, manipulation, and resistance to our interventions. It is important to realize that such reactions result from our missing the subtleties and nuances of the immediate situation, and from not understanding how to respond effectively. One who is confused and unsure of what to say is easily swayed by feelings of inadequacy, anger, boredom, competitiveness, frustration, and so on. One who sees what has to be done and involves himself in the appropriate interventions is somewhat protected against these unconstructive attitudes and feelings. We become more comfortable as we learn to effectively manage the interpersonal difficulties which would otherwise undermine, confuse, and frustrate us.

Those considerable insecurities and frustrations so common in the initial stages of psychotherapy training are too often interpreted as idiosyncratic personality issues of the trainee. As a trainee in a position of responsibility with troubled persons, your insecurities and frustrations are understandable as reactions to your situation: you are in over your head, and you know it! The main objective of supervision should be to help the trainee to understand the clients and find better ways to intervene with them. Personal feelings should be understood and acknowledged, but individual idiosyncrasies need not be a major focus unless they interfere with the trainee's abilities to learn from consultation and supervision.

Unconstructive emotions which do occur find easy expression in an unstructured situation, but are less troublesome when we have guidelines to help structure what we are to be doing and how we go about it (cf. Wachtel, 1980). The use of intervention guidelines gives us some protection therefore against the effects of unconstructive attitudes and feelings.

Suppose, for instance, that in a first interview with a young man you explore his attitude that other people are stupid, shallow, and only interested in themselves, that they are unimportant, and that he is smart to do without them. It appears to be a good first session, and you mention toward the end of the session that he seems to have dealt with important issues and that you feel he has gotten a good start with them. But the young man comments that it has been a waste of time because you did nothing for him. "What would you know about any of this?" he accuses. "You study your stupid books and get your credentials, but you cannot understand what I am going through. You are just acting interested because that is your job!" The client thus casts you as an adversary, and as an incompetent one at that. How do you respond?

This is the sort of situation which can evoke in a therapist feelings of inadequacy and frustration, as well as anger at the client for his unjust accusation and for his unwillingness to acknowledge the attempt to help. If the therapist should miss the significance of his comments or have no appropriate response, he could easily get caught in these feelings and might act on them in unconstructive ways.

The client in this case casts others as stupid and shallow, and in so doing he does not allow them to be important to him. It is a reasonable bet that he is doing the same thing here with his therapist; so we might respond as follows: "When you see others as so shallow and unimportant, you keep them from becoming too important to you. There are some good reasons for doing that: other people may indeed hurt and disappoint you. Seeing others as unimportant may be your way to keep from getting too involved with them, so that you cannot get hurt by them. You may be concerned here, as well, that if you get involved, it may come to nothing and you will feel hurt and disappointed. That is surely possible, for nothing can be really guaranteed. It seems safer to stay uninvolved with people, but at the same time we do need people, so we cannot really get away from them. It seems you are up against a hard choice here. . . ."

The response shows the sense it makes for the client to see things the way he does and so legitimizes his views. The client, by his comments, has invited an adversary relationship because he challenged and tried to discredit the therapist. It would be easy in such a situation to want to defend ourselves or to fight back. Note here that the therapist does not take his own side in the conflict, but rather takes the client's side. The therapist acts as a supporter and consultant to the client in figuring out his problems with his therapist. The need to stay unentangled with our own positions and to be genuinely committed to our clients is at the heart of the "Be on the client's side" guideline.

Knowing how to interpret and to intervene is essential, for it protects us against unconstructive emotional reactions and generates good feelings. The issue then is not merely to attend to and attempt to resolve our feelings, but also to involve ourselves in the sorts of interventions which tend to generate constructive feelings. "Be on the client's side" was suggested by Ossorio as a policy for psychotherapy.

The remaining guidelines structure our responses, involve us in constructive and often satisfying tasks, and thereby give us some protection against unconstructive attitudes and feelings. The guidelines can provide some assistance, therefore, in improving our attitudes and feelings about our clients and about doing psychotherapy.

2. MAINTAIN AN ALLIANCE

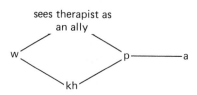

Client's perception of the therapist

sees therapist as
an ally

w   p ———— a

kh

Psychotherapy is most importantly a *collaborative* activity. The overall aims and objectives are most readily accomplished when therapist and client cooperate together and assist each other, and the maintenance of a cooperative alliance yields real benefits in almost every aspect of the therapeutic process. It is important and in some ways essential, therefore, that we act as allies and that our clients come to see and to accept us as allies.

The client's experience of an ally is in itself therapeutic, it is generally agreed, for the sense that the therapist is accepting and supportive conveys that the client is an acceptable and worthwhile individual and that he matters to someone of some significance. It also invites the client to identify with and perhaps emulate the therapist's supportiveness and strengths, and thus learn to better manage his own interpersonal relationships.

An alliance is also an important condition for further influence since it enables a therapist to effectively utilize a range of candid or forceful interventions which would otherwise lead only to trouble: it enables us to gain leverage from interpretations and suggestions which would otherwise cause argument and resistance. Suppose that a therapist comments, "Might I hazard a guess that you are sometimes more than just a little bit stubborn?" to a client adhering obstinately to an untenable position. If the therapist is already seen as an ally, this has a good chance of evoking from the client a smile of recognition and some inclination perhaps to consider further the issue of stubbornness. But if the therapist is viewed as an antagonist, the interpretation stands to be seen as an uncomplimentary insinuation which may evoke argument, resistance, and further stubbornness. As a general axiom, one is more inclined to accept hard truths and difficult suggestions from someone who is seen as an ally. One is on guard and often opposes as unfriendly intrusions these same comments from someone who is seen as an adversary.

Client-centered, humanistic, analytic, object relations, and psychodynamic orientations see the client's relationship to the therapist as itself therapeutic, while behavioral orientations see it mainly as an instrument for effective influence. We do not have to choose between these positions: it is both.

Psychotherapy is described as a collaborative partnership by Strupp (1978), who stresses the importance of establishing an alliance. All indications are that expectations for progress should be markedly lowered for clients who are unable to see their therapists as allies. The establishment of an alliance thus has high priority. To establish an alliance, we act as an ally to the client—as a supporter, a confidante, a consultant, and a collaborator. Furthermore, we must act in ways that enable the clients to see us as allies. Some principles for doing this are suggested here.

Begin Where You Are Welcome

Particular problems may involve issues which are relatively safe, and other issues which are threatening and uncomfortable. It is best in such cases to begin with those issues in which you are seen most easily as an ally, and to save for the moment those issues in which your position is open to misinterpretation.

One woman, for instance, continually mismanages and screams at her children, and condemns herself relentlessly for her failings as a mother. The situation allows one to begin either with the child management issues or with the self-condemnation. It is better to begin where you are most readily seen as an ally, for instance: "It is not going as well as you would want with your children, and you condemn and harass yourself for each and every failing. You are so tough on yourself, it seems, that it would be difficult for you to feel comfortable at all with your children and to enjoy being with them. The excessive self-condemnation may be itself a major element in your problems, for it prevents you from doing your best. Let's begin there—shall we?—and see what we can figure out."

An attempt to begin instead by suggesting better child management procedures would run a good chance here of failure. The woman is too touchy, and would too easily interpret any suggestions as further evidence that she has done things wrong and that she has indeed ruined her children by her many mistakes.

The mother begins in an impossible position—both wanting to improve as a parent and unable to tolerate the existing failings in herself. An initial focus on the self-condemnation shows a sensitivity to her position, and establishes the therapist as a supporter and an ally. It is easier then from the position of an ally to deal with the complex issues of better child management.

The same issues are seen again in a second illustration: A young woman is excessively invested in, and continually upset by, her relationship with her mother. Both daughter and mother appear to be contributing equally to the general malaise, for each deals with the other in the same underhanded and manipulative manner: each uses upsetness and sulking to intimidate and gain advantage over the other. The situation thus allows one to begin either with the young woman's manipulativeness or with the ways in which she is herself manipulated by her mother. The "whose side are you on?" issue is critical in these sorts of situations, and it is best to begin where you are most readily seen as an ally, for example: "Your mom continually shows you how miserable her life is and how much you upset her when you do not comply with her wishes. The implication is that your mother's feelings are entirely your responsibility, and that you are a rotten person and it is entirely your fault when she is so upset. . . . Is all that upsetness really authentic? Do you ever wonder if she *uses* it to make you feel guilty and to manipulate you into doing what she wants?"

An attempt to begin instead by showing the young woman that she is herself manipulative would invite unnecessary difficulties. The mother contends that the daughter is at fault in the relationship, and an initial interpretation of the daughter's manipulativeness would appear as agreement with the mother's position. The young woman would see the interpretation as yet another accusation and would see the therapist as yet another adversary.

In beginning as he does with the unfair influences against the client, the therapist thus establishes himself as a supporter and an ally. It is easier then as an ally to interpret the young woman's own manipulative contributions. The issue of influencing through being upset is already understood and can be used in the next step: "As a youngster growing up, you learned naturally enough from your mom that being upset and refusing to speak are the effective ways to gain advantage in an argument. It is understandable enough that you too learned to use that strategy in order to hold your own against your mom. As a youngster, you saw no other ways available to you . . . As an adult, you are now in a much better position. Let's look at some more effective ways of holding your own with your mother, which do not involve investing in that same old pattern."

The interpretation thus legitimizes the young woman's current manipulative patterns, for it shows that they were acquired honestly: the manipulative tendencies are now seen as understandable reactions to ongoing manipulations and not merely as indications of bad character. The therapist thus establishes an alliance by his initial support against the mother's unfair manipulations and he maintains the alliance by legitimizing the daughter's own similar manipulative strategies.

Maintaining an alliance is a first priority. We focus initially on establishing an alliance, and then continue with other objectives in ways which tend to further the alliance and with an eye out for signs of trouble. Should some of our interventions seriously weaken our alliance, then we must soften or alter the intervention, and take measures to repair any damage and to reestablish the alliance.

Sessions with several family members present introduce the sometimes troublesome requirement that we maintain an alliance with each of the often antagonistic intimates. One writer suggests that the adult who is less involved with the problem be spoken to first, and the person with the most power to bring the family back be treated with the most concern and respect. Often we can maintain alliances with each of several quarreling family members by understanding and legitimizing each of their positions, and by working for fair play and equitable compromises.

Counter Transference!

Clients who have felt neglected or mistreated in other important relationships may anticipate the same or similar mistreatment in their relationship with their therapists. Some tendency to see a therapist as too similar to a parent or other intimate is only natural and has been termed "transference" in psychoanalytic parlance. The tendency is easily understandable from a general principle: a person takes the world to be as he has found it, so he expects to be treated as he has been treated in previous similar situations. Such misinterpretations weaken the therapeutic alliance and impede constructive collaboration. We should act to minimize transference reactions, and should troubleshoot and intervene to counter transference reactions which do occur. To maintain an alliance we must counter transference.

One client is initially guarded and uncooperative: he gives only minimal comments, and those in response to questions, and he withholds anything important about himself. One gets the initial impression that he is mistrustful of the therapist and of the relationship. The following is an attempt to troubleshoot the problem:

Therapist: You give little or no information on your own, and only the minimum when I share my thoughts or ask questions. It seems that maybe you are feeling that you do not entirely trust me, or you are wondering if I might have some advantage over you if you do say too much about yourself.

Client: Well, maybe. It takes me a while to open up, I guess.

Therapist: Have you had some experiences where you have told someone about yourself and found that he or she used it against you?

Client: No, not really.

Therapist: Never? Has there not been maybe a time when someone understood you, and used this to criticize or manipulate? Your parents, for instance, how do you get along with them?

Client: I get along with them OK now, I guess.

Therapist: And when you were growing up?

Client: Well, my father was unhappy a lot of the time, and moody.

Therapist: And how did he treat you?

Client: When he was frustrated, he would yell at me, often for things I could not really do anything about. I felt criticized a lot, I guess. I remember that I would stay out of the way, and not say anything, because I was afraid of making him angry.

Therapist: So you learned quite naturally that some people cannot be trusted, and you learned to stay back until you find out a bit more about whom you are dealing with. . . . It makes some sense to do that here as well, at least until you find out more about me and about how I respond to the information you do offer. . . . Gradually, I expect, you will find that there are at least a few differences between me and your father.

Client (laughs): There are a few differences, for sure.

The young man was expecting about the same treatment from the therapist as he had received from his father and was responding in one of the ways he had learned to respond in such situations. The therapist's initial comments are attempts to understand and to legitimize the fellow's guardedness and reluctant participation. Since no explanations had been volunteered, the therapist's initial comments are necessarily estimates of what *might* be going on. These comments are attempts to understand and legitimize the problem: although sometimes incorrect, they come across nonetheless as supportive and so cast the therapist as an ally. The therapist in these interpretations shows that he can understand and accept the young man's minimal participation; thus he contrasts in this important way with the moody and often critical father.

As a principle, we should clarify the actual relationship, and establish sufficient contrast between ourselves and the parties in those other relationships which are seen as so unsatisfactory. Many schools are in agreement here, notably Adlerians, who are themselves anything but anonymous; reality therapists, whose first principle is to be personable to the clients; and family therapists, who bring those other contrasting relationships into the therapy sessions. The psychoanalytic and psychodynamic traditions straddle the fence, in that classical analytic practice encourages transference—and so stands in opposition—whereas the current psychodynamic practice which emphasizes reconstructive emotional experiences and the early resolution of transference is thus in agreement.

The rationale in classical analytic practice is that transference must be encouraged so that it may be explored and analyzed at length, and, through the course of analysis, resolved. The analyst remains anonymous—a so-called "blank screen"—and thus invites in the patient fantasies and misinterpretations, which occur unfortunately in confused combination with realistic anger and insecurities over being unsupported and ignored. Advocates of encouraging transference note the importance of a working alliance, but they assume rather uncritically that one can both encourage transference reactions and at the same time maintain the stability of a working alliance. The plausibility of a client's seeing a therapist as a critical and abandoning father figure and at the same time as an accepting and trustworthy ally stretches the imagination. It is possible to alternate between suspicion and trust, but the client cannot have a full measure of each of them at the same time.

We must choose, therefore, between encouraging transference or maintaining an alliance. An average client already has more than his share of what he perceives as unsupportive or otherwise unsatisfactory relationships and does not need one more with his therapist. When we are seen as supportive and trustworthy, we stand in contrast and are in a better position to explore those other relationships and to promote more satisfactory ways of relating. As a general principle: In order to counter transference, be personable and participate actively, and interpret and challenge transference reactions which do occur.

The principles and guidelines here are general considerations for practice and not particular techniques which can be memorized and performed blindly. We must weave the guidelines appropriately into the ongoing therapeutic procedure. The means by which we try to maintain an alliance may be complex and quite varied, and may call upon the full sensitivity and experience of the individual practitioner. Nor is it always possible to form an alliance, for some clients remain suspicious and uncooperative in spite of our best efforts.

Any number of additional principles and considerations may be involved in maintaining an alliance. The issues of maintaining and utilizing an alliance continue to weave through our remaining assortment of therapeutic guidelines, and several additional principles will be presented which serve to cast us as allies.

3. MAINTAIN CREDIBILITY

Client's perception of the therapist

sees therapist as
sensible and competent

Being seen by the client as competent and sensible contributes measurably to the impact of our interpretations and suggestions and, therefore, to our overall effectiveness as therapists. A number of considerations improve our credibility with our clients and thereby help maintain our opportunities to influence them.

Showing the sensibleness of our interpretations and suggestions provides a good beginning. Clients deserve an explanation anyway, and a well-communicated rationale for what we are doing instills confidence in the programs we undertake. Psychotherapy need not be a secretive or esoteric procedure which is conducted on clients without their understanding. Indeed, clients are generally appreciative when we share with them the secrets of what we are attempting to accomplish, and are in a better position from there to collaborate and contribute. Some evidence indicates that physicians who explain the medical problems and procedures inspire greater cooperation and confidence in their patients than those who attempt to maintain their credibility as experts through looking important and keeping the information to themselves. The principle is clear enough, and we in counseling and psychotherapy need only to heed the lesson.

Explaining our rationales does not lock us to them or require that we never change our minds or never acknowledge misdirections. When we do change directions, we can explain whatever new considerations are operative so that the changes make sense, and such changes are generally accepted with few problems. Changing as we consider things further may itself improve our credibility because clients, like anyone else, have more respect for those who are flexible than for those who consider themselves infallible. Also, acknowledging misdirections may give the client a needed invitation to do so himself without undue strains on pride and ego.

Our ideas need not always be better than those of our clients, for a cooperative give-and-take with our clients speaks well of our flexibility and good sense. Competitiveness and one-upmanship with our clients over who is right are clearly out of line.

Oftentimes clients find themselves feeling better, but do not see the connections to the seemingly minor changes that we have worked on with them. When our interventions result in improvements, it is good to link the two together in the client's mind, both to establish the credibility of our programs and to further motivate the client to continue with them. Thus to one who is feeling better we might comment: "Be sure to note that you started feeling better shortly after you made those important stands with your husband; and that when you did that earlier you felt better, and when you forgot to do it you started feeling worse again. The things we are working on do make a difference, and it is important to stay with them."

Some long term orientations are wary of providing quick relief for fear that the client who is no longer suffering will not be sufficiently motivated to work on the more fundamental characterological problems. The suggestion here, in contrast, is to attack first those problems which appear easiest in order to gain leverage and improve things. Showing that our programs really can and do improve things improves our credibility immeasurably, and generally increases rather than decreases the willingness of clients to stay with therapy. Those who do choose to leave with the quick fix at least know that we know how to do something which works. We invite them back should further problems occur, and we have not really lost those clients either.

Explaining expected problems or relapses prior to their occurrence helps maintain the credibility of our programs. Along with suggestions for parents to more strictly manage their troublesome youngster, we might explain that he will be mad about it and fight them, and may look considerably worse before he looks better. If this were not explained, then the youngster's objections and escalating troublesomeness would be taken as indications that our therapeutic program is wrong and has failed. However, the same problems, explained and even predicted in advance, can be cast instead as further confirmation that we know what goes on and that the program is working as expected.

If we were to say things which are untruthful and get caught at it, then that quite obviously would undermine our credibility. The ways in which our clients interpret our comments matter considerably, for saying things which appear to be untruthful or wrong can undermine our credibility every bit as much as saying things which actually are wrong. As therapists, we introduce new ideas, and we explore and weigh them with our clients so that they can attain more realistic understandings. Ideas too far from what our clients accept already can overshoot the mark and result in the clients' discrediting our statements rather than changing their opinions. Some cautions are in order therefore against committing ourselves to statements which are correct in fact but which we cannot get our clients to see as anything but wrong.

Those clients convinced of their own worthlessness who cannot accept those who approve of them present for us a subtle problem in maintaining our own credibility. Include here those who are convinced they are stupid, ugly, bizarre, trashy, or in any of the range of ways worthless and socially unacceptable, and who cannot and will not accept any opinion contrary to their own convictions. One who is so thoroughly convinced of his flaws does not consider the opinions of others who try to reassure him that he is intelligent, attractive, or an otherwise acceptable human being. A classic Groucho Marx quip portrays the position well, along the lines that: "I would never belong to any country club that would have the likes of me as a member." Any club unselective enough to accept him thereby discredits itself in his eyes. A person such as this figures that others who try to reassure him either see his flaws, but are pretending otherwise as a social courtesy, or do not see his flaws because they are naive and gullible or because he has fooled them for the moment into seeing him as normal. Either way their statements count for nothing because those who are nice as a courtesy do not really believe their own words, while those whom he has fooled will find out sooner or later about his awful character and the charade will be exposed. He discredits as false or naive the reassurance he receives, and discredits similarly those who attempt to reassure and support him.

The only relationships these persons accept as genuine are antagonistic ones because antagonists, they feel, see their undesirableness and are real enough to treat them accordingly. Such persons frequently wallow in abusive relationships and are too easily mislabeled masochistic. The person is not there because he loves pain, but rather because like anyone else he is more comfortable with those he feels are being real with him.

As therapists we act generally as allies and supporters, but the subtle problem here is that in appearing supportive with these clients, we would seem false or naive and discredit ourselves in their eyes. The requirement then is that we be supportive while skirting the problem of discrediting ourselves by appearing supportive. With an intelligent young man who is convinced that he is fundamentally stupid, for instance, we cannot merely reassure him or even point to the good marks he makes in graduate school, for those were flukes and anyway he has the instructors fooled too: he is really an impostor masquerading as a smart student. But conversely, it would be wrong to agree with him that he is stupid, for he is not and there are traps waiting for one who argues untruths. Remaining silent is also not a good option, however, because by remaining silent one fails to be supportive and comes across either as above it or as stuck, which is not helpful. So where do we go? What we can do is clarify and legitimize the client's position, and from there avoid being caught by it and perhaps move on to challenge it.

We clarify the inclination to discredit supporters as a first step to enable the client to accept support. We might mention the Groucho Marx quip and draw the parallels: "You are a lot like Groucho and the country club—you discredit anyone who is undiscerning enough to accept you." The particulars must be elaborated and the problem hashed through as much as is necessary. Once the problem has been clarified, we can use it to cover ourselves when we are being overtly supportive, as in the following compliment: "Actually you are doing quite well, but if I were to tell you that you would lose respect for my judgment." It is a compliment, but it stays one jump ahead of the client's tendency to discredit: in the same motion, we make the pitch and cover the bases.

We might also interpret the client's tendencies to present himself as so stupid: perhaps he does this to avoid the possibility of being disappointed, or to evoke reassurance and involvement from his friends, or for other reasons. We legitimize and make sense of those tendencies, and only then go on to challenge. By clarifying the inclinations to discredit, we remain credible ourselves and so remain in a position to be taken seriously.

One who argues forcefully that he is stupid makes an obvious contradiction, and we might challenge that, as by saying: "Everyone argues that you are plenty smart enough, but you are sure that you really know you are stupid and they do not. For one who sees himself as so stupid, you sure have a lot of confidence in your opinion. I realize you are arguing that you are inferior, but you come across as quite sure of yourself: you are sure that you are right on this and that nobody else knows anything at all.'' The comment is challenging in appearance but supportive in substance. Because it is challenging, the client cannot assume we are just being nice to him or that he has us fooled; yet the thrust of the interpretation is that there is more to him than he is admitting.

Ostensibly the client has an inferiority complex, but note the shades of superiority and aloofness in one who discredits so easily those who appear supportive. One who ostensibly sees himself as so inferior nonetheless remains in charge of his attitudes and has the satisfaction of feeling superior to those who are so foolish as to accept him. In interpreting the control he exercises, we accredit the client as someone in charge already of one critical aspect of his life—a principle elaborated in later guidelines.

Those who are reserved and aloof maintain their status as objective observers above the client but are not sufficiently supportive, while those who are too overtly supportive offer something important but chance being discredited in the process. The artistry is in being supportive and remaining credible at the same time. The credibility of the healer is suggested by Jerome Frank as an essential factor to all forms of psychological treatment, and credibility is emphasized as a major factor in attitude change in the social psychological approach to treatment (cf. Strong, 1978).

4. COMMUNICATE AN UNDERSTANDING OF THE CLIENT'S POSITION

An individual's feelings and concerns are too often overlooked or misunderstood in ongoing, everyday communications. One who understands and acknowledges another's position shows an interest and concern, and is seen more readily as an ally and a supporter. It is important then for a therapist to convey that he does understand and accept the important aspects of the client's communications.

Specific techniques for expressing one's understanding are emphasized in client-centered and related counseling orientations, and in parenting communications training. These techniques are variously termed empathic responding by Rogers, reflective listening by Haim

Ginott (1965), and active listening by Thomas Gordon (1970). Any of these terms seems satisfactory.

The main principle is to listen carefully to the feelings and concerns being communicated, and then to share our understanding of the important elements. An empathic listening response may grasp key words or phrases, but it should not be a mere paraphrase of the person's statement. Any response qualifies which adequately conveys that we understand and accept the important feelings and concerns.

Empathic listening responses convey understanding and acceptance, but they should not imply agreement on anything which appears inaccurate or false. Suppose a woman expresses strong anger over the way her husband is treating her; compare the following empathic responses:

1. "You feel he is being really unfair, and you find yourself angry over the way he is treating you."
2. "Sounds like he is being quite inconsiderate and unfair, and you are really angry about it."

The first acknowledges the sense of injustice and anger, and the second includes agreement that the sense of mistreatment is accurate and realistic. Both convey an understanding of the client's position, for we need not be in agreement in order to convey understanding and acceptance. We can express an understanding even when the client's position seems problematic. But only when the client's position appears accurate and appropriate should our response include agreement.

An empathic response may sometimes pass over a manifest question, and focus instead on the implicit issues and concerns which are being expressed. A mother, for instance, asks anxiously about her troubled youngster: "I want to know if I am the cause of the problems he is having." A good response is: "Sounds like you are feeling responsible, and you are wondering if you are to blame for literally everything that is going wrong." The response makes explicit the underlying concern and suggests an important issue for further consideration. The initial question the mother asked may be answered as well, if it remains important. But the major focus should be on what appear to be the primary issues and problems conveyed in the client's communication.

Empathic statements may help clarify the issues for client and therapist alike: empathic responses focus the client's attention on important aspects of his feelings and concerns, encourage him to understand and accept aspects which otherwise may have been overlooked or avoided, and tend to increase the richness and complexity with which he understands himself and his relationships. Empathic responses also focus the therapist's attention on understanding better what is being communicated and give us an opportunity to improve our understanding as a client confirms or questions our initial impressions. Empathic listening tends to facilitate further client communication: it conveys an interest in what the client is saying, and it helps us avoid asking too many questions or giving easy advice based on too little understanding.

Showing that we understand should not be seen as incompatible in any way with any of the range of further interventions. The sequencing of therapeutic interventions is important. One who acknowledges another's position is more easily seen as an ally, and is in a better position from there to challenge and restructure. Expressing an understanding is thus an initial intervention which prepares the groundwork for later, more forceful strategies for change. In general, as each issue is introduced, we should convey that we understand the client's position on that issue, and then continue from there to interpretation and redirection.

The empathic response is given an exalted position in classical client-centered counseling: it is the answer to everything, and anything else a counselor might do is just plain wrong. Most eclectics use empathic responses but reject the restrictive ideology. We see the empathic response as but one of a range of available therapeutic responses.

Empathic communication is thus an initial therapeutic response which encourages an alliance, clarifies issues, opens communication, and thereby prepares the groundwork for further, more forceful or elaborate therapeutic interventions. Empathic statements are those recurring nickle-and-dime interventions which each contribute only a smidgen of therapeutic movement, but without which the course of therapeutic progress would be markedly slower.

5. SHARE RESPONSIBILITY FOR IMPROVEMENT

Psychotherapy is a collaborative activity in which client and therapist both contribute: each should share, therefore, in the responsibility for making things go as they should. By everyday conventions, some measure of responsibility is generally assigned to each of the participants in any collaborative activity, and we build here upon these commonsense conventions.

Being responsible for something involves the complementary aspects of being in charge and of being accountable. These two aspects usually go together, since one who is in charge of something stands to be held accountable for the outcome. Sharing responsibility thus involves sharing control of the activity and also sharing accountability for the results. As therapists we take control so that our clients learn to better control their own lives, and we emphasize compassion and openness to learn rather than condemnation as we assess our own accountability. Some practitioners avoid taking control for fear of taking control away from the client, or to avoid being accountable. Issues of control and accountability are dealt with here in turn.

It is common for clients to fail to take responsibility for their lives, and to contend instead that it is others who are causing the problems and who should be expected therefore to provide the solutions. Such persons do not seek cooperative solutions. Instead, through passivity, misery, resentment, and accusation, they attempt to transfer the full responsibility to others. "It's up to you, not me" is their attitude and also their intended message. An inability to accept responsibility is itself a major limitation, for it undermines self-initiative and impedes any collaborative efforts to seek solutions.

It may be tempting for a therapist to counter the "it's up to you" attitude through a similarly passive "no, it is up to you" attitude of his own. A client who refuses to accept responsibility thereby invites the therapist to take over. In remaining passive, the therapist foils the invitation, thus forcing the client to take some initiative or to endure the silence. A passive stance is therefore a means to avoid accepting the wrong sorts of responsibility. It is generally ineffective, however, as a long run approach. Passivity by a therapist leaves the client feeling unsupported and thus further impairs the already fragile therapeutic alliance. Troubled clients, furthermore, are not merely unwilling but generally and in important ways unable to take appropriate responsibility. A passive countermove is therefore counterproductive, for neither therapist nor client generates solutions, and both are stranded together in a muddle of entangling inactivity.

It is better in such cases to deal actively with the issues of responsibility, as in the following illustration. A young woman complains about her marriage—her husband neglects her and refuses either to acknowledge his contributions to the problem or to make the changes she requires. The therapist tries to explore some obvious alternatives: she might consider ways to adapt herself to the marriage, try on her own to improve the relationship, or leave. But the woman is uninterested in any of these alternatives. Her husband is making her life impossible, she contends, and it is intolerably unfair therefore that she should be expected to have to make the changes; it is up to him, and not her, to make the necessary changes.

She also brings the same attitude into her approach to her therapy. She is uninterested in changing herself and is waiting for the therapist to redress the gross unfairness that life has perpetrated upon her: it is not up to her but up to her therapist to make things better for her. This woman is entrapped by her failure to take responsibility and has only the vaguest understanding of her self-generated bondage. There are two separate but related problems, one in her understanding and the other in the thrust of her actions. She misconstrues and overestimates her husband's contributions, for although he contributes to the problems, she contributes also, so that he is certainly not the sole cause which she has convinced herself he is. The thrust of her actions is more subtle and complex but extremely important: she is attempting to make him responsible; to do so, she presents herself as miserable, accuses him of causing her problems, remains passive, refuses to try to change herself, and thus commits herself to the miseries she claims he is causing. Her objectives are to show him he cannot get away with neglecting her, to make him feel responsible for her feelings, and to force him to become more considerate. Her objectives are understandable enough, but her use of miserableness is not particularly effective and carries too high a price. As a means of getting him to be more responsible, it is clearly cost ineffective.

There are any number of ways to begin to intervene, such as: "You have issues of whether he should change and issues of how to get him to change, and you must distinguish between the two. We can both agree that he is contributing to the problems and that therefore he should change, for a husband should be more involved and considerate. But you have yet to deal with the issue of whether he will change and what you might do to get him to change." The comment distinguishes between ethical questions as opposed to practical means to improve the situation. Agreement here that the husband should make some change conveys supportiveness and casts the therapist as an ally: although certainly not the whole story, it is nonetheless a place to begin. The means by which the husband actually might change is presented then as a separate and further issue.

Perhaps the husband is most annoyed by her continual upset and ongoing insinuation that it is all his responsibility, so that an improvement in the wife's attitude might yield real improvement in the entire marriage. The therapist explores these relationship factors and suggests how she might contribute to a solution, but she is too committed to her current position to accept the reinterpretation. The impasse continues.

We might better focus on the pragmatics of the wife's statements. The "you are responsible" messages to her husband are attempts to force him to accept the responsibility; thus, the following intervention: "In holding your husband responsible, you invite him to take responsibility and to treat you better. Your premise, it seems, is something like this: 'If only I could make him see how upset he is making me, then he would feel responsible, and he would have to treat me better, as he should.'" Once the woman understands and acknowledges her approach, then the issue of its effectiveness can be raised: "Is your premise valid? Is your strategy going to work?" The outline provides a beginning, and we might elaborate and expand on the themes.

Suppose that further conversation reveals that this woman grew up with parents who were overconcerned with her feelings and who took responsibility themselves for her every unhappiness. The information can be used to further understand and legitimize the pattern: "When you got upset as a youngster, your mom and dad would do almost anything to make you feel better. You learned naturally enough that when things go wrong, it is someone else's responsibility to make you feel better, and all you need to do is to show them how upset they have made you. Your problem here is that your husband does not react to you the same way your parents react. When you get upset and angry, your husband does not take responsibility. Rather, he becomes annoyed and ignores you even more. It seems as though the rules have changed, and nobody told you. You were taught that being upset gets you some cooperation, and now here it does not. That must seem unfair."

The experience as a youngster thus makes more understandable the woman's pattern of being upset and moody, and of requiring someone else to make things better. It also enables the woman to see better why her current approach is a failure, for the rules have changed and she did not notice it. In acknowledging the apparent unfairness, the therapist appeals to her belief that things are unfair and thereby makes it easier for her to accept the interpretation. When she understands, it is no longer so easy to continue the same blind pattern. Holding others responsible thus loses some of its appeal, and she becomes more inclined then to look for other alternatives.

Note in this case that the therapist takes responsibility in order to enable the client to take responsibility. To share responsibility we take responsibility in ways that enable the client to begin to take responsibility himself, but not in ways that take *away* responsibility. We do this most readily not through remaining passive, but through various courses of active interventions.

Note also that the therapist adapts and alters strategies to gain the appropriate impact. It is not sufficient to conduct a standard therapeutic approach and to make it the responsibility of the client to benefit from it. When a client fails to benefit from one approach, we should make it our responsibility as therapists to figure out the problems and to change and implement alternative approaches. We need to tailor interventions to fit the particular inclinations and abilities of each individual client.

A client unwilling to take responsibility generates a major problem, but not necessarily an insurmountable one. Some argue that the client has to really *want* to change and thus hold the client accountable, but that is too simplistic and notoriously ineffective. A troubled individual who is unwilling to change is also in some important manner unable to change. Our task, as in the case just described, is to figure out why the person is unable to change and to address the issues involved. It is our responsibility as therapists to enable the client to better assume responsibility for his own life.

Managing issues of responsibility in therapy is often quite challenging, for there are complexities and considerable room to wrangle over who is responsible for each particular aspect. We try to contribute that which the client is unable to contribute, and we invite and require a client to contribute in every way he is able. Therapist and client must complement and assist each other.

Being responsible involves being in charge, and it also means being accountable; thus blame and recrimination are possible when things go wrong. It is this latter issue of accountability and recrimination which makes responsibility so uncomfortable and troublesome. Many clients may avoid taking charge of their lives in order to avoid being accountable. Should we not recognize that therapists too might avoid being in charge of therapy sessions in order to avoid being accountable for the outcomes?

In my own training, I consulted with a schoolteacher to help her more effectively manage an extremely difficult and unruly class of students. The consultation was ineffective because of the inherent difficulty of the class, the inflexibility of this particular teacher, and my own limited abilities as a consultant trainee. Imagine the worst possible outcome of such a situation: over a Christmas vacation the teacher committed suicide, leaving fellow teachers, students, and others involved to figure it out as best we could. While the main impetus appeared post mortem to be loneliness and adversities in her family relationships, the daily frustrations of that unmanageable class undoubtedly worsened the situation. I was devastated and, in what I now realize is a typical reaction, I indulged myself in feelings of inadequacy, guilt, and self-recrimination over what I should or could have done but failed to do.

I sought my training supervisors for assistance and support. A first supervisor listened briefly to the situation and then told me that I was not responsible: it was a situation over which I had no control, and the teacher as an adult and professional was responsible for her own actions. Students, he concluded, always take these things far too personally. While the information may have been correct, it was not particularly helpful. I surely felt responsible, and those feelings could not be ignored.

A second training supervisor listened carefully to the situation, and then commented that I did indeed share some responsibility, as did everyone else involved, but that my own responsibility was probably much less than I was imagining it to be. What I needed to do for myself was to sort through the extent to which I was and was not responsible, and to find some reconciliation which I could live with. That I found was extremely helpful. In my inventory, I noted that I was merely a consultant and not a therapist. A consultant, according to the approach we were learning, does not intervene in the teacher's personal affairs, for if he does he is soon seen as an in-house shrink and is excluded by other teachers from their classroom concerns.

Nevertheless, the issue was still emotionally laden. I explained to a third supervisor that I was only a consultant, and therefore it was not really as bad as if I had been her therapist and had been intimately involved with her personal issues. "It's even worse," he replied, and I held onto my chair as I felt my foundations give way. "Because then you didn't even get a chance to try to help." This last comment rearranged my views of responsibility for the better. There can be actual satisfactions in the willing acceptance of responsibility, even without guarantee of a favorable outcome.

It is too easy to assume that by being less involved we are thereby less accountable when things go poorly. Active involvement is advocated here, and thoughtful attempts to assist by whatever means are appropriate. "Share responsibility" implies that we share accountability, but it is not a recipe for self-recrimination when things go wrong. We need to see ourselves as accountable, but in ways which avoid excessive self-recrimination for mistakes and failures. We must rely on compassion and gentleness toward ourselves, and on an openness to learn by our mistakes. In so doing, we convey by example an important lesson in responsibility: we show that it is possible to be committed and involved, and to be nonetheless accepting of oneself when things go wrong.

"Share responsibility" is suggested here as a guideline for effective collaboration, and responsibility is apportioned on the basis of practical considerations. We are to take charge in ways that move things forward, and to place our clients in charge in ways that they are able to manage. We should hold ourselves accountable to the extent that it is within our reach to make changes and hold our clients accountable when that would benefit them. Likewise, we do not hold our clients accountable when they are overly conscientious already and would be overwhelmed by further accountability.

The guideline to share responsibility comes from considerations of therapeutic impact. Telling a client "you are responsible" is not merely a statement of existing realities, for words are deeds, and telling someone he is responsible is usually a way of holding him responsible. This we should do when it moves things forward and not otherwise.

The issue of responsibility for psychotherapy is often approached from one or the other of two supposedly competing positions. One position, seen commonly in analytic, psychodynamic, client-centered, humanistic, and existential approaches, is that the client is responsible for session gains because it is he who must choose his course and who must live finally with the consequences of his own actions. The contrasting position, seen commonly in behavioral and in many family systems orientations, is that the therapist is responsible because it is he who is engaged to find solutions which the client on his own is unable to manage. Communications strategist Jay Haley is widely appreciated for his tongue-in-cheek satire on professionals who abdicate responsibility for therapeutic progress. The guideline here draws from the two positions, although somewhat greater importance is given to the responsibility of the therapist.

In taking our share of the responsibility, we cast ourselves as allies, for we actively collaborate with the client in seeking solutions. The remaining guidelines are ways of taking our share of the responsibility for therapeutic impact.

6
Affirmation and Accreditation

Their confusions, inadequacies, and failures are all too obvious, and most clients emphasize these and fail to see the many strengths they might have which exist alongside their problems. The person who sees few or no strengths in himself and considers solving his inadequacies faces a sadly unmanageable task: How does one make oneself into an adequate person when there is so very little to work with? It is not surprising that so many lose heart or never attempt the struggles of psychotherapy in the first place. One of our major initial tasks is to introduce and affirm the client's existing strengths so that these can be acknowledged, accepted, and used as a more suitable basis for realistic attempts to improve existing inadequacies.

The following guidelines are to affirm existing strengths and to accredit the client as someone who already makes sense, is acceptable, and in important ways is in control of his own life:

1. Legitimize (show the client the sense he makes).
2. Make it acceptable.
3. Confirm the client's control.
4. Don't buy victim acts.
5. If it works, don't fix it.

1. LEGITIMIZE (SHOW THE CLIENT THE SENSE HE MAKES)

There are ways in which clients are rational and make sense in what they do, and ways in which they are confused and mistaken. We have choices, therefore, as therapists on where we begin and what we emphasize. There are important reasons to begin with and emphasize the ways our clients do make sense, and to use these as a foundation to troubleshoot and resolve the mistakes and errors. We legitimize as we show the client the sense he makes.

The importance of legitimizing is seen over and over in almost every clinical issue we encounter. In one case, a man complains bitterly that his wife does not care enough for him to fulfill his legitimate needs, that other women he has known have not given him what he needs, and that more generally life itself is niggardly and unfair to him. From other things he says, however, it appears that his wife is nurturant and reasonably concerned with him, and that while she does not give everything, she does give considerably more than he acknowledges and as much as might be reasonably expected with so little appreciation. The therapist mentions some of those things she does contribute to him, but he argues the more strongly that she gives him nothing at all, or nothing of real importance. Thus, he is grossly mistaken in how little he is being given and critically restricted in his ability to appreciate any of the good things that life is offering him.

We cannot merely continue to suggest that women can be nurturing and supportive or that he should appreciate what they give him, for he argues the more strongly that it is not so and that nobody is giving him enough of what he really needs. His argument is far from reality, but before challenging it, we must analyze the argument so that we can understand the sense it makes. He wants more from women, and as we explore further, it becomes clear that he feels that since women give him so little, they owe him more and should be expected to give him more. He continually complains and is unappreciative in order to show the inequity and thus require women to treat him better. To maintain his position he discredits anything he is given, so that he experiences himself as receiving nothing and thereby further confirms his argument.

Our intervention is to legitimize his position: "You want more from women, and by arguing that women give you nothing at all, you are making a case that you have been mistreated and that they owe you something better than that. You make this argument in order to get a woman to see your side and to realize that she should treat you better. It seems that if she could only see how little she is giving, then fair is fair, and she would realize that she better give you the things you really need. The flip side of this is that if you were to acknowledge and appreciate the things that you are already getting, then she would no longer be obligated to you, and you would have to settle and not get anything else. So that leaves you with no reason to appreciate her, and lots of reason not to.''

After showing the sense it makes, we can go on to better challenge the misconception: "The argument makes some sense, for there are those times when you have to really justify yourself to get anything. But not always, and in this case the argument is failing to get you anywhere. Sometimes it works the other way around. As you do appreciate what you are given you receive more, because others want to give more when they are appreciated and because you are more open to what is given. And as you fail to appreciate you receive less, because others tire of hearing all the complaints and so they give even less, and you are closed to whatever is given. . . .'' "With many women it works just backwards from the way you were figuring it works, which would explain why you are winding up with so very little. . . .'' "Appreciating what your wife gives would not mean settling for less, as you figure it would. My best bet is that it would encourage her, and you would find yourself getting much much more.''

Perhaps this man grew up in a family in which he was ignored most of the time and only got his share of anything when he complained loudly enough to intimidate his mother. We might use that information to legitimize his unconstructive pattern: "When you were growing up things did work that way, for by complaining enough you obligated your mother to do things for you; otherwise, you were ignored. Naturally, you might take for granted that it works that way with other women as well and continue with what you learned to do. But what works in one situation does not always work in another, and your wife does not respond the same way your mother did.''

His operating premise here is that by arguing how unfair a woman is, he justifies himself and forces her to give him more. By showing him the sense in his position, we construct a framework from which its inherent mistakes become more apparent. The continual complaining is in order to gain something quite intelligible, but loses for him what it is intended to gain.

This same dynamic is frequently operative in marriages, in which each person fails to appreciate what the other is contributing and complains instead about what he is not getting. It is easy to suggest that each should be more appreciative and complimentary, but the good sense of the suggestion is too frequently ignored. Each spouse is making a case that the other owes him something more, and to appreciate the other is to ruin the case. Anyway, one who is mad at someone does not want to make him feel better by appreciating the things that person gives. In clarifying the sense it makes to not appreciate the other, we bring forth critical issues and from there attempt to resolve them so that each can appreciate the other without feeling that by so doing he is losing ground.

Any action occurs in a framework of multiple considerations and complex social competencies. Considerable which is right and good may be involved even in misunderstandings and in inappropriate actions. Most important, we fully understand the source of the errors only as we locate them in the context of everything else that the client is doing which does make sense: the errors make sense themselves only in the context of the ways the client makes sense. In the case just discussed, the husband's obvious error in misjudging his wife's contributions makes sense only in the context of what he is trying to accomplish through his argument and the reasons he has for doing so. To fail to understand the sense behind the mistake is to leave ourselves with too few options for effective interventions.

When one wants to change someone's mind, it seems only natural to explain how the other is mistaken: show how he is wrong so that he can see the errors and correct them. Emphasizing instead the ways the person makes sense runs contrary to a deeply ingrained everyday tendency, for most people feel that to emphasize the good sense involved in someone's mistaken views is to strengthen those views and weaken their own counterargument. It is unusual indeed in everyday conversation to see anyone legitimize someone else's views and then use that as a basis to challenge the mistakes. Legitimizing may require considerable study and practice because it is sometimes complex and because it runs so counter to deeply ingrained everyday tendencies. It takes some getting used to.

Consider as an everyday case a parent whose daughter has gotten into trouble for talking in class. She says that one of her classmates asked her about a problem, and she was just answering him when the teacher yelled at her for talking: it all seems so terribly unfair. The inclinations of most parents either would be sympathetic with the daughter and in opposition to the teacher, who it seems should be more understanding, or would be sympathetic with the classroom authority and in opposition to the daughter, who should learn to conduct herself more appropriately in a classroom. Either position has its problems. Siding against the teacher supports the daughter but fails to resolve the classroom problem, for more trouble awaits the youngster who continues to talk in class. But by siding with the teacher, the parent comes across to the youngster as insensitive, callous, and not to be trusted; the chances are that the youngster will not listen and the problem will continue.

The issue is problematic only when one sees it as a choice between supporting the youngster and requiring her to change; it makes good sense to do both. The best solution is to legitimize the youngster's position and show her the sense that she makes, and from there to recommend or even require alternatives. One might begin by saying, "It does seem unfair, because you were just answering a question and you did not mean to be causing trouble. When someone asks you something it is really hard to know what to do. Should you just ignore him (but that doesn't seem right because he is your friend) or should you answer him (but then the teacher is going to get mad)? I can see how it's a real problem. Anyway, when the teacher yells at you that makes it hard to want to do anything to please her." One is in a better position after legitimizing to work out a solution and expect some compliance: "It may not seem quite fair, but you still have to get along there. Could you talk to your friend before class and tell him that you are not going to answer his questions because you cannot afford to get into any more trouble?" There is no need to choose between being sympathetic and understanding as opposed to being challenging and directive. Sequence the responses, and there is ample room to do both.

Legitimizing accredits the client as one who makes sense, for by showing time and again that one view after another and one action after another make sense, we show that the client himself makes sense and we make the case airtight. Indeed, within the context of the therapeutic relationship, everything the client does is considered to make some sense, even prior to our understanding the sense that it actually makes. The client is simply ineligible to not make sense, for there is nothing he does or could possibly do which we would see as making no sense at all.

Consider a young woman who accepted a ride from a stranger, sensing full well she was inviting trouble, and barely slipped away from him without being physically harmed. She is puzzled by her action and sees no reason why she might have done it: she considers herself not merely unwise but entirely irrational as well. Our initial comments should affirm that she, like other persons, acts on reasons. Beginning with "that is puzzling" confirms the good sense the woman has in realizing that something is quite amiss. From there, we might go on: "I don't know what your reasons were for what you did, but surely you had some reasons. You are not the sort of person who would do something for just no reason at all." Perhaps further inquiry might reveal that the young woman has been bound by stifling moral conventions in which any affections at all were considered improper and indecent. In accepting the ride, she was rebelling against the constrictions of her upbringing, although in a manner that ensured she would find few pleasures and would receive her just punishment for it. She accepted the ride then in order to slip outside her moral conventions without abandoning them altogether.

The "you are not the sort of person who would do something for just no reason at all" statement accredits the woman, for—despite her puzzling behavior—she is held to make sense in the same general ways that everyone else makes sense. The comment is an easy move, for it requires only that we understand our common language concept of persons: persons may or may not be conscious of the reasons they have, but to be a person is to be the sort of being which has reasons on which he acts. No person is the sort of being which does things for just no reason at all. While obvious, the move is also essential. It introduces making sense as a logical requisite for any action and so invites us to find the reasons the woman has, to make sense of them for her, and from there, to help her to reevaluate them. In this way, our clients are simply ineligible to make no sense, for the logic of our common language concepts requires that there be some sense to anything they do.

Legitimizing might involve the use of any of the common language concepts. Generally, to legitimize the observation or action, we might mention the reasons a person has and then use situations, individual characteristics, or past experiences by which these characteristics were acquired.

Legitimizing interpretations are generally nonpejorative and often quite sympathetic, and so are readily accepted by the client. Because they convey the inherent sensibleness in the client's position, they come across as quite empathic—often more empathic than active listening statements which merely rephrase the client's statements and feelings. By legitimizing we show that we really understand the complexities of what is involved.

Legitimizing contrasts most obviously with standard rational-emotive interventions, in which Ellis argues to his clients that their views and beliefs are irrational. In sharp contrast, we show our clients that their views and actions make sense—indeed often more sense than they ever considered they might make. In so doing, we accredit the person as rational and sensible.

Clients are often puzzled by their actions and see themselves as making little sense or being generally irrational. One who sees himself as irrational has little reason to attempt to apply his irrationality to solve his own problems, for he sees that the application of further irrationality is no way out. By legitimizing, we challenge the clients' views of themselves as irrational and show the inherent sensibleness in even the most puzzling of actions. By so doing, we instill in our clients some confidence that they make sense and legitimate expectations that they can profitably apply their good sense to solve their problems. Support for legitimizing is given by attitude change research which indicates that when we thoroughly and adequately address the rationales supporting the client's initial positions we markedly increase our therapeutic influence (cf. Hass and Linder, 1972; Jones and Brehm, 1970).

Many theories of psychopathology ignore altogether the fabric of human sensibleness and begin instead with mechanistic interpretations or with irrationalities. Psychoanalytic and psychodynamic traditions see man as irrational; behaviorism holds that one's so-called reasons for actions are unimportant in understanding human behavior. Humanistic traditions challenge these mechanistic concepts but do not elaborate adequately the alternatives; client-centered therapists avoid any evaluation whatsoever of their clients. Gestaltists, who also avoid evaluation in their sessions, nonetheless emphasize in their theories the irrationality of human perception. Rational-emotive therapists emphasize the irrationality of troublesome views and begin interventions with strong argument to the client that his views are irrational. The underemphasis of the ordinary sensibleness of problematic actions may be due to the everyday tactic of beginning with what is wrong and also to the tendency in social sciences theorizing to sideline commonsense explanations in favor of the theoretical alternatives. Much of the good work on the fabric of everyday human reasoning is left to the fields of philosophy and logic (cf. Angell, 1964).

While prevailing theories underemphasize ordinary human sensibleness, it should not be assumed automatically that those who identify with these theories fail similarly to take into account the sensibleness of their clients. Practitioners from most orientations show something of the sensibleness of their clients' experiences and actions. But legitimizing can be carried much further than is commonly done, for we can do it more frequently and can increase the impact by using terms that the clients themselves are familiar with and can intuitively understand. "Legitimize" was suggested by Ossorio as a general policy for therapeutic influence and stands here as one of the most salient characteristics of the current pragmatic psychotherapy approach.

By showing the ways our clients make sense already, we gain a considerable advantage. Playing somewhat with the words, we can expect to do considerably better with our rational clients than others do with their irrational or nonrational clients.

2. MAKE IT ACCEPTABLE

Troubled persons conclude too readily that whatever is wrong is unacceptable, intolerable, and inexcusable, and is to be condemned, concealed, rejected, and squashed out of existence. Even the most commonplace mistakes and failures may be taken as evidence of intolerable inadequacy. This indicates a broad-ranging inability to accept the weaknesses and limitations of life as a fallible human being.

Too frequently, the client holds that he is absolutely unacceptable as he is and that he must change before he or anyone else can tolerate him. The task as he sees it is to take an inexcusably inadequate individual and alter him enough to change him into an acceptable human being. We must avoid any implicit agreement with this formulation, for it is a sure invitation to failure. One might attempt any number of alterations and make only minimal headway, nonetheless, in changing an unacceptable failure into an acceptable human being.

We do well to begin instead with a reformulation of the problem. Our essential therapeutic position here is that the client is in important ways *already* acceptable but is unable to see himself that way. The issue then is no longer one of making an unacceptable wretch into an acceptable human being. The issue rather is one of convincing the client that he is already acceptable, and of beginning there in understanding and changing troublesome characteristics.

A client who sees that his therapist places the best light on whatever characteristics of his are revealed comes to expect that other sensitive issues will be similarly understood and interpreted in a favorable manner. Making personal characteristics acceptable thus tends to improve the therapeutic relationship and to further open the channels of communication.

Clients often feel that by accepting their troublesome characteristics, they would resign themselves to them, whereas by condemning and rejecting these characteristics, they can expect to make them vanish. Generally, it works just the other way around, for by rejecting troublesome aspects of themselves, people merely lose conscious awareness of the nature of those problems, and leave themselves in no position to puzzle things through and to generate alternatives. The gentle tolerance of existing foibles and failings is not a resignation to continuing the problems, but rather a first step in generating alternative solutions. Sometimes it is useful to explain this directly: "As we look at these things, you condemn yourself so harshly and make yourself so uncomfortable that you are going to force yourself to forget all about them as soon as you can. To remain conscious of these factors you must be gentle with yourself when you see them, so that you can keep them comfortably in mind and work with them."

We make things acceptable by creating an atmosphere of comfortableness and acceptance, and by presenting things in ways that the client can most readily accept. We should structure the interview so that it is as comfortable as possible for the client. The individual entering therapy has been unable to manage well on his own, and oftentimes is troubled and embarrassed by his lack of independence and self-sufficiency. In many cases, he is unsettled also by the expected unsavoriness of whatever might be revealed about himself: he is sure that the therapist sees through him and that his multitude of sins, embarrassments, inadequacies, and failures will be exposed. Such an individual might be set at ease by restructuring the relationship in the following manner: "It sounds as though you feel I am here to evaluate you. Some concern is understandable, of course, for everyone has some initial apprehension about what is going to happen. You are forgetting, however, that you are the one who is here to evaluate me. You use the first session to see if I am someone whom you are comfortable talking to, and who can understand you, be supportive, and offer you some constructive thoughts and suggestions. If I meet your requirements, then you continue with me. If I do not meet your requirements, then you seek somebody else. So I am the one who is being evaluated, and you are the one who is doing the evaluating. You need to keep that in mind here in our first interview."

We thus reinterpret and restructure the relationship to make being in the position of a client more acceptable. The reinterpretation reaffirms the right of the client to choose his therapist, and thus eases somewhat the problems of unequal status between client and therapist. Usually it lessens the tensions and invites the client to continue in the relationship on a more equal footing.

Be comfortable: A client naturally gauges the acceptability of what he reveals from the responses he receives from the therapist. The comfortableness of the therapist is a critical indicator for the client of whether the issues are tolerably comfortable or socially uncomfortable and inappropriate. Continuing warmth and acceptance suggest that the client is quite acceptable already and thereby invite the client to see himself in a similar manner. He counts as acceptable, at least to this one important person. Thus, it is essential that we maintain an easy comfortableness and set our clients similarly at ease.

Use humor: Humor is extremely important. A message which is otherwise ignored or resisted may be more easily accepted when stated in a humorous manner. One woman, for instance, is married to a chronic alcoholic, but ignores the realities and clings tenaciously to her wishful fantasies. "If only he would stop drinking," she argues again for the fifteenth time this session, "then I'm sure together we could work out the rest of the problems." The therapist has been trying throughout the session to challenge the "if only" reasoning but has failed even to get her attention, and she continues persistently. Some humor in the challenge might turn the trick: "Exactly," we might begin "and if frogs had wings then they wouldn't bump their asses." This breaks the tension and allows her a moment off the drivenness of her argument.

Humor adds sparkle and intrigue, and allows one to enjoy issues which would otherwise appear mundane or ugly. Humor thus is one way of making existing problems and foibles at least minimally acceptable. A sense of humor cannot be introduced artificially, for one must genuinely appreciate what is intriguing and enjoyable about a situation so that it comes across as natural and supportive. Sessions which are effective are often characterized by a strong note of enjoyment and humor between therapist and client. The message is that there is something worthwhile and appealing in even the dreariest of circumstances.

The introduction of humor is foreign to many therapist trainees, who are understandably concerned with showing respect, not offending their clients, and avoiding making errors in the sessions. Some precautions might be noted, of course, for humor relies on social relationship and context, and an attempt at levity inappropriate to the relationship is simply not funny. But training programs which stress so strongly the seriousness of psychotherapy and fail to mention the enjoyment and humor do everyone a disservice. Sessions without humor can be dreary indeed and too familiar for clients who already take themselves far too seriously anyway. We should establish a respectful relationship, then introduce humor, and use the clients' responses to gauge its appropriateness and effect. Humor, successfully introduced, can go a long way to challenge and alter the drab and humorless views many clients have of themselves and of their lives.

Select acceptable phrasing: The phrasing of an interpretation may make an essential idea more or less acceptable. We should phrase interpretations so that the essential ideas are conveyed in a manner least offensive and most acceptable to a particular client. Consider the following interpretations of a husband's continuing hostile and antagonistic actions:

1. "You are trying to get even with your wife for the way she is mistreating you."
2. "You are trying to show your wife that she cannot get away with mistreating you that way."

The first interpretation may evoke considerable resistance, for one would not want to accept that his motive is retaliation and vengeance. The second interpretation is considerably more acceptable, for one will easily agree that he should not allow someone who mistreats him to continue getting away with it. The two interpretations are alternate descriptions of what is in many ways the same essential motivation. The interpretation which is most acceptable invites the client to accept and understand the issues. We go from there to reevaluate the issues and to consider alternate courses of action.

Emphasize positives: One who fails or wrongs others in spite of his good intentions may indulge in self-recrimination for his failure, and can miss or ignore entirely the importance of his good intentions. We may make such incidents more acceptable by introducing and emphasizing the importance of the intentions: "You see only the failure. Your intentions, however, were good ones, and you are missing entirely the importance of what you were attempting to accomplish. You see only the outcome which follows your actions and are absolutely blind to what you yourself are contributing. What you contribute is the attempt to make things go well, although the resulting outcome is not always in your control. You need to be more aware of your own contributions to your actions." The individual who emphasizes failure is shown here that his is a failure to see and understand his own good intentions. The recognition of good intention is generally comforting, for it enables one to accept more easily one's own actions in the face of uncertain outcomes. Emphasizing the positives creates a supportive atmosphere and makes it easier to accept other interpretations which are challenging or otherwise uncomfortable.

Underplay negatives: We may underplay the strength of a portrayal to make it more palatable. Suppose we suggest to a client that he was angry, and he feels that this casts him in a poor light and so objects to the interpretation. To underplay, we comment: "I'm not saying that you were really angry but perhaps just slightly angry—as anyone would have been." The milder interpretation would be easier for the client to accept, and the underinterpretation is all we really need anyway, for once the client acknowledges that he was angry at all then we can discuss the causes of the anger and how to rechannel it. We need only a foothold, and the acceptance of any anger provides an entryway.

Introduce norms: Persons too often see their own inadequacies as extraordinary and fail to see that others too have similar problems. Information about others' experiences in similar situations may invite the client to alter unrealistically high standards and expectations, and to accept otherwise unacceptable aspects of himself. An individual going through separation and divorce may find himself confused and frazzled much of the time, and worry that in addition to failing at a marriage he is now on the verge of losing his sanity. Anxiety and embarrassment about his emotional instability further complicate an already difficult condition. Some basic information about what is generally experienced by others in such situations should give him a better sense that such experiences are normal and expectable, and would enable him to tolerate better the painful process of separation. Uncomfortable and unstabilizing emotions are the normal course in divorce experiences, and one who understands that is in a better position to accept and to struggle through the experience.

Comparisons to others and a lowering of unrealistically high standards may be some of the major benefits of sensitivity and personal growth groups, in which participants often mention relief in finding out that others have problems too; they become more comfortable with the vagaries and imperfectibility of human nature.

When we do present unfavorable interpretations, we should present them as possibilities or as completions of an otherwise favorable picture. We should avoid unfavorable character assessments as primary accounts of personal difficulties.

It is not necessarily sufficient for a therapist to merely accept what the client says. A therapist who avoids condemning but expresses no opinions invites uncomfortable suspicions about where he really stands and inadvertently may even convey agreement with the client's own self-condemning attitudes. One who intervenes actively makes it clear where he stands, and encourages confidence and trust in his position. Therefore, we must be more than merely accepting in order to promote greater self-acceptance in our clients.

In a friendly manner, we may interpret, challenge, banter, and even humor a client to a more self-accepting attitude. Consider the client who is giving exaggerated importance to relatively minor transgressions and is squirming under the weight of his own self-recrimination. Merely accepting the self-recriminative statements would do little to encourage self-acceptance and might convey implicit agreement with the acid of his comments. Some alternative is needed. We might playfully exaggerate and dramatize the client's position: "Sounds like 'what a great sinner I am.' You're saying, 'My sins are not the sins of ordinary mortals, but are exceptional, grand, extravagant, unique, and tremendously important sins.'" The effect here is to jostle the client out of his self-indulgence and to make the case forcefully that he himself is the agent ascribing exaggerated importance to his own relatively minor misdemeanors. The intervention is a good-natured challenge to the client's position, and it invites him to accept his own transgressions as relatively minor.

Thus, we encourage the client to accept things by being comfortable with them ourselves, by presenting them in a supportive manner, and also by challenging directly the client's tendencies to condemn and reject himself. Analysis of and challenge to the client's self-critical tendencies are dealt with more thoroughly in chapter 10 on self-critical tendencies.

Some contend that merely talking about feelings and concerns in a supportive atmosphere leads to greater self-acceptance and to therapeutic improvement. It does sometimes, but oftentimes it does not. We should ask whether these issues are all that unacceptable to begin with and whether the client has concealed these concerns previously or talks about them freely. Concerns that are frightening secrets might become more acceptable just by being brought out in the open. Someone who had been sexually molested or had an illegal abortion, and was then required to remain silent, would stand to profit greatly from talking the experience through in a supportive atmosphere. Revealing such secrets and having them accepted make them more personally acceptable, and can be extremely therapeutic. In major personal losses, expressing grief is especially important in helping to accept the loss. In contrast, other concerns are not particularly unacceptable to begin with and have been talked about too much already. For instance, a woman who complains about her neglectful child or alcoholic husband to anyone who will listen will not profit from merely going through the same dreary story again and again in a supportive atmosphere. The concerns have been thoroughly covered, and now need to be reinterpreted and challenged.

Good interventions are those which deal with significant issues in a manner which encourages comfortableness and which involves and intrigues the client. "Make it acceptable" sets a standard for therapeutic interventions and for the nature of a therapeutic experience. Interpretations should assist the client in understanding issues in a way which encourages acceptance and appreciation of oneself. An overall effect of a therapeutic session should be an awareness that one is acceptable already; from there, further possibilities are available for making life better. In general, a client should leave the sessions feeling better because of the therapeutic experience. While we are not able to achieve this in every session with every client, it is nonetheless an important objective. When too many clients leave their sessions more confused, unsure, troubled, or miserable with themselves, it indicates that insufficient attention is being paid to making the experience an acceptable one.

It is wrong to use the amount of uncomfortableness generated by an interpretation as an indication of the depth or significance of the interpretation. Sometimes some interpretations do hurt, but we do not argue that they should hurt and we should not use the number of tears or the amount of pain in a session to gauge the quality of the therapeutic experience.

Encouraging the client to better accept himself is an important objective of perhaps a majority of psychotherapies, but the *means* used to encourage self-acceptance vary considerably from orientation to orientation. Psychoanalytic and psychodynamic emphasize timing as the way to make interpretations acceptable. Client-centered holds that being warm, real, and empathic enables the client to accept what he shares of himself. Transactional analysis uses picturesque terms and stories to make its interpretations fun. Behavior therapy makes things acceptable by attributing problems not to personal choices but to conditioned response patterns, and in systematic desensitization by giving soothing suggestions to relax and then presenting the tough stuff a little bit at a time. Cognitive behavioral teaches control of pejorative statements about oneself. Rational-emotive argues that to not accept oneself is irrational. "Reframing," popularized by Milton Erickson and Jay Haley, and widely used in communications and family systems approaches, involves redescribing, relabeling, or reinterpreting an action, usually to make it more acceptable to the client. The "positive connotation" technique in other family therapies is similar. Note the contrast between client-centered counseling, which seeks to promote self-acceptance by accepting everything the client says, and rational-emotive therapy, which seeks the same objective by challenging forcefully the client's beliefs that he is unacceptable.

3. CONFIRM THE CLIENT'S CONTROL

An automobile rental company advertises, "Let us put you in the driver's seat." If we were to attempt that strategy with our clients, some would step compliantly into the driver's seat only to step out again when conditions got rough or when it suited them to abandon the journey, and others would not want the responsibility of being in control of their lives in the first place. Our strategy instead is to show the client that he is now, has always been, and always will be in the driver's seat. Once one acknowledges that he exercises control anyway and resigns himself to it, then he goes on from there to learn to control things more advantageously and so get where he wants to go with fewer accidents. We might use the image of being already in the driver's seat to convey to clients that our task as therapists is not to talk them into taking control of their lives, but rather, since they are in control already, to confirm it for them and from there to look at ways to control things to suit them better.

There are ways in which one is a passenger in his life, and ways also in which one is contributing to and controlling the course of that life. We do well to begin by emphasizing the control the person is exerting and from there to fill in the picture with the ways he does not have control. We must confirm the ways in which the client is not undirected, but misdirected; not weak, but inept in how he is using his strengths; not adrift in life, but paddling crosswise and backwards against the current.

When a person cannot seem to decide something, we could see this as an inadequacy or weakness, which it is, and we could also see it as a way the person has of controlling things by not deciding, and thus as something more than mere inadequacy. As an example, take the perhaps too familiar situation of a man (it could as well be a woman) who is married and having an affair, and who worries about it continually but cannot seem to decide whether to leave home or to terminate the affair. The failure to decide can be seen as an inadequacy on his part, for it is causing considerable turmoil and pain for himself and everyone else involved, but it is more than just a failure to make up his mind. Quite probably, the man has fears both of leaving his wife and of losing his lover, and fears also that either choice he makes may be the wrong one. Thus, he has reasons for not deciding, for by not deciding he avoids making the wrong choice and he also keeps both women. Without acknowledging it to himself, he is acting on these quite intelligible reasons, so he is genuinely in control of his own apparent confusion in the matter.

To convince the client that he is in control, we must do more than merely state that he is in control. The best way to confirm for the client that he is controlling things is to make explicit the reasons he has for the control he exercises and then if necessary to legitimize those reasons. In this case, we could mention that there are ways to go wrong with either choice and that since he fears making the wrong decision, he stays clear by making no decision at all. To legitimize those fears, we could mention the pressures he feels from his wife and family and from his lover as well, the advantages of each, and the pain there would be in losing either woman.

He seeks safety by avoiding the wrong decision, but there may also be real satisfactions from being involved with two women. We could mention such satisfactions in order to complete the picture and suggest that since he gains something from each and the attention is flattering, he has that further reason not to give it up. Interpretation of his fears of making the wrong decision is the more sympathetic of these, but interpretation of the satisfactions involved in having both worlds completes the picture, for it includes the ways his own appetites contribute to his problems. The thrust changes then from "Are you able to decide?" to "Are you willing to give up those satisfactions?" Both interpretations are accurate enough, and both have their place in our pragmatic approach.

Making explicit his reasons for not deciding spoils the innocence of his acting on those reasons without responsibility for the actions. By bringing to consciousness his reasons for not deciding, we force him either to continue to act on those reasons, but now consciously and by choice, or to reassess his reasons and do something else. He must then either choose between the two women or choose not to choose, but either way he is shown to be in charge.

By emphasizing the ways the client controls things, we may even recast apparent failures into modest successes. Some clients are attempting to achieve particular objectives that are intelligible enough but too easily missed in the light of other obvious and more socially important objectives at which they are failing. In such cases, we do well to emphasize the individual objectives which are sought after and successfully attained.

One young man has a history of job failures, and ambivalent attitudes toward his parents who are themselves quite successful and who expect from him nothing less than outstanding achievements. The young man comments: "I cannot even hold a job. My parents put a lot of pressure on me and are always after me to accomplish something, but nothing does any good. I guess I am just a big failure."

Our therapeutic response is to recast the failure as follows: "It strikes me that not holding a job in the face of that sort of pressure is more than merely failing to hold a job. We would better describe it as refusing to be pressured into something, as holding your own against the pressure. You are not the sort of person who buckles under pressure, and you have been holding your own with your folks, and quite successfully."

At doing something socially or personally acceptable he is a failure, but in resisting parental pressure—which to this individual is paramount—he is a modest success. Were a therapist to begin instead with the failure, he would be accepting at face value the proclaimed inadequacy and would have a poor foundation indeed for further interventions. How much time might be spent trying to convince the fellow to get up on time instead of sleeping through the alarm, and just how much could one expect to accomplish anyway with a young man who is so thoroughly inadequate that he cannot even make it to work on time? But by beginning with the success, we are in an excellent position for further interventions. The young man has reasons for resisting parental pressure, and through an understanding of these reasons, we can help him to reevaluate and find other less costly ways to hold his own and exert his independence. Perhaps he complies overtly with his parents while resisting covertly, and encouragement toward overt independence would affirm his self-respect and free him from such costly passive ways of resistance. Perhaps we could interpret his having to resist as itself an indication that he lacks real freedom and, to the extent that he values independence, encourage him to break away and chart his own course. The beginning interpretation of the ways the client controls and is successful opens these and other strategies for practical interventions. This illustration has been adapted from Allan Farber's (1981) exceptional essay on accrediting successes.

In the two cases just discussed, showing the reasons for the actions is a basic method of confirming to the client that he is controlling those actions. Showing the sense the actions make supports the argument that he is actually making those actions. As a general principle: showing the reasons for the behavior and legitimizing serve as a solid foundation for confirming to the client that he is indeed in control of that behavior. By confirming the ways the client is successful, we construct again the familiar therapeutic double bind: should the client continue in the same manner to resist his parents, then he is acting on intelligible reasons and being successful; should he discontinue the pattern, then he is cured.

One might say that the young man is succeeding at being a failure, which is not incorrect but is so abbreviated as to miss the essentials entirely. What the young man is succeeding at is resisting his parents, and being a failure is merely the way he goes about it and the price he has to pay. Failure is the means to success and the price of that success, but it is not of itself success.

We confirm that the client is in control by interpreting the ways he takes control and also, importantly, by treating him as someone who is in control. Merely telling someone repeatedly that he is in control of his life belies the argument, for one who is in control is most certainly in control also of whether he is going to see it that way. It would be more consistent to mention that he is in control, and from there to point out that he has the choice of whether or not to see it that way, and then to support the point by showing the reasons he has to avoid acknowledging his contributions. Similarly, reassuring someone repeatedly that he can do something is a way of treating him as someone badly in need of reassurance, just as avoiding challenging someone when it is called for is a way of treating him as fragile or too easily thrown off course by a challenge. Too much reassurance can come across as patronizing. The message is "You are weak, but with my continued reassurance you can make it anyway." Indeed, we may do better instead with constructive challenge, for that is a way of treating our clients as persons who are sturdy enough to take it.

While interpretations and challenges should be constructed to be as readily acceptable as possible, some issues are particularly sensitive and some clients particularly touchy, so that with some interpretations we lose ground and find the client upset and angry that we would say what we did. Should the interpretation be a poor one we are free to withdraw it, but what about an interpretation which is as gentle as we can make it and really important? The client may be controlling the conversation through his anger and upset, and a good move here is to confirm that control: "By becoming so upset and angry over my comment, you give me the message that I am upsetting you and that I better not say those things any more or I might be responsible for causing you real harm. By becoming upset, you effectively stonewall my comments and prevent me from saying those things it seems I should not be saying." We could go on with the original interpretation at this point if the client permits it, or we could withdraw it if necessary or water it down to something more acceptable. In any case, we confirm that the client is strong enough to exercise control over what he permits us to say. We thus interpret the control that he is exercising and also treat him as someone who has the control that he does indeed have. Being treated as in control gives him that status in the therapeutic relationship, and is one important step in his seeing himself as in control and beginning to use it more suitably.

Along these same lines, Gestaltists change "I can't" statements to "I won't" statements to stress oppositional motivations, and game interpretations in transactional analysis stress the control and resulting satisfactions in apparent weaknesses. Ossorio suggests as a therapeutic policy that we choose anger over fear interpretations, for anger interpretations implicate the force and control the client is exercising while fear interpretations convey the weakness. Analytic and dynamic orientations interpret anger and resistance motivations in apparent weaknesses. But some orientations are weak in this area, notably the behavioral orientations, which focus too exclusively on how one is controlled by situations and by past learning, and overlook the subtleties of how one is in control already.

4. DON'T BUY VICTIM ACTS

Appearing persecuted and victimized might seem at first glance bereft of real satisfactions, yet persons do cast themselves as victims by choice and for a variety of basically intelligible reasons. Persons may cast themselves as victims in order to appear noble and gain support, to avoid responsibility themselves, or to cast others as ignoble persecutors and oppressors, thereby making others responsible. A person might have one such reason or several in combination together.

Challenging victim acts is complementary to confirming the clients' control. By recognizing that they actively cast themselves as victims and by legitimizing the reasons they have for doing so, we accredit our clients as contributors and participants rather than mere victims in their lives, and so confirm the control that they do have.

Acknowledging the clients' contribution to victim acts affirms their control in their scenarios, but it also ruins their acts as victims and is thus one of the touchiest of interventions to bring off successfully. The exploration of victim acts is as essential as it is complex and sensitive, for the client must see the contributions he can and does make to his condition so that he might be in a position to redirect his contributions to better uses. We must interpret and legitimize the reasons clients have for presenting themselves as victims, and only from there attempt to challenge the acts.

In many relationships, the one who hurts the most gains all the attention and concern, and others who are doing well are always responsible. These folks accept as fundamental the ideology that the one who is the most miserable therefore merits our concern the most—an ideology that has been termed "victimism" for its unfaltering faith in the goodness of the apparent victim regardless of the causes of his sorry state. The contributions of misconceived views of Christian suffering have been explored elsewhere (Driscoll and Edwards, 1983). When someone casts himself as a victim to involve others, we should interpret the advantages of being the sufferer, challenge the ideology, and invite the person involved to try other ways of gaining concern and managing responsibilities.

One may cast himself as a victim in order to avoid responsibility for many aspects of his life. Some see power itself and those who exercise power as oppressive, hurtful, and wrong, regardless of the uses of the power. Lord Acton stated as a political maxim that "Power tends to corrupt, and absolute power corrupts absolutely." In essential agreement and applying it to their own lives, these persons squelch their own personal power in order to maintain their innocence and to avoid being corrupt. For apparently ethical reasons they avoid power, and accept and cherish positions of powerlessness, from which they find themselves angry victims of others who wield power.

The misconception here is that oppression belongs exclusively to those in positions of overt power. That may be mainly so in economics and in politics, but in close interpersonal relationships it does not hold at all. One may be every bit as much the oppressor from an inferior position as from an apparently superior one, for the apparently weaker position justifies and camouflages the retaliatory manipulations toward the apparent persecutors. Those who seem strong are held accountable for their actions, whereas those who seem weak are ignored or excused. If you think power corrupts, try powerlessness!

One may cast himself as a victim in order to cast others as the callous perpetrators of the problems, and thus to condemn and punish others for their misconduct, and to pressure them to change. The "sons of bitches" have made his life miserable, and he is going to hold them fully accountable. There are no incentives here for solving one's own problems, and there is at least one major reason for not solving them: one can blame others only so long as things remain miserable, but were one to show that he himself could make things improve, he would ruin his case against those culprits who he contends are responsible for his miserable condition.

Some people are indeed victims, for they have been mistreated and abused in various ways throughout their lives: there are neglected childhoods, alcoholic husbands, nagging wives, meddling in-laws, ungrateful children, financial problems, and so on. Many people are also victims of their own misconceptions and maladaptive tendencies. But there are very few people who are *merely* victims, for they are also participants in the lives they live, and their choices and actions do contribute for better or worse to their fortunes and misfortunes. Victim acts cast one as merely a victim and not a participant. Our task in challenging the act is to emphasize the manner in which the person is also a participant, and so to encourage him to understand and redirect the nature of his own participation.

One who is running a victim act is not interested in solving the hardships or even in making the best of those that cannot be changed. Rather, the interest is in what he might gain through being the victim, and any real effort to change things or to make the best of things would ruin the course of action.

Claims to being a victim may be true enough as far as they go, for life can be harsh and oppression real. We might try to sort through how much of the problems result from genuine oppression and how much from manageable hardships and maladaptive inclinations, but such questions become too readily confounded and unresolvable. Those who are mistreated also mistreat others in turn, and each contributes to the overall problems of the others. It is better to focus on the pragmatic or "in order to" aspects of the argument: What is the client attempting to gain by investing in his claims to being a victim, and what sorts of outcomes are to be expected? We can even agree that one has been treated unfairly in particular ways and still make a case for not pursuing the claim against those who have no interest in listening.

A young adult who was neglected or mistreated by his parents might feel quite reasonably that they owe him more than they gave him, and argue continually that he was wronged in order to convince them and make them give him the love and consideration which is his right. We can agree that he does have a case, for children should be treated better than that, and then from there use the concept of a bad debt to show how he is investing his energies and wasting his life in something that is quite clearly uncollectable. "Your parents really did not give you what they should have when you were growing up, and it is quite understandable that you feel they messed up your life and that they ought to make up for it now. But it is a bad debt, for there appears to be no way to collect it. You argue that they owe it to you, and that they ought to recognize your rights and be more considerate of your feelings. But in doing so you merely waste your time and mess yourself up. It is like driving across town every day to collect from somebody who owes you some money, finding every time that the person doesn't have it to give to you, and then doing the same thing the next day. You get insulted and angry all over again each time; you waste your time and deplete your energy. It is better to write off the bad debt and go on with your life. That is what you need to do with you parents: they ignore you and get angry when you expect things from them, for they see you as accusing them and have no interest in listening."

In agreeing that others are not living up to their responsibilities, we come across as supportive and sympathetic, and from our position there as supporters and allies, we can more easily challenge the client to write off the bad debt. We hold him not entirely accountable for his problems, but then point out how his current attitudes contribute to and maintain these problems, and show him how to make changes.

We identify problems as victim acts by an exaggerated miserableness in the face of rather everyday hardships, by a staunch commitment to arguing the victim position, and by an unwillingness to accept alternative solutions. These persons must relinquish their commitments to being victims before they have any real interest in considering alternative solutions.

Social conventions are more understanding and sympathetic to women who are oppressed by men than to men who are oppressed by women, and thus offer more opportunities for women to benefit by casting themselves as the abused or neglected victims of their lovers or spouses. A woman who contends that the bastard she is involved with is ruining her life gains sympathy and support, and turns her friends against her oppressor. In contrast, most men avoid casting themselves overtly as oppressed and victimized by women, for men strive to see themselves as strong and superior, and they feel humiliated rather than supported when abused or abandoned by women. While there is more support for women who present themselves as victimized by their men, there is little real long term benefit for either men or women in casting themselves as victims. We benefit persons of either sex by challenging the acts.

In challenging victim acts we attempt to take away something that may be a cornerstone for a person's whole way of life, and because of this we should be prepared for quite a contest. Several tactics make the message easier to swallow, including legitimizing the reasons the client has for the act, making our interpretations acceptable by acknowledging that others do the same things, avoiding generating resistance by accepting the justifications the client offers, and so on. To make the challenge work, we must also offer something better as a replacement. A woman who has invested so much in blaming others might be complimented on how well she has managed nonetheless, and asked to consider all the energy she has invested in holding others responsible and to imagine how remarkably well she might do were she to use that energy to her own benefit. The message must be one of optimism, confirming existing strengths and indicating a better life ahead as those strengths are put to better use.

Victim acts might easily be termed manipulations or games, but since these labels appear pejorative there is practical reason to avoid using them with our clients. Our task is to describe the nature of what the person is doing, and to legitimize and make sense of it: we should avoid using general category descriptions which indicate that the actions are inauthentic or wrong without indicating exactly what is going on. Thus, we might state that the client is acting to hold others responsible and legitimize his reasons for doing that, but we avoid the pejorative connotation of manipulation or playing games.

We should watch out whenever we find ourselves feeling sorry for our clients. In general, we feel sorry for others when we have no therapeutic plan of action, and so see only the hopelessness and pain. In contrast, when we are actively engaged in finding solutions, we do not dwell on feeling sorry for someone but invest in the promise for change: we are too involved with what we are attempting to contribute. Feelings of sorrow and pity for someone convey that the situation is hopeless, and may even encourage a client in his own indulgence in misery and self-pity. Feeling sorry for oneself is a primary aspect of a victim position and need not be encouraged by a complementary position on the part of the therapist. Compassion for our clients is important, but sorrow or pity indicates that we have been taken in by victim acts and that we have too few ideas for therapeutic interventions.

Most therapeutic orientations are wary of victim acts. Transactional analysis uses games interpretations to challenge victim acts by indicating the satisfactions attained through the appearance of being a victim. "Wooden Leg" portrays social lameness as a manipulative self-presentation constructed to avoid responsibilities—after all, what can you expect from a man with a "wooden leg"? When one allows others to take advantage, "Now I've Got You, You Son of a Bitch" (NIGYSOB) portrays it as a ploy to gain the final satisfaction of proving how very much they wronged him. The clever humor makes games interpretations such as these easier to accept. Behavior modification suggests that attention reinforces and thus maintains the complaining, and several orientations—including existential and humanistic—focus on the avoidance of responsibility. "Don't buy victim acts" was introduced by Ossorio as a policy for psychotherapy.

5. IF IT WORKS, DON'T FIX IT

Special care must be taken to maintain the sometimes subtle distinctions between characteristics which are strengths and those which are failings, in order to continually affirm existing adequacies. "If it works, don't fix it" is a reminder to avoid introducing uncertainties into areas which are functional and to reserve our tinkering for that which is dysfunctional already.

It is too easy, when frustrated by subtle and perplexing issues, to fail to uphold strengths, and to analyze and challenge those more obvious characteristics which seem to conceal the elusive problems. It is better in such cases to acknowledge that problems are not always apparent and to have patience with the investigative process. Problems are most easily seen within the structure of existing strengths, so any failure to uphold strengths serves only to conceal from us the important issues. It is better in such cases to have no answers than to be satisfied with the wrong answers.

Tinkering with strengths is considered a mistake in most orientations, but not in all. An opposing position holds that what appear to be strengths and virtues may instead be covers and defenses against underlying pathologies, and as such impede therapy. Such underlying pathologies are held to have been determined by experiences and conflicts of early childhood, and to be nonetheless of fundamental importance to present character. Long term regressive approaches attempt to strip away present functional characteristics to regress the patient to states which are developmentally earlier and less mature, so that childhood conflicts may be reexperienced, analyzed, and defused of their pathological potential and character may be reintegrated in a healthier manner. Involved here is the peeling away of present adaptive characteristics, in the expectation of being able to reassemble the patient later along healthier lines. The approach is patterned on a surgical analogy: as a surgeon cuts through a healthy abdominal wall to remove an infected appendix, so too should a psychotherapist slice through apparently healthy characteristics to expose and exorcise those otherwise concealed internal pathogens.

Yet once present adaptive strategies are diminished and a regressed state is achieved, is there any guarantee that the patient will be reconstructed in a healthier and more integrated manner? What about the lost opportunities and mishaps which may befall the patient while he is so regressed? Psychotherapy practice sometimes produces detrimental outcomes, and undermining adaptive functioning is one of the ways in which such casualties can occur. Characteristics which are assets, strengths, or virtues should be seen as such and not merely as defenses against underlying pathologies—they should be affirmed rather than undermined. Personal difficulties may be appraised and treated in the presence of such adaptive characteristics, and often all the more easily because of them. Any program to undermine adequacies in order to uncover and treat weaknesses should be undertaken only with the utmost precautions and only after every available alternative has been attempted without progress.

A number of characteristics usually do cushion the emotional impact of stress and adversities, and these are often subject to interpretation as escapes or defenses, perhaps from the infusion of psychoanalytic themes and terminologies. One client, for instance, has a tremendously fast wit, which she uses as a cushion against emotional trauma and also to enjoyably entertain herself and her friends. In the midst of a painful separation and divorce, she questions her adequacy and worth, and her sense of humor is included in the trial by fire: "Oh yeah, I've a great sense of humor, always there with a laugh. It's my way of fooling myself into surviving—old Jannie is easy enough to fool, but a grand lot of good it's doing me." A therapeutic response to this necessarily distinguishes between the source of the difficulties and everything else which is being thrown out to burn: "Be careful! Things go wrong, you're in a squeeze, and your impulse is to question everything about yourself. Something's wrong, granted, but the sense of humor is not a very likely candidate. Your humor enables you to stay involved, to stay alive, even sometimes to sparkle in the midst of the worst. It's a source of stability, an ally—you're taking a cheap shot at your most obvious characteristic. Whatever's going wrong, that's not it, and you had better resign yourself to some serious personal sleuthing."

The same may hold for religious beliefs, commitments to family, or a variety of generally stabilizing social and individual characteristics—any of which might be interpreted as defenses against underlying pathologies. Those characteristics that are generally constructive must be affirmed and not interpreted as obstacles in the search for the underlying pathologies.

7
Assessment

We conduct assessment procedures in order to gain the information we need for our therapeutic interventions. The following guidelines are suggestions for gaining practical information:

1. Assess what matters.
2. Use ordinary language concepts.
3. Collaborate.
4. Learn as you go.
5. Don't expect the client to be somebody else.

"Assess what matters" is the objective of pragmatic assessment, and the four additional guidelines are the means by which we pursue that objective.

1. ASSESS WHAT MATTERS

The objective of assessment is to gain the information we require for most appropriate therapeutic interventions. The information in the assessment must be true rather than false, but its practical utility is most important. It should be self-evident, that all truths are not created equal, nor endowed with inalienable relevance to life, liberty, or the pursuit of happiness. Some information is important or even critical, and other information is tangential or absolutely irrelevant to the conduct of effective psychotherapy. Pragmatics stands as the essential criterion, for the principle standard for adequate assessment is that it contain what is required for the tasks at hand.

Assessment must reveal those factors which contribute to the problems, and also factors which are strengths and might be brought to bear on the problems. Contributing factors might include behaviors, situations, or individual characteristics: most generally there are many identifiable contributing factors, woven together as configurations of behaviors, situations, and individual characteristics.

The *key factors* that we should attempt to alter are those which (1) *can contribute to major changes in the overall pattern* and (2) *are most readily altered through something we are in a position to do.* Sullen passivity in the face of obvious provocation would be a key factor with a generally passive client who feels continually taken advantage of: becoming more assertive could change social relationships and break several aspects of the pattern, and we should try to encourage it. Implementing assertiveness in turn might involve changing the individual's concepts, attitudes, motivations, and skills, all of which maintain the passive stance. There can be numerous key factors which might be altered in a case and many other factors which must be altered to change these key factors. Our assessment must identify these key factors as targets for interventions.

Key factors are necessarily present factors, since changes can be made in present factors only. Assessment might cover some past experiences as well, for the past might help to make sense of and legitimize the existing patterns. But the main thrust must be toward those factors which are to be changed and others which are to be used to create the changes, and those are necessarily in the present.

Although psychotherapy is not itself physiological intervention, it falls upon us as counselors and psychotherapists to assess and identify cases in which psychotropic medication or nutritional or other physiological changes would be appropriate, and usually to refer appropriate clients for those treatments. Often, we must also help monitor the effects of medications, to assess whether they continue to be appropriate or whether changes might be called for. So we must also be alert for indications for physiological interventions.

Stay with the Specifics

The most practical focus in any assessment is on key behavioral patterns. We want to know how the persons involved see things, and what they are doing, and what they might do instead which would work out better. The patterns should be given as specifics and not as broad general psychological categorizations. Describing a woman as "continually complaining to justify herself and to hold him responsible" is more useful than describing her as "rigid" or as an "hysterical personality." Describing each of two family members as "using upsetness to show how much he or she cares and to bind the other to him" is more useful than describing them as "fused together" or as an "undifferentiated ego mass." The specifics provide an indispensable basis for therapeutic interventions. Complaining to justify herself is something the woman is actually doing and so might change: we might legitimize and explore her reasons for justifying so much, and from there suggest alternatives. "Rigid" or "hysterical" are global personality categories and not something she is doing—she is not acting in order to be rigid or hysterical. One who focuses on these global categories would not be speaking to anything she might recognize as her own actions and choose to change. Similarly, using upsetness to influence is something that each is doing for understandable reasons and that might be changed; "fused" is something they are but not something they are doing, and it does not suggest practical interventions.

Psychotherapy tries to get persons to change how they see things and what they do and, by affecting these specifics, to promote general changes in personality and social relationships. We must stay with the specifics, for we must tie into these in our attempts to promote changes. Staying with specifics runs contrary to a general trend in our field to underplay simple description and to focus instead on global explanatory formulations.

Omit Extraneous Information

Case analyses too frequently include a clutter of particulars which have no real bearing on the interventions that one might choose. Such extras are padding and have no real business in the assessment, but are included anyway to make the assessment appear thorough or because the assessor was not sure what was important and what was irrelevant, and so included everything to cover his bases. One who is unsure of what is important does not want to omit anything at all and so collects a trash dump of information in which there are a few essentials covered over by everything else. Such extraneous information is not wrong in the sense of inaccurate, but neither is it entirely innocuous. Extraneous information causes problems because it draws attention away from the essentials, and thus confuses and obscures the picture.

Distinguishing between what is essential and what is extraneous may require considerable sensitivity and judgment, but the ability to do so is essential in clinical practice. It is well worth the effort to improve our abilities to make these distinctions.

It is perilous to try to specify categories of information which will invariably be irrelevant, for conceivably even the most tangential information might be relevant somewhere in some circumstances. But some sorts of information are tangential enough to be relevant to few, if any, therapeutic interventions. For instance, a "genogram" assessment, in its focus on the birth order and family lineage of the client and of his mother, father, aunts, uncles, cousins, in-laws, and so on, is going far afield of what matters to the tasks of psychotherapy. Birth order and family lineage are not things that can be changed through psychotherapy, nor are they resources to be used to promote changes. Such information may be interesting, but it is not a key factor for therapeutic intervention.

The case illustrations presented throughout this book give only the information essential to understand the grounds for choosing the suggested interventions. The point of limiting the information given here is not merely to save space: the conciseness is an attempt to give a sense of what an analysis looks like uncluttered with extraneous material, and so to familiarize the reader with this format and perhaps encourage similar conciseness among others.

Most active therapies gear their assessments to what they need to know to intervene, and this is especially so in the behavioral schools. The pragmatic standard for information is an alternative to the principle familiar in liberal arts education that all learning may be important and that concern for its practical utility belongs elsewhere.

2. USE ORDINARY LANGUAGE CONCEPTS

We use ordinary language concepts to structure our own observations and descriptions, and also to interpret and sometimes reinterpret or translate the client's observations and commentary.

Include Norms

Assessment must focus on that which is noteworthy and unique about the case at hand, for that which is human nature or found in all cases can be taken for granted and need not be assessed anew each time. It is those factors which are unique and distinctive that are so essential in tailoring our interventions to the particularities of Joe or Sally.

Our ordinary language concepts are used generally to distinguish the characteristics of one person from another and are well suited to make these distinctions. Ordinary language descriptors portray someone as being a particular way in contrast to other ways which might be expected. When we describe someone as anxious, intelligent, naive, loving, vain—or whatever—we portray him as that way in comparison to how he might have been instead. Someone who is properly described as anxious must be anxious in comparison to others: he might be anxious in comparison to other troubled people, to the average person, to those who are better adapted, to others in stress situations, to others in more ordinary situations, or to other women or other men; he might be more anxious than some or anxious, at least, compared to a yogi who achieves absolute calmness. Points of reference must be stated when they are not implicit from use and context. Descriptions loosed from their points of reference become unmanageably ambiguous. It would be misleading to describe someone as straightforwardly "anxious" who is merely mildly anxious, for the implicit comparison is to our expectations or to average persons. It would be better to describe him as "mildly anxious" or as "anxious, but no more than most."

Ordinary language description distinguishes between cases and contrasts in this important way with those general explanations which are expected to apply across cases; the latter may actually interfere with comparative assessment. Some formulations become standard stock explanations applied by those who rely on them in any and all mental health problems: for some, anxiety or insecurity is the cause of mental health problems; for others, it is an inferiority complex or a poor self-concept. One who relies on such general explanations might observe an aggressive youngster who boldly rules the roost at home and pronounce him insecure, anxious, or suffering from inferiority feelings. But consider the norms: he is not manifestly as insecure as another troubled youngster who stays to himself because he is afraid of people or as insecure perhaps as his "well-adjusted" sister who complies with everyone's expectations for fear of offending. Stating that he is "insecure" might pass as an explanation, but it is misleading for it has no point of reference and does not distinguish this child from other children. It becomes clear that it is no explanation at all when we specify that he is less insecure than others who do not have his problem. It would be better to describe him as bold, aggressive, or insufficiently socialized and to reserve "insecure" for those who are manifestly insecure when compared to other persons.

Stock general explanations which clump problem cases together may be misleading. If the youngster were comparatively insecure, we might suggest support and reassurance, but if he were overly aggressive, then continued reassurance would come to naught and we should rely instead on better ways to control him. Aggressiveness must be described as aggressiveness and not reinterpreted as insecurity, for otherwise the assessment can serve to mislead us.

The objective is to describe the particular characteristics, not to reinterpret them by substituting explanations broad enough to apply to everybody. A wide range of ordinary language concepts is available, and we try to sort through them and choose the right concept from among the many. Assessment requires a sensitivity and alertness, for we must wrestle with the phenomenon and not simply squeeze it into the same tired categories.

Descriptions may apply to a person in some ways in some situations but not in other ways. A man properly described as jealous might be jealous of the fellows who show interest in his attractive teenage daughter, but not jealous at all of other men who talk to his wife. A woman who lacks confidence with anyone who is a potential sweetheart might have considerable confidence with friends or business associates. It is important to specify the range of situations in which the descriptions apply or do not apply. Our initial impressions may be quite skimpy, and we should elaborate on them as more information becomes available.

See through the Client's Concepts

Many words may have more than one meaning, and we must consider what the client means by what he says. A young man confused by his fiancee's actions might say that she is really sensitive, leaving it to us to interpret this. The term "sensitive" has two distinct meanings in ordinary language: it translates as empathic (understanding others and being concerned for them) and also as touchy (thin skinned, easily upset, and too involved with one's own insecurities to be really concerned with others). Perhaps the young man could see that she is really touchy but calls her "sensitive" instead as a euphemism to avoid seeming too harsh on her. It is easier for him to remain ambiguous, and we must clarify the situation for ourselves and for the client as well.

Someone who says he did not "intend" to do something may mean that it was quite inadvertent and accidental, or he may mean that he was not conscious of wanting to do it, that he had not planned to do it, that he wishes now he had not done it, or simply that he should not be held responsible. We must interpret the statement in the light of the client's own semantics. Also, we should avoid saying to a client that he did something intentionally if he would interpret this to mean that he was wrong and we are holding him fully responsible. We might better say that he had legitimate reasons for doing it and was acting on those reasons.

We may need to translate somewhat when clients are using concepts which are confused, faulty, or merely at variance from standard usage. Ordinary language or our explicit common language system provides the template against which the clients' concepts can be readily compared and clarified. The use of ordinary language concepts facilitates communication, for the concepts we use and those of our clients are indeed quite similar. Clients are familiar already with our assessment categories, and we with theirs. By conducting psychotherapy in ordinary language, we facilitate those clarifications which are needed and maintain a mutually understandable basis of communication.

3. COLLABORATE

Assessment, like other aspects of psychotherapy, involves close collaboration between therapist and client. The client has been unable to understand himself adequately on his own; yet we must rely closely on his involvement and judgment in our attempts to understand him.

Ask for the Particulars

Even clients with their own quite unrealistic interpretations of things can often relate the actual statements in a conversation accurately enough for us to get a more realistic flavor of what is going on. The clients are seeing the statements but misinterpreting the significance of the actions. The client gives his interpretation of the events, and we ask, "What did you actually say to him?" or "What did he actually say which made it seem that way?" Often it becomes clear that the client is drawing conclusions which follow only tenuously, if at all, from the actual interaction. We use the particulars along with the situational context to better estimate the significance of the actions in question; then we take our conclusions back to the client.

In this way, therapist and client each contribute something essential which the other would otherwise be unable to attain. The client, since he was there, can contribute the particulars that would otherwise be inaccessible, and since we are more experienced and are in a position to be more objective, we can better interpret the meaning of the acts.

Suggest Plausible Interpretations

Most clients can conceive of only a limited range of possibilities on their own. Their conclusions reflect the limited possibilities they consider: they arrive at these conclusions not because these square with their observations better than the alternatives, but because they do not even consider the alternatives. We can see other possibilities, but we must enlist the clients' aid to weigh and evaluate them. We suggest alternative interpretations, and invite our clients to give their impressions and to bring forth whatever information they have for or against these interpretations. Clients who would not think of these possibilities on their own can nonetheless contribute a great deal to help sort through and evaluate them when we suggest them. We, as therapists, contribute the alternatives which the clients have overlooked; the clients contribute further information which is essential to weigh those alternatives adequately.

A woman client is hurt by a friend's turning against her and concludes automatically that it happened because she herself had been rude or had done something wrong. She assumes that others' intentions are always good and has not considered that the friend might be jealous of her new lover. We introduce jealousy as a possibility and ask then if it fits. Is this companion a foul weather friend who stands solidly behind you when things go wrong but turns nasty when you start to win? Does she have obvious reason to be jealous? Is she jealous of others? The client contributes the additional information, and together we try to figure out whether jealousy is the answer. There might be other interpretations of the incident as well, and we suggest any which seem to fit. We need not be sure of an interpretation before we introduce it. We introduce interpretations which are plausible and then rely on a collaborative process to evaluate their adequacy. Our participation is essential, for answers given by clients without our assistance may be narrow and quite inadequate to the tasks at hand.

Agreement is not taken as a final indication that an interpretation is adequate, nor disagreement as a final counterindication. Those clients who try to be cooperative might agree sometimes without having really weighed the ideas, and clients usually disagree when interpretations appear threatening, prejudicial, or otherwise unacceptable. We must weigh these factors in evaluating their responses. We may minimize spurious objections by legitimizing characteristics and by crafting our interpretations to make them as acceptable as possible to the clients. Understanding, objection, or a puzzled expression to an interpretation properly legitimized can be a good indication of its accuracy.

By introducing the possibilities, we structure what the clients will consider, and we must recognize that it is possible thereby to prejudice their answers. But we need not ensure that the clients' answers remain completely unaffected by our interpretations, for we have an ongoing relationship in which artifacts so introduced can be identified as such and steps can be taken to correct them. The purity of our assessments is not as important as their adequacy. We must collaborate to reach adequate formulations of the problems and manage as best we can any wrinkles introduced by our assessment methods.

Monitor Judgment

To assess judgment we look at the ways the client sizes up things and the reasons he has for his actions. We see how his understanding fits the available information and note apparent errors. We see his reasons and compare them to reasons which would be appropriate to someone in such circumstances. The client might weigh factors too heavily which should not be that important or miss factors which truly need to be considered. Poor judgment is shown when someone acts on considerations which are inconsequential or inappropriate to the existing circumstances and ignores more essential considerations.

We monitor judgment as the client tells of what he has done, and we explore with him the reasons he has which weigh into those actions. Some actions which initially seem questionable might be seen as more appropriate in the light of the ways he is viewing things, and others might be seen as more problematic. Our own personal judgment is involved, of course, for we must make estimates of which considerations seem important enough and should weigh into appropriate action. While no one is conscious of all his reasons, most clients are able to contribute many of the considerations that go into their actions. We make better sense of our clients as we listen to the ways they make sense of themselves.

Some schools expect the client to generate the answers on his own and avoid introducing any information into the process for fear of prejudicing the client's answers, like the opinion pollster who avoids saying anything which might suggest an answer to the respondent. Others, in contrast, make their assessments independently and avoid sharing their impressions with the client, anticipating that the client would have little to contribute and might misunderstand the information or be offended by it. The collaborative methods suggested here stand midway between these two extremes.

Recreate Episodes

We may gain more information by having the client involve himself more fully with the situations, experiences, and actions of interest. We promote this by having the client play out particular experiences and by watching him interact in a session with family or friends.

We might invite the client to actually enact a scene which he has been concerned about. Perhaps he would speak to a parent as if that person were actually there and then play the response he would expect from that person. Perhaps he could enact the scene including what he might say and also what he would want to say but could not say under the actual circumstances. Enactment involves someone more fully and may bring forth more information than merely talking about the concerns.

Recreating episodes is the mainline procedure in psychodrama, and is used extensively in Gestalt and related dramatic techniques such as family sculpting. Some orientations which rely heavily on recreating things may see this as therapeutically complete in itself and not consider anything more directive to manage the wealth of issues which are brought forth. The suggestion here is to recreate episodes for assessment purposes, and then feel free to use a range of other procedures to manage what is uncovered.

We can also recreate key episodes by inviting intimates into the sessions and having them address key issues. A husband who complains that he and his wife do not fight properly might not be aware how things go wrong when they try to argue. He knows things are going wrong, but there are critical actions that he is overlooking and thus does not understand and cannot tell us. He can give his limited observations and we can estimate other factors from those, but such an assessment might remain too sketchy. To really see what is going wrong, we should invite the wife into the sessions: we might ask what they have disagreed about recently and invite each of them to state his or her positions on the matter. We find out immediately what happens when they attempt to fight. Perhaps each accuses the other and complains about how miserable he is, but neither is willing to risk saying what he wants from the other. We can clarify what is happening and ask each to say what he wants, instead of what he feels he must endure. From there, we can see quite quickly how willing each is to go along with the other and find out what objections stand in the way of change.

Having both parties present allows us to recreate what happens when they fight, but cautions are in order against allowing the fight to continue as it would outside the session. Being accused and condemned raises insecurities and anger quite rapidly, so that clients become too interested in protecting themselves and retaliating against their antagonist to focus seriously on finding mutually compatible solutions. Our strategy is to allow the fight to continue only for the few moments it takes to see what happens, to stop the fight before anyone is seriously harmed, and then to take control and redirect attention to finding solutions. Recreating an argument is a way to assess, but it is not generally therapeutic by itself. The parties who are present can be enlisted to contribute to the solutions.

Friends in a session can be extremely helpful—it is surprising how much a best friend can enrich our understanding of what is going on.

Sometimes close friends offer highly accurate observations, and sometimes confused or distorted statements which indicate that the friends are themselves part of the problems. In either case we know better what is going on, and friends as well as family can be enlisted to contribute to the solutions.

Behavioral and of course family therapy orientations include the family as a standard method of assessment. Those who do not invite family or friends to at least one session are missing out on a valuable source of information.

4. LEARN AS YOU GO

There is a sensitive interplay between assessment and intervention: some initial assessment provides a basis for choosing appropriate interventions; and the way the client responds to those interventions yields further information and suggests critical questions for additional assessment. The interplay between the two is continual throughout any sequence of therapeutic sessions, so that assessment and intervention are not separate phases but co-occurrences relying, supporting, and building upon one another.

Interweave Assessment and Intervention

The position of assessment suggested here contrasts with what is familiar from medical practice in which assessment and treatment are usually separate phases, with assessment completed before treatment begins and little further assessment required unless something unexpected is uncovered. Assessment in psychotherapy belongs not as a stage separate from and prior to therapeutic interventions but as an integral aspect of the entire psychotherapy process. The present chapter on assessment is placed as it is here in the middle of the chapters on intervention guidelines to underscore the position of assessment across the psychotherapy process.

Our main objective in the first moments of an initial session is to make the client comfortable and to establish an alliance. We begin this prior to any formal assessment, and keep an eye out for what creates a comfortable atmosphere and casts us as allies. The client soon brings up some of what is going wrong, or we inquire, and the focus turns to exploring the problems. But as we assess we also work to make things more acceptable to the client, to further establish the alliance, and also to legitimize and in other ways accredit the strengths the client reveals. Thus, from the very beginning and as strongly as possible, we blend in therapeutic statements as we begin our assessment procedures.

We should begin to intervene to clarify and resolve issues as soon as we have a good sense of where to go with these sorts of interventions. We require information sufficient for the initial interventions, but not thorough and complete information on every aspect of all the existing problems. As we play out those initial interventions, we are free to turn again to assessment to pick up additional information which might suggest further or alternate interventions. When the initial interventions are successful, we look to further problem areas, and when unsuccessful, to further or alternate interpretations which suggest to us alternate strategies.

Too many practitioners shy away from early interventions for fear of making some frighteningly irretrievable error. Some caution is appropriate, but one can too easily become overly cautious. Small mistakes are usually not serious unless a therapist becomes stubborn and continues with them too long. Interpretations and interventions should be offered as suggestions anyway rather than as the final word from on high, and those which are not accepted by the client can be sidelined or altered with no harm done.

Most clients appreciate early therapeutic interventions, and it increases their confidence in the therapeutic process. Sometimes clients offer minor problems initially to see if we understand and can help with those problems, and then open up with their more major concerns after sufficient confidence has been built. In crisis intervention cases the immediate problem is readily revealed, but some crisis clients do not continue after the initial crisis is resolved, and there are many clients with little commitment who do not continue past a few sessions anyway. It is especially important with these people to intervene early so that something of value might be attained in the first sessions. Those who do not return may benefit nonetheless, and others who are uncertain might be swayed by seeing that therapy does indeed do some good. It would be an obvious mistake with these clients to devote the initial sessions entirely to assessment.

Supervisors and case conferences too frequently expect a complete assessment of the case, thus pressuring the presenting therapists to spend their first sessions gathering sufficient information to answer enough of the possible questions to avoid appearing unprepared. It would set a better atmosphere in case conferences to ask the presenting therapist what he did in the first session that was effective or at least therapeutically promising, so that trainees learn to sort and grasp promptly some key factors in a case and to move quickly into therapeutic interventions.

Assess through Interventions

We can learn from the interventions that others have tried. With a woman who complains continually that nobody understands her, we might ask how her husband or her friends respond when she tells them about the problem. Perhaps they ask her why she feels that way, or sympathize and try to reassure her, or perhaps they become frustrated themselves and tell her it's not so and not to talk that way. The responses which others are already giving are not doing a great deal of good, and by finding out the ways others are failing we can avoid falling into the same mistakes ourselves.

It is becoming more common to see clients who have been seen previously by other therapists, and we should learn from those earlier interventions. Some obvious questions include, "What are some of the things that your previous therapist talked to you about?" "What did he (or she) say which you thought was most helpful?" "What did he say which you felt was insensitive or wrong?" Perhaps some of the previous interventions have been helpful, but others have not gone far enough or have miscarried and caused problems. Through questions such as these, we gain some understanding of what the clients benefit or fail to benefit from, what they approve of, what they find objectionable or intolerable in a therapist. Perhaps a couple terminated with the last therapist because he did not seem to listen to what they were saying or perhaps because he listened all the time but did not talk. Maybe they left their last therapist because he felt they were badly mismatched and should separate; from this we learn that they are not ready to accept that sort of suggestion and will not tolerate a therapist who has that in mind. We do well to look at previous therapeutic attempts so that we might avoid repeating the same mistakes.

Many aspects of problems reveal themselves only as we begin to intervene. Current maladaptive patterns indicate restrictions in the client's ability to do something else which would work out better, but how embedded are those restrictions? Is it just that he has not thought of something better but would jump at it when he saw it, or is he so firmly stuck in his current patterns that he would be unable even to consider what would appear to us to be fairly obvious alternatives? We find out as we suggest that the client try out adaptive alternatives. A husband fails to compliment his wife, but could he do so relatively easily? We ask that he turn to her and compliment her on something she has done. If he cannot think of anything, then we suggest something and ask that he try it. If he is yet unwilling or unable, then that indicates a more stubborn problem. Perhaps he feels awkward complimenting her, or unmanly and weak; perhaps he is angry and sulking at her for neglecting him sexually, and so is strongly disinclined to appreciate her or pay a compliment. Perhaps he agrees and does give her a compliment, but she remains reserved and complains that he is just saying that because he is supposed to, but he does not really mean it. In this case, our attention turns next to what would it take for the wife to accept his compliments.

We sometimes phrase our suggestions to make them assessment questions as well. We might vary the standard "You might want to tell her more of how you are feeling" to make it a question: "What would it take for you to tell her more of how you are feeling?" The latter phrasing is both a suggestion to do something and acknowledgment that the client may be unable as yet to follow the suggestion, and an invitation to talk about the difficulties.

The nature and severity of the impediments to change can sometimes be "guesstimated" ahead of time, but they show themselves most easily, and are most readily explored, as we suggest changes and then continue by finding out what is holding things up. Therapeutic interventions are one of the major ways in which we learn what is holding things up and thus are primary methods of assessment. In many cases there is simply no way to find out ahead of time, and we must rely heavily on what we learn as we intervene.

Everything need not be included in our initial assessment—only enough to suggest an initial therapeutic direction. We should begin with the simplest plausible assessment of the problems and gear our interventions to address those problems. We introduce elaborations and further complexities into the assessment as additional leverage is needed. Initial impressions are sometimes altered, but almost always elaborated upon and expanded continually, over the course of psychotherapy.

The key factors that we should attempt to change are those which have a major impact on the overall pattern and which are most readily altered through something we are in a position to do. But often we must begin interventions aimed at several different factors before we come upon one or more which yield readily and which make an overall difference. We learn which factors are the key ones through our interventions as we try in a number of areas and see what works. Failures provide further information, and therapeutic successes provide some pragmatic validation of our assessments and complementary intervention strategies. We must learn as we go, for much of the critical information is simply not available prior to initial interventions.

Early interventions are characteristic in crisis intervention and in several of the more active therapies. Brief assessment, early intervention, and assessment through intervention require quick judgment and considerable confidence, and may be more characteristic of experienced than of inexperienced therapists (cf. Haley, 1971).

5. DON'T EXPECT THE CLIENT TO BE SOMEBODY ELSE

The problems clients have are oftentimes subtle and complex, and not adequately grasped by our initial assessments or overcome by our initial interventions. It is only natural to want the client to respond to our programs in a constructive manner, and it is too tempting to hold him responsible when he fails to do so. The reminder here is that we must adapt our programs to fit the capacities and inclinations of individual clients, rather than expect them to be the sorts of persons who are to benefit from our most standard intervention tactics. It is up to us to work with the sort of persons the clients actually are, rather than to expect them to be the sort with whom it would be easy for us to work.

Any expectation that clients should understand, readily agree to, and cooperate with whatever we suggest is simply unrealistic. Clients may indeed be quite impossible when one tries to manage them in the standard ways and they will frustrate therapists who cannot adapt. Persons do not sign on as clients in order to fulfill our expectations. Clients become clients in the first place because they are not adapting well to the ordinary conventional ways in which things are done. Their confusions and uncooperative attitudes are not merely impediments to solving the problems—in real ways they are the problems. In treating maladjusted people, the limitations caused by the maladjustments surely must be considered.

We may contribute perfectly good interpretations and suggestions, and find that a client fails to accept our interpretations or follow our suggestions. It is too easy here to become vaguely annoyed and to expect the client to get with it by showing that we really mean business, but if he were the sort of person who could profit from those interpretations and suggestions, then he would not be who he is but someone else better suited to profit from those interpretations and suggestions. We must see therapeutic failures not as indications of bad faith but as opportunities to reevaluate our assessment and to further understand the client's problems.

Many programs appear excellent, but the clients do not respond as expected. It is too easy to continue to expect clients to respond anyway and then consider it their own responsibility when they do not. When apparently excellent programs fail, we must reassess and adapt or alter the programs to suit the clients. A standard *quid pro quo* marriage approach suggests that husband and wife should each agree to give something, in exchange for getting something they really want. It is a good program, but many clients do not comply. Many of those who feel wronged and mistreated are motivated so strongly to get even that it is anathema to even consider a cooperative program which benefits their antagonists. The major motivations are toward retaliation and against cooperation. Rather than continue to expect such a person to cooperate anyway, we would do well to acknowledge the failure and to explore its basis. We might legitimize the problem by saying: "After the way he has treated you, why should you want to do something that would benefit him? That must feel like letting him get away with it." The retaliatory interests can be explored, and perhaps resolved or rechanneled, but it is foolish to expect cooperation from husbands and wives whose main interests are in getting even.

Preconceptions can contribute to unrealistic expectations. A humanist who sees persons as wholly good may fail to acknowledge that persons do purposeful harm to others. Everyday experience teaches us that persons are complex enough to intend ʋoth good and harm to others, and a preconception of simple goodness restricts one's ability to see the darker side of human action. One who expects clients to be always motivated to cooperate and make things work out is expecting them to be other than how they really are. Ideally everyone should be willing to cooperate to make things work out best for everybody, but not everyone conforms to these ideals.

One who expects others to be some other way may be attempting to require them to live up to his expectations. It is a way of exerting social pressure. But clients do not straighten out merely because we expect them to do so, for they have limited capacities which must be overcome. One who expects clients to overcome limitations they cannot overcome may be doing so in order to avoid responsibility himself for figuring out what would make things work. Requiring clients to do things they cannot do is a sure path to therapeutic failure.

Questions are too often asked which are well beyond what the client can reasonably answer, and we should avoid asking unanswerable questions. One way to estimate whether the question is answerable is to ask yourself what would qualify as an answer and then ask yourself if the client can come up with something like that himself. We should be able to see at least one plausible answer to any question. Should the client find the question too vague, we can suggest plausible answers, and invite him to weigh and choose between them. If you cannot come up with anything that would qualify as an answer, then that indicates that the client probably cannot either. Suggesting plausible answers is the major way to avoid asking unanswerable questions.

The following exchange between a frustrated psychotherapist and an inveterate alcoholic provides a parody of an unanswerable question:

Therapist: So what are you going to do to stop drinking?
Alcoholic: Gee, sir, I don't know.
Therapist: Well, think about it, and tell me in the morning what you figure out.

Therapist and alcoholic have not "figured it out" in the entire session together, and it should be quite clear that the alcoholic is not going to produce the answer magically on his own. The therapist expects the client to do something he has already shown himself incapable of doing, perhaps to avoid facing squarely the obvious impasse. It would be better to acknowledge that they have failed to find a reasonable facsimile of a solution.

It is our responsibility to adapt our programs to our clients rather than expecting them to be properly adaptable to our programs. This is not to advocate that we try to work with any and all clients, or even that we struggle forever with those clients we do take on. Not all clients can respond to the things we know how to do, for there are limits to our personal competencies as therapists and limits to the art of psychotherapy regardless of who is conducting it. Some clients show themselves to be unresponsive to everything we know how to do, and we should not continue and expect them to respond anyway when they have shown they cannot. Acknowledging the limitations to our competencies is not the same thing as holding the clients responsible for the failures. In addition, cost effectiveness and personal preferences must be considered: we might choose to work less with those who respond slowly if at all and to focus instead on those who respond more rapidly to therapy. We might focus on those with whom we are more personally compatible. As therapists, we should take responsibility for improving our competencies, but nobody should expect to treat every client successfully. We must accept responsibility for our choices of where and to whom we commit our energies.

8
Clarifications

The following guidelines are to clarify for the client existing situations and to clarify the means by which he attempts to change these situations:

1. Clarify situations.
2. Clarify concepts.
3. Use illustrations and images.
4. Deal with the reality basis of emotions.
5. Clarify operating premises.
6. Clarify alternatives.
7. Familiarize (bring it home).
8. Structure carry-over.

1. CLARIFY SITUATIONS

Actual situation and perceptions of the situation

What you understand or misunderstand contributes directly to your experiences and actions. What you take to be real provides the boundaries for what you might be concerned with and want to do something about, and also for what you consider as opportunities for possible actions. It is an essential aspect therefore in every experience and action, and in the overall way of life you might lead. Inadequate or mistaken observation is a basis for inappropriate responses and is found to be a contributing factor in most psychological problems. Clarification for the client of the situations in which he lives is essential in the therapeutic process.

Remove Confounding Factors

In many cases the client is contributing so much to foul up relationships that it is impossible for him to assess properly how others would behave under more ordinary conditions. A wife who complains that her husband does not speak to her and then ices him every chance she gets leaves us with an open question about him: Is he incapable of a more involved relationship, or is he simply responding to her aloofness and resentment? Sometimes an answer can be estimated from available information. Is the husband more involved with others than he is with her, or is he generally uncommunicative with everyone? Has he ever been more involved with her; if so, under what circumstances? Has he responded when she has been warm to him, or has he remained silent? Oftentimes, however, the answer is best attained by having the client clear up his or her contributions to the relationship problems and from there seeing if the partner is capable of changing. In this case, the woman might be coached to be warmer and see if it does make a difference. Changes can be suggested for each partner should both of them be involved in the sessions, so that the process seems fairer and more palatable. In this manner, we clarify important relationships by having the clients change and then seeing how others respond. If the wife here is unwilling to make such changes, she limits how much she will know about her husband: she cannot know how he would be to a warmer wife. And proper caution suggests that we too wait for real evidence before drawing conclusions about what sort of person he would be in a warmer marriage.

The same issue is seen in various forms. A client who is himself unassertive is often taken advantage of by family and friends. If the client were to stand up for himself, would those others become more considerate, or would they simply ignore the assertive requests and fight harder to stay in control? One good way to find out is to encourage assertiveness and see how others react. With those who accept your rights when you state them forcefully, there are opportunities for improved relationships, but not with those who are unyielding. An assessment principle introduced earlier is to intervene actively and see how our clients respond. The same principle is applied here to help the client see clearly those persons who are important in his life: encourage the client to act in improved ways so that he can see how others respond.

Weigh Alternatives with the Client

Often single observations can be interpreted more than one way, so that one needs to consider alternate interpretations and weigh several observations to piece together what is going on. Involved here is a process of reasoning from available observations to arrive at conclusions best fitted to the overall configuration of information. Our objective as therapists is not merely to arrive at the answers, but to improve the abilities of the clients to reason through similar problems in similar ways. The process requires considerable sensitivity and judgment, which are best transmitted by having the client participate actively in the entire reasoning process. It is a mistake to figure things out ourselves and then lay on the client our startling and ingenious conclusions. We should go through the reasoning process step by step in collaboration with the client and thus arrive jointly at some reasonable conclusions. In so doing, we familiarize our clients with the steps it takes to arrive at good conclusions and thereby improve their abilities to do so themselves.

When family or friends are included in the sessions, the process is made easier for we can see directly what those persons are saying and doing, and can share our impressions. By so doing, our clients see what we consider as important and how we interpret things.

Legitimize Misunderstandings

We clarify the specific paths by which the client is arriving at his wrong conclusions and so make sense of his misperceptions. In so doing, we accredit the client as rational despite his errors and gain further advantage: as the structure of sensibleness becomes clear, the particular errors stand out in contrast, and can more easily be analyzed and reevaluated.

The client may have a vested interest in particular views or may be threatened by more realistic alternatives. In some cases our conclusions are literally unthinkable to the client, for were things that way then familiar pillars of security would be shaken and foundations would have to be constructed anew. We can lend some credibility to our conclusions here by mentioning the limitation: "To you, it is unthinkable that this could be so." By this simple move, we avoid confrontation on whether or not it *is* so, and direct the conversation instead to that which limits the client's ability to consider it even as a possibility. In so doing we legitimize the client's failure to consider an alternative viewpoint.

Emphasize Understanding over Misunderstandings

Alternative approaches are available to try to redress misunderstandings: one might comment first to clarify the situation itself, so that the person can get a more realistic view of the situation and from there see that he had been misunderstanding it; or one can comment first that the person is misunderstanding things, so that he can look at his misunderstandings and change them. Several considerations suggest that we begin by clarifying that which is to be understood.

Identifying something as a misunderstanding is generally a two-step process: one who understands something a particular way attains an apparently more reliable observation, and then identifies the first view as less reliable and mistaken in comparison to the second. The most apparent quality of a misunderstanding is that is falls short by comparison to some other view which is taken to be more reliable.

Consider the issue in seeing others as trustworthy or untrustworthy. With a husband who is suspicious of his wife and sees her as untrustworthy, we begin in our assessment with an obvious question: Is she untrustworthy? Only as we answer that can we understand whether he is misperceiving his wife's actions or perceiving them accurately. Suppose she is faithful to him and concerned with his best interests, so that his failure to see her as trustworthy shows him to be an overly suspicious individual. It is on the basis of viewing her as less conniving than he sees her to be that we conclude he is misperceiving the matter.

In what ways might we best enable him to overcome this problem? An initial tactic is to take the client through the same reasoning processes that anyone must go through to identify a misperception. We might analyze with him the wife's actions, weigh plausible interpretations, and draw the conclusion that her actions in themselves do or do not suggest unfaithfulness. Whether agreeing or disagreeing with our conclusion, he can see that we have taken the issue seriously, and he generally appreciates the consideration and thoroughness of the analysis. Often the person can understand the reasoning but is unable to actually see things that way; in such cases, he can see his own perceptions as misperceptions, and is more apt to cooperate with the sometimes lengthy task of changing those perceptions.

The overall objective must be to clarify the situation itself, rather than to clarify misunderstandings of the situation. Should the husband come to see his wife as trustworthy, then whether or not he understands his suspiciousness he has resolved his problems. Should he come to see that he is excessively suspicious but still perceive his wife as unfaithful, then his problem remains in full force and his insight that he is suspicious is of little consequence. Improvement occurs as he comes to see the situation more accurately and not simply as he understands his misunderstanding. It is the ability to see clearly one's situations and relationships which must stand as the critical objective; interpretations of misinterpretations are only one of the ways of accomplishing that objective.

The client here is too untrusting, but the issue is broader and more complex than that. Aside from whether he should trust more or take more risks, the issue is primarily one of judgment. Whom should he trust, in what circumstances, and to what extent? What sort of risks are involved, and how does he recover without too much grief if someone fails him? Focus on the relationship factors for or against trusting invites the client to look beyond his introspective inadequacies and to begin to see the real world complexities so essential for good judgment. The issue is whom and when to trust, and that must be answered whether or not someone identifies himself as too untrusting. It is important to look at specific relationships and understand them on an individual basis. Some persons may be found to warrant more trust than one is giving; others, less trust. The major issue is in making the distinctions, and extremely suspicious persons have as much or more difficulty as anyone else in telling the difference between trustworthy and untrustworthy companions.

One might analyze situations and thereby clarify misinterpretations, and one might analyze misinterpretations and thereby clarify the situations which are being misinterpreted. Each has its place so long as they are the means to the primary objective, which is to enable the client to see clearly the situational realities that he is facing.

The principle here to first clarify situations is suggested by several orientations but contrasts to that of other familiar schools. Behavioral orientations emphasize objective measurement, reality therapy clarifies the reality of existing situations, and family orientations look firsthand at what actually happens in the intimate relationships. A good many eclectics tend to focus first on situational realities and from there try to redress confusions and misunderstandings about those realities. In contrast, analytic and dynamic traditions interpret misperceptions but underemphasize situational realities; Gestalt unfolds the complexities of the client's views but does not suggest more realistic views; client-centered accepts without questions whatever interpretations the client makes; and phenomenologists emphasize individual experiences over the actual situations. These latter schools focus primarily on what the client sees and experiences, and secondarily or not at all on what is there to be seen.

2. CLARIFY CONCEPTS

Concepts used to structure observation

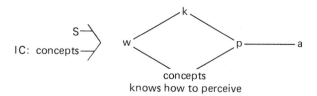

concepts
knows how to perceive

The clarification of everyday concepts provides a sturdy foundation for our common language approach to psychotherapy, and we naturally advocate the same good foundations for our clients. Concepts are those distinctions we use to order our world. Clients who are using concepts which are inadequate or confounded by extraneous meanings are restricted in their abilities to figure things out. Progress is often gained through clarification and improvement of key concepts. Such concepts may be simply impoverished or confounded by extraneous meanings, and these will be dealt with here in turn.

Elaborate Impoverished Concepts

Troubled persons tend to use concepts which draw distinctions in queer ways and thus misstructure reality. The concept of "selfishness" provides a good example, since it is an important issue in social relationships and is often misunderstood. Selfishness for many troubled persons means standing up for oneself, taking care of oneself, or merely finding enjoyment in something. Thus, finding satisfaction in life means being selfish. Such persons, to avoid being selfish, restrict themselves to patterns of miserableness clearly void of observable pleasures.

Too frequently, practitioners attempt to challenge such problems by telling the client that it is good to be selfish and that he should feel free to be selfish. This sort of solution accepts the existing misconstrued concept and turns it backwards: it accepts that enjoyment is in itself selfish, and then argues that selfishness is right and good rather than wrong. The solution violates our commonsense understanding that selfishness is wrong and so invites confusion, failure, and possibly narcissism or, in plain language, selfishness.

A better solution clarifies the key concept. We might begin with a simple statement of what selfishness means, such as, "Selfishness means taking more than your share at somebody else's expense," and from there apply the concept appropriately to the client's situation: "When you do things you enjoy you feel it is selfish, but in order to qualify you must take more than your share so that somebody else misses out. There is no such thing as more than your share of enjoyment, for there is enough for everyone who seeks it. When you enjoy yourself you are more pleasant to be around, but when you are miserable you make others miserable too, so in that sense there is even some social good in enjoying yourself." Applying the concept to the client's situation is helpful. One young woman, for instance, feels that it would be selfish of her to ask her husband to do things in their lovemaking especially to please her, but she resents his inconsiderateness. He, on the other hand, would love nothing better than to please her. One might comment: "You feel it would be selfish to ask for what you want, but it would please him greatly for you to do just that. When you find pleasure in your lovemaking, you give him pleasure. It would be generous of you, and not selfish, since by asking for what you want you would please him as well as yourself."

Sometimes by looking out for ourselves we might cheat others, but this is not generally so, and in many cases we even enrich the lives of those around us. A failure to see the difference is a clear limitation. By enabling a client to make distinctions such as this, we open up new possibilities for more sensible actions.

Untangle Confounded Concepts

An individual may include extraneous meanings in the distinctions he makes and thus confuse critical issues. Concepts which include extraneous meanings might be termed confused, overinclusive, or confounded concepts: the extraneous meanings obscure the critical distinctions.

One might have a concept for instance of marriage as entrapment, of success as selling out to the establishment, or of suffering as a sign of love. In confounded concepts the one thing means the other, so that there is no separating them: marriage means entrapment, is always entrapment, and cannot be seen otherwise. Appropriate concepts in contrast allow one to make the available distinctions: some marriages are entrapping, and others are quite freeing. Confounding is involved when an individual sees *all* marriage as entrapment and is unable to conceive of marriage which is not entrapment or to see it that way when it is in front of his eyes. Marriage means entrapment, and the concept is binding upon his view of reality.

Confounded concepts such as these are frequent sources of problems. A young man, for instance, who has made plans to marry might find himself beset with insecurities, and feeling that the freedom and joy of life are gone. Little does it matter that he and the woman have spent many enjoyable hours together, that she loves him dearly, or even that they have been living together in a relationship which is marriage in all but formal legal sanction. The same woman who has been so pleasant as a sweetheart and companion is now to be a wife—an agent of the oppressive system of entanglements—and he, who so enjoys his freedom, is to become a husband. His concept of marriage is binding on the participants. Anticipation through misconstrued concepts casts a sense of gloom over the coming changes and tends to reconstruct the relationship so that it fulfills his expectations of it.

We begin here in the most obvious manner, by making explicit the misconstrued concepts: "To you, marriage means entrapment. Your concept of marriage is that it is entrapment, and you cannot see it any other way." We attempt to clarify the concept for the client by outlining variations that marriage might take and by asking the client to look into them: "What would a marriage be like in which there was warmth and love?" "What except your own expectations keeps you from continuing as marrieds with the same friendship you shared as lovers?" "Have you ever seen a good marriage? Would you recognize one if you saw it?"

Legitimizing the confusion is usually a step in untangling it. Suppose the young man grew up in a family in which his parents sulked, moped, and appeared miserable but stayed together, as the story goes, for the children. The upbringing might be used to legitimize his perceptions, as follows: "Your main exposure has been to your parents' marriage; you saw the miserableness and entrapment, and that there was no escape. It is not so surprising that you have come to see marriage as entrapment and are wary of it." By legitimizing the misconception, we show the client the sense he makes to have the views he has and also open the way for reconsidering those views. One marriage is not a good enough sample for all marriages, and other possibilities can be considered.

Confounded concepts such as these are common. Steps to clarify them are to make explicit the extraneous meanings, to suggest a clearer concept and draw attention to supportive considerations, and to legitimize the original misconstrued concept. The clarification of confounded concepts opens possibilities for the client to better structure reality. The clarification of inadequate concepts resolves problems in some cases, although in other cases the problems are more embedded and do not yield. Either way the clarification is a good beginning in that it provides an initial understanding of the problems and suggests some further paths to explore.

The clarification of the client's concepts is included in some cognitive approaches and is the major focus in personal construct psychotherapy (cf. Landfield and Leitner, 1980). But there is too little concern generally with the analysis and clarification of those everyday concepts used by the clients, perhaps because so many orientations push their own theory-based concepts as replacements for everyday concepts.

3. USE ILLUSTRATIONS AND IMAGES

Images and illustrations can construct critical distinctions in a way that entertains and intrigues the client, and so maintain rapport and avoid generating resistance.

Take the concept of avoidance motivation. Some actions are performed in order to get what you want, and others to avoid what you do not want. Avoidance motivations have two interesting characteristics: merely avoiding adversities is less satisfying than getting what you genuinely want, and seeking to avoid something can be readily confused with actually valuing its opposite. Avoidance motivations can be problematic, since they involve fewer satisfactions and are easily confused with strivings for things.

The following *Poor No More* image introduces and clarifies some of the issues of avoidance motivation: "A middle-aged man comes into my office, and he is unsatisfied with his life. What matters to him most, as he tells it, is money. He is an executive and so makes a considerable amount of money, and he has all the accoutrements of the good life that money can buy. At this point, we want to say, 'Wait a minute. If you care so much for money and you have so much of it, then why are you so unsatisfied?' We investigate further, and find that the fellow grew up dirt poor, humiliated and contemptuous of his poverty, and swore at an early age that he would not stay poor. He was smart enough and worked hard for many years, and so finds himself now with considerable money. Even though he has so much money, the possibility of poverty still frightens him, so he continues to struggle for more and more money, in order to avoid that possibility. So at this point, we know why he is so unsatisfied. It is not wealth that means something to him, but rather the avoidance of poverty. And running your whole life in order to avoid poverty cannot yield all that many satisfactions."

Poor No More can be applied to a variety of avoidance motivation problems. Consider for instance a young woman who is continually trying to please everyone and to avoid doing anything which might cause disapproval. She is outgoing and considerate, and indeed everyone does like her, or at least almost everyone. Yet life is unsatisfying; she lives in continual fear of others' opinions and does not enjoy the friendships which she does have. Her problem, as she sees it, is that she cares too much about others' approval.

Note first of all that there is something amiss in her assessment of her problem. She gets considerable approval from others, and if that were what she really cares about, she should find this satisfying and find herself feeling good about others instead of continually frightened by them. A better estimate is that what she mainly cares about is avoiding disapproval.

Poor No More can be used to introduce and structure consideration of such avoidance motivation issues in the following manner: "Your problem, as you see it, is that you care too much for others' approval. My impression, however, is that you do not really have your eye on the approval you are getting. My impression is that what you really care about is avoiding disapproval. Let me outline an image which we use to clarify these issues." The image is then presented to the client, and from there it is applied to the specific situation: "In your case, it is not poverty but rather disapproval which is of concern. It is not Poor No More but *Unacceptable No More*. But the issues seem to be the same. You say you care too much about approval, but you have plenty of it, and if it really matters to you then why does it not make you happy? One answer is that it is not approval but avoiding disapproval which matters so much. Does that fit?" "This helps explain why you find so little satisfaction in the friendships you do have. When what matters is avoiding something, then the best that you can do is to break even: on a wrong day someone disapproves, while a perfect day is one in which you do not get any disapproval. Either way you do not get ahead, and there is little satisfaction."

Often the concept applies in some ways or to some extent, but does not apply in other ways. Perhaps the client strives to avoid disapproval from most acquaintances and from members of her family, but has a single close friend whose approval she sees and counts on. The image introduces the concept, and from there we confer with our clients on where and to what extent the distinction pertains. Where there are some areas of attainment motivations rather than avoidance motivations, then these provide an important contrast. The client can see that approval really can matter, and can use that to contrast and better understand the avoidance of disapproval.

The issue from here is to find ways for the avoidance of disapproval to become less significant as a life motivation. One way is to analyze directly the importance of the disapproval. How much disapproval is involved, and how much should it affect your life? A complementary approach is to suggest that gaining approval should be more important than the client allows it to be. The approval and love of others should give you satisfactions and build your esteem, so that as you gain good feelings from those who do approve, you are thereby fortified against times when someone disapproves. One who sees the problem as one of caring too much about approval has reason thereby to try to make approval matter less in her life, and that is what most persons have been doing who present the problem in these terms. Our therapeutic strategy then is to challenge directly the motivations to downgrade approval and to show the clients good reasons to upgrade it instead.

Avoidance motivations can take a variety of forms, and the image can be adapted to any of them. Poor No More became Unacceptable No More in the adaptation just discussed. One might strive to appear smart, sophisticated, or attractive but really care mainly about avoiding appearing stupid, graceless, or unattractive; one might strive to be popular and included but care mainly about avoiding being unpopular or lonely. A person might strive to win but care mainly about avoiding losing: It is not the sweetness of winning which is on the person's mind—it is avoiding the anguish of losing. The therapeutic image gives the sense of what is happening, how it might have come about, and what is wrong with a life constructed that way. It has implications for what to do to correct the problem.

An image plants the essential concepts in the mind of the client, and also serves to organize and hold the concept for us as therapists. Read over this image again, use it once or twice, and you should find it easy to catch avoidance motivation issues and to remember what to do about them. Will you ever hear another client say that he cares too much about others' approval without wondering if what he or she really cares about is avoiding disapproval? Some images are constructed for an individual client, while others are used over and over to present common issues with a variety of clients. Poor No More was suggested by Ossorio as a standard way to introduce avoidance motivations.

There is a natural sequencing of presenting and then applying imagery which works to our advantage. We present the image and elaborate on it so that the client understands the critical issues, and from there, we apply it to the client's situation. Presentation of the image itself is intriguing to most clients and invites them to ponder the issue before personally sensitive applications have been raised. It does not generate resistance, since it is about things in general rather than specific to the particular client. Once the image has been presented and the concept understood, it becomes easier from there to talk about where and to what extent it applies in the client's life.

Aphorisms, analogies, metaphors, mottoes, parables, poems, rules of thumb, stories, jokes, witticisms, and so on can all carry information. The use of any or all of these is appropriate to imprint information on clients' minds.

Several orientations are noted for using imagery and illustration, including modern Adlerians; adherents of transactional analysis; hypnotherapists in trance induction procedures, à la Milton Erickson; humanists, and advocates of guided fantasies. Imagery and illustration have been suggested recently to augment standard rational-emotive procedures (Wessler and Wessler, 1980). Many eclectics make liberal use of images and illustrations. It may be something of a neglected art nonetheless, for it is a complex skill, and there is too much emphasis in texts, journals, and training programs on condensing ideas, and too little attention is paid to bringing them to life. Writers frequently ignore the very stuff that makes information come alive, in the interest of saving space and perhaps also appearing serious minded. In clinical practice we have ample time to elaborate and embellish, and clients appreciate relief from the seriousness with which they too often conduct their own lives. The point is to communicate effectively so that clients see and maintain the ideas: for this images and illustrations are indispensable.

4. DEAL WITH THE REALITY BASIS OF EMOTIONS

Situational realities in emotions

The client's situation as he sees it is a major contributing factor to the feelings and emotions he experiences. There are really two factors involved here: the situation as it actually is, and the client's perceptions and misperceptions of his situation. One reacts to the way things are, but one reacts more specifically and immediately to the way one perceives things to be. Perceptions themselves are understandable from the actual situation and from the individual's distinctive ways of seeing and interpreting things.

An individual's situation as he sees it is a major contributing factor to his feelings and emotions, and also to the actions he takes to deal with his situation. So one major way to influence someone is to influence what he perceives, and to accomplish this, there are two major therapeutic paths. (1) To the extent that the client misperceives his situation and sees it as worse than (or merely different than) it really is, our task then is to clarify with him the existing situation and enable him to perceive it more accurately. (2) To the extent that the client is in an uncomfortable situation and is accurately perceiving how things are, our task is to clarify ways in which he might more effectively manage the situation and perhaps change it to suit him better. The objective either way is to deal with the reality basis of the emotions: in the former case, we clarify what the reality basis actually is; in the latter, we clarify ways to change it.

With a client who is lonely we might convey that we accept and understand the feelings of loneliness, but there is only so much that can be accomplished with this response. The major focus should be on the reality basis of those feelings, so that the essential question is, "In what sense are you really alone, and what can you do about it?" One who is lonely generally sees himself as having no close friends or as being separated from those who are important. Perhaps there are others near who have friendly feelings about him, but the person is wary or considers others beneath him and himself above them, so that he fails to appreciate available friendships: he needs to see more clearly that there are friendships available and that it is his attitude toward others which causes his loneliness. Perhaps, on the other hand, the person is socially introverted, knows few people, and is afraid to meet anyone: in such cases the person needs encouragement and perhaps training to become more active socially, in order to meet others and make friendships. The therapeutic task either way is to deal not merely with the feelings but also with the perceptions and situational realities which are the basis of those feelings.

There is a logical connection between perceptions of situations and feelings and emotions. Perceptions of being friendless or socially isolated go with feelings of loneliness. Anxiety and fear are associated with being threatened or in danger. Anger goes with being provoked or mistreated. Feelings of guilt go with the perception of having done something wrong. These go together because of the logical connections between seeing things in particular ways, and the feelings and emotions one generally has toward those sorts of things (cf. Ossorio, 1976).

Situations, perceptions, and emotions in issues of anger and guilt are explored in the following illustration. A young woman is being confused by a highly manipulative relationship with her mother. The young woman fears that she has failed her mother and, more specifically, that she is ungrateful, neglectful, and inconsiderate toward the woman who has given her whole life to raise her. She feels insecure, worthless, and guilty over all the trouble she is causing. She lives with her mother, is conscientious and attentive, and does everything she can to avoid hurting her mother and to make up for everything. She does not understand why she is so fearful and depressed so much of the time. Yet she acquired the attitudes she has through direct inculcation. Her mother complains continually about how much she gives to her daughter and how little she receives in return, most probably in order to obligate and maintain control over her daughter. The mother figures that her daughter owes this to her and fears perhaps that her daughter might abandon her if she allowed her to go her own selfish way.

In brief, the young woman is passive, insecure, and being run over by an angrily manipulative and long-suffering mother. Passivity and compliance in the face of such obvious mistreatment are clearly contributing to the problem, and one major therapeutic objective is to enable this woman to confront her mother, challenge the mistreatment, and take some steps toward normal independence. At the outset, however, suggestions to challenge her mother would be unsuccessful, because she sees the conflicts with her mother as caused by a failure on her own part, and not as caused by manipulation and mistreatment by her mother. The initial step must be to clarify with her the reality basis of the feelings she is having. She needs to understand clearly that she is not inconsiderate but is herself being mistreated, and to see this, she must come to perceive her mother's accusations accurately as inauthentic and manipulative.

The initial step, therefore, is to enable her to see through the suffering and accusations, and to understand them for what they are—manipulative attempts to obligate and subordinate her. As long as she perceives the accusations as legitimate, then the acid of those accusations binds her, and she sees herself as guilty and has strong reason to capitulate. When she sees the accusations as manipulative rather than legitimate, then her reasons to capitulate are no longer so strong, and she gains reason to resist. Capitulation makes sense when you are in the wrong, but making a stand makes sense when someone else mistreats and wrongs you. In seeing more clearly the reality of the situation, the young woman gains reason to act more appropriately toward the problems. Clarifying with her the realities of her relationship with her mother may require considerable time and energy, for she would have some investment in the current way of seeing things. Nevertheless, this is an essential objective: she must perceive what is really going on if she is to see the sense in an appropriate way to deal with it.

Assertive stands are generally therapeutic to the extent that they affirm your rights and prevent others from ignoring or mistreating you. But they are not particularly therapeutic when others ignore them and continue to run over you anyway, for that further confirms your impotence. Assertive stands are therapeutic to the extent that they deal effectively with the reality basis of the problems.

Since the woman does not acknowledge or express anger, one might consider that she needs to be able to do so. But at the outset, our interpretations of underlying anger or suggestions that she express anger would gain little. Were we to look only at the mistreatment she is receiving, we would see that she has every right to be angry, and we might assume therefore that she really is angry. But it is important to look not merely at the situation but at her perceptions of the situation, and to match her emotional states to her perceptions. As she sees it, her mother is justified and she herself is the one in the wrong. She says she feels guilty rather than angry, and in recognizing her perceptions, we see that it makes sense for her to feel the way she says she does. She feels guilty because she sees herself as in the wrong, whereas she would feel angry if she were to see herself instead as provoked and mistreated. Perhaps she alternates between feeling guilty and feeling angry, as persons sometimes do, seeing herself alternately as the wrongdoer, then as having been mistreated, and then again as the wrongdoer. Should she get angry, she might take that as further indication that she is ungrateful and in the wrong; so she would quickly suppress the anger, feel guilty about it, and try to make amends for it. When she can see better the reality of the relationship, she will be in a better position to feel emotions that are more appropriate to that reality: when she sees that she is being manipulated and abused, she will feel angry rather than merely guilty and will be able to accept the anger. The anger can then be channeled into assertive counterresponses to the manipulation and intimidation she is facing, for justified anger over the mistreatment would provide additional motivations for assertive stands with her mother.

Note here that the problem is not simply a matter of being unable to express her feelings. It is a matter rather of seeing more clearly the realities of the situation, so that she will have more realistic and appropriate feelings which can serve as motivations for more appropriate actions. The perceptions a person has of his situation contribute directly to his emotional states, and as he comes to see better the realities of his situation, his emotions should become more appropriate to that situation. As he sees things more clearly, he is in a better position to respond to them more appropriately, and feelings and emotions are but one aspect of a more appropriate response. Seeing existing situational realities and dealing appropriately with them go hand in hand, for accurate perceptions and the corresponding appropriate emotions are proper bases for effective action.

Expressing feelings may affect for better or worse the reality basis of those feelings. One who expresses anger over being mistreated may find that others listen, that problems are clarified, and that relationships improve. In other circumstances, one who expresses anger may find that others see him as unjustifiably antagonistic and counter with further antagonism of their own, so that relationships deteriorate and one has more problems than before. Like assertive responses, expressions of anger are therapeutic to the extent that they contribute constructively to the reality basis of the emotions, and not otherwise. Orientations in the analytic and humanistic veins uphold expressing feelings as essential to adequate mental health, whereas others in the behavioral, rational-emotive, and reality therapy traditions see it as vastly overrated and often problematic. Our analysis here suggests a way of integrating the countermanding voices: the expression of feelings is therapeutic when it clarifies and improves the reality basis of those feelings, but not when it confuses or exacerbates things. It is not a matter of freeing oneself from the emotions by expelling them through their expression, but of freeing oneself by dealing constructively with the factors which contribute to and cause the emotions.

Thus, in advocating the expression of emotions, we should be clear about what issues might be clarified and what situations improved in the process. Blind expressions of emotions such as anger, without regard to their effects, may generate too much heat and too little light: it is better to realize what we are getting into. The pragmatic considerations suggest that we encourage expression of feelings when it helps the client accept his feelings, clarifies situations, and improves relationships, but not when it commits him to confused or indulgent positions, antagonizes others, or jeopardizes relationships. "Deal with the reality basis of emotions" was introduced by Ossorio as a policy for psychotherapy.

To deal with the reality basis of emotions we clarify the situations contributing to those emotions and also clarify the ways to change those situations. The two guidelines following explore further the pragmatics of attempting to change situations: the first focuses on the approaches the client is currently using; the second, on generating more effective alternatives that might be used instead.

5. CLARIFY OPERATING PREMISES

Client's understanding of how to do it

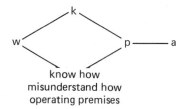

know how
misunderstand how
operating premises

Some understanding how or misunderstanding how you might accomplish your objectives is an aspect of each attempt to accomplish something. This know-how or competency aspect of the action is appropriately termed an operating premise: for any purposive action, the operating premise is that that act is a way of attaining the objective of the act. The actor has as a corresponding individual characteristic the tendency to utilize that particular premise: he takes it that such acts are ways of attaining those things he is after.

For instance, punishing a child in order to make him work harder has as its operating premise that punishment is a way to make someone work harder; punishing a child to show that you are superior to him has the premise that punishment is a way of showing you are superior. Showing upset feelings in order to gain special consideration has as its premise that showing these feelings is a way to gain special consideration; in sulking in order to get even, the premise is that it gets you even. More generally, for any action there is always the premise that the act is a way to accomplish what it is being done to accomplish.

One of the important quirks of everyday operating premises is that they are most generally implicit: as with any know-how or competency issue, you are not generally conscious of the nature of your operating premise or conscious for that matter that you even have a premise. There is this important contrast between knowing *that* something is so and knowing *how* to do something: you are generally quite well aware of the former, but the latter is usually quite inarticulate (cf. Ryle, 1949). As long as premises remain implicit, they are not subject to change through conscious consideration and reevaluation.

The effectiveness of various ways of acting is the concern here. Some actions are appropriate to what they are done to accomplish, whereas other actions are ineffective or dysfunctional, perhaps even losing for the actor his objectives. In the former, the individual knows how to bring about what he wants, and his operating premises are valid ones. In the latter, he misunderstands how, and his premises are invalid and cause problems; acts such as these are not effective ways to attain the desired outcomes. When a person has insufficient know-how and invalid operating premises, he goes about things in the wrong ways and so fails to attain what he is after. One who acts in ways that cannot gain for him what he seeks is in the grips of invalid operating premises.

Our task is to recognize the premises on which the client acts, to clarify and make them conscious for the client, and to evaluate their validity with the client. Where the premises are invalid, our task further is to have the client see this himself so that he no longer uses these ineffective means to get what he seeks.

Some sensitivity may be required to correctly identify implicit premises, and considerable effort may be involved to convince the client to let go of premises which are invalid. One mother becomes extremely upset when her daughter misbehaves, and the mother fails to exercise appropriate authority. An initial therapeutic objective is thus to diminish the mother's upsetness and enable her to exercise authority over her daughter. Straightforward justification of the use of authority and instructions on how to do it have little impact with this woman: the mother contends that the daughter should care more for her and be more considerate. The argument here is that the daughter should see how much her misbehavior is upsetting her mother and should show her love by correcting her conduct. Additional leverage is thus needed, and we might focus on the apparent commitment to being excessively upset. The mother argues that if the daughter realized how much she was hurting her mother, she would not continue to act that way. She thus reveals her operating premise: "Showing her how she is upsetting me should cause her to realize her responsibility for my feelings and to improve her conduct." The upsetness, as the mother sees it, should evoke in the daughter some caring and sense of responsibility, and should cause her to regret her mistakes and act properly. Instead and quite understandably, the daughter sees the weakness, loses respect for her mother, is angered by the manipulation, and uses the opportunity to do as she quite well pleases.

The operating premise is explained to the mother with the daughter present. The mother agrees that she expects her being upset to control her daughter's misbehavior, and she sees that it has not had the expected effect. But she continues to argue that her feelings should mean something to her daughter and seems genuinely baffled that the daughter misbehaves anyway. Our task at this point is to show the mother that her operating premise is invalid, and we might pursue this in one or more of several ways.

We might legitimize the invalid premise. Suppose that when the mother was a youngster, she and her family and friends were compliant and concerned with their parents' feelings, and would go to considerable lengths to avoid hurting their parents' feelings. She learned naturally enough that being upset merits, and indeed gains, special consideration from others and causes others to improve their misconduct. We use her experiences as a youngster to legitimize her premise, for at that time consideration of mother's upset feelings did indeed cause one to correct misconduct. But families change, and youngsters today are more involved with their friends and with television, family authority is weaker, and upset feelings no longer command the compliance they once did. We thus show the mother that she acquired the premise honestly enough, but that it no longer has the same validity in the current modern patterns of family relationships.

We might challenge by inviting her to consider the available evidence: "You feel that a youngster who sees how much hurt she is causing, if she loves you, would have to change. Yet you have been upset with her for many years—quite openly and conspicuously upset. Could you conclude that it is not doing the job for you?" We might continue: "If showing how much she upsets you were the golden path to raising responsible children, then Julie would be one of the most conscientious children on the block, for you are certainly one of the most long-suffering of parents."

Finally, we might invite the mother to continue to act on her premise—perhaps even in an accelerated or exaggerated manner—so that through further observations she invalidates for herself her misconceived approach. Such tacks have a paradoxical appearance and are best done with a touch of humor, for example: "Perhaps being upset should cause your youngster to realize her mistakes and change, but maybe you have not yet really given it a fair chance. My opinion is that it will not work, but you are not going to take my word for it. You might want to give it a try for a few more weeks, but this time really do it right. You might show that you are extremely upset by the way she is treating you and lay it on with extra exuberance. Have you tried suggesting that she is going to cause you to have a nervous breakdown? Perhaps something exotic might get her attention."

In addition to controlling misbehavior, several motives may be involved in the commitment to showing upset, such as appearing to be a concerned and loving parent, presenting oneself as so undone already that nobody would dare accuse you of messing up your daughter, or transferring responsibility for failures from yourself to your daughter. Each additional reason for being upset must be addressed on its own.

Clarification of operating premises has important commonalities to some of the philosophies and methods of Eastern enlightenment, in which unexamined premises are seen as major barriers to be reexamined through the requirements of the training. In one "koan," or training problem, the master holds a brick over the apprentice's head and tells the apprentice, "If you speak to me, I will drop this brick on your head. And if you do not speak to me, I will drop this brick on your head." The situation seems impossible: the apprentice reveres the master and wants ever so much to show himself worthy by solving the problem, and in so doing to protect his cranium. Yet either of the alternatives is a sure loss. So what is the apprentice to do? Note that there is an implicit premise here and that the situation is problematic only so long as the premise remains implicit. The premise is that staying seated under the brick is the way to attempt to solve the problem. Once you recognize the premise, then you are in a position to reexamine it. In this case, you easily see that your premise is invalid, and you have solved the koan: you get out from under the brick. The problem is resolved when the premise can be consciously scrutinized.

Many everyday situations appear to offer similar unacceptable alternatives: continue your efforts, or try harder, and fail; or quit and fail. In such cases there is an invalid premise so that efforts are wasted in unconstructive directions, and failure is a constant companion. In some cases, as with the koan, merely mentioning the invalid premise is sufficient. But in most cases considerable effort is required to clarify and adequately reevaluate the premises. Identifying the operating premise is in all such cases an essential first step in the solution of the problems.

Where the premises are implicit, the client can face failure, and even repeated failure, but remain unable to connect it to the source of the problems. He sees things are going wrong but sees nothing about what is making them go wrong; the result is that he profits not at all from his failures and may be harmed by them. In contrast, when the premises are explicit, the client can connect observed failures to the operating premises and, through such experiences, evaluate and perhaps alter his premises. There is considerable advantage in clarifying the operating premises in our search for solutions to seemingly intractable problems.

In Eastern enlightenment, the method is often to encourage the student to struggle with seemingly intractable problems until he stumbles upon the operating premises which narrow his vision and make solution of the problems impossible. Alan Watts (1961) in *Psychotherapy East and West* compares the Eastern process to insight-oriented psychotherapies, and focuses on the prevalence of invalid premises:

But what is the *guru* or therapist to do? . . . almost the only thing the *guru* or therapist can do is to persuade the individual to act upon his false premise in certain consistent directions until he sees his mistake. . . . For this, as we have seen, was the essential technique of liberation: to encourage the student to explore his false premises consistently—to the end. (pp. 106–107, 78)

The method of Eastern enlightenment is to force the student to struggle on his own until he finds his premises, so that he can reexamine them. Our approach here is tailored to Western ways, in which there is less patience and we are expected to resolve many misdirections in a finite number of hours. Our approach is an abbreviated version of the Eastern approach: we do not require our clients to struggle for the years it might take to recognize their invalid premises on their own. We clarify and make explicit their operating premises so that they can begin to examine them and go on from there. When clients see the failings of their premises but are still committed to them, we too can recommend that they continue to act on the false premises consistently and with increased effort—to the end.

There are practical advantages in favor of clarifying premises in our search for rapid solutions to particular maladaptive tendencies. We contribute as we can to clarifying operating premises and, from there, consider with the client the appropriateness and validity of those premises. Convincing the client to give up his invalid approaches goes hand in hand with introducing him to more effective alternatives.

6. CLARIFY ALTERNATIVES

Improved understanding how to do things

know how
improved competencies

What might the client do instead? Existing approaches are not working, and alternative, more practical ways to approach things are needed. Our task is to find alternative ways to make things work and to clarify for the client how he might approach things in these more effective ways. Clarifying invalid premises and introducing better alternative approaches go hand in hand, for together these clarify the practicalities of how things are and are not to be done. Each contributes to helping the client change.

Treating the parent who uses being upset to control thus involves two complementary tacks: we convey that being upset is not a viable approach, and we involve the parent in alternatives. In so doing we give her reasons for not continuing to use upsetness and reasons for using something else instead. We might alternate focus between the two in any single session. In order to generate alternatives, we might support the parent and improve her confidence, teach her more effective ways to manage the youngster and to exercise authority, suggest negotiations with the youngster, and so on. It is easiest to give up an invalid approach when one has a more effective alternative to try instead.

Alternatives are best sought cooperatively, by inviting our clients to puzzle through with us what is or is not a more practical way to do things. But we must be willing to introduce the more practical alternatives ourselves, for clients are often unable to do so on their own. Clients who could see for themselves the more effective alternatives would be well on their way already to using them. That clients do not act more expediently already is in itself a good indication that they do not know how to do so.

Suggestions for more practical alternative actions are used in most active psychotherapies. Behavior therapists suggest positive behavior patterns, including assertive actions to affirm one's rights and cooperative actions better suited to gain positive responses; rational-emotive therapists order assertive actions to correct problem situations; planning for more successful action is one of eight major principles of reality therapy; and family orientations suggest complementary changes simultaneously for several members of the family.

Deal with Objections

Clients generally have some reasons against trying available alternatives. The suffering parent who fails to take charge might feel that if she did exercise authority, she would lose control of herself and harm her youngsters, that she would suppress their individuality, or that they would not love her anymore and she would be alone. One who fails to make assertive stands might feel that it is inconsiderate to be so forward, that in doing so he would hurt others' feelings and be responsible for their suffering, or that he would lose their friendship. Such considerations give the person reasons for avoiding the suggested alternatives. These objections are not invented on the spot to foul up our excellent plans for changes. Such reservations have been operative all along, often severely limiting the alternatives the client has been able to consider. Too many stock "yes, but. . ." counters to our suggestions may indicate that we have paid insufficient attention to the client's legitimate objections. To make alternatives viable, it is essential therefore to clarify the client's objections and to answer them sufficiently so that they no longer weigh so strongly against change.

Our task is to address the objections so that we can clarify how many unfavorable outcomes are to be realistically expected and convince the client of the safety of the suggested alternatives. When some unfavorable outcomes might be reasonably anticipated, these need to be weighed against the advantages of the action, and preparations should be made to contain the problems. What if someone does get icy when you take a stand—what do you do then? How long will the chill factor last, and how do you manage it while it is there? We need to take such reservations seriously and construct some answers. Where problems are to be realistically anticipated, an essential question is, Is it worth it? If the alternatives are to make sense, the advantages of the alternatives need to be weighed favorably against the risks.

Often the client is overestimating adverse consequences and needs to view them more realistically. When you make a stand with your children, they are indeed angry at you, and may say you are unfair and mean—nobody enjoys being told he cannot have his way. But such outbursts are not enduring feelings or wisdom about real injustices. These outbursts are merely countermeasures to undermine parental authority. We need to clarify this and enable the parents to see them as such. We try to enable the parents to stand on a fair and reasonable position, and to avoid overestimating the significance of the youngsters' attempts to undermine them.

Our task then is to clarify that there are more effective alternatives and that, no, these alternatives do not get you into more trouble than you are in already. Reality therapy suggests as a major principle that we should not accept excuses. The suggestion here is to treat the excuses seriously, use them to troubleshoot the problems, and answer objections or adjust our programs to meet the objections.

It is essential as we clarify things to enable the clients to thoroughly accept and integrate the new understandings, and to maintain them so that they are continually available for use in their everyday lives. The next two sections focus on integrating and maintaining these understandings.

7. FAMILIARIZE (BRING IT HOME)

Surface understanding matters little, and new information must be more than merely heard and acknowledged to be of real benefit. It is essential that the client fully understand, accept, and integrate new viewpoints, and be able to apply them in everyday situations. The client must become familiar and comfortable with new understandings, and accomplished in recognizing when and where to apply them, and how they fit. As we clarify we give the client new ways to see and do things, and these must be used as a foundation for new competencies to see and act. Our objective is that the client gain the competency to apply new understandings in appropriate ways. To do this we have the client participate actively in the new viewpoints, and we go over new information as much and as thoroughly as is needed to understand and integrate it fully.

Have the Client Try It On

One excellent way to involve someone is to invite him to state aloud his apparent position or to rehearse a suggested position or action. Actually stating the position has more impact than merely hearing us interpret it for him. Suppose we discover that a young woman is showing her husband how much misery he has caused her in order to get him to see his responsibility and treat her better. Her operating premise is that showing he is causing her problems is a way to make him treat her better. We interpret this, and to bring it home, we have her say aloud to herself, "I am trying to make him recognize how miserable he is making me, in order to make him feel responsible so that he has to change." What does saying that bring forth in her? We ask, "Does it sound right to you?" Where it does sound right, the client is consciously recognizing an already existing operating position, is more involved, and is in a better position to reevaluate.

Involving someone more fully in his position corresponds to the Gestalt principle of having him "own" his position. Strategic therapy, in an interesting twist, has family members pretend the family symptoms in order to bring home the view that current patterns are an enactment.

Trying out alternatives is beneficial, for it enables the client to gain experience and confidence, and to identify with new ways of doing things. We support the person and approve of the actions, conveying that he is someone who does have the right to do that sort of thing and is doing reasonably well with it.

One advantage of having someone rehearse a new action in the session is that any problems or reservations he has about it become apparent quickly. The client tries out making a stand, for instance, and we ask, "How did it feel when you did that?" Perhaps it felt scary, awkward, or just plain rude. Problems with conducting the action readily become apparent, and we can attempt to correct them before they cause problems in everyday relationships. We must answer any reservations about alternative actions, for residual objections undermine confidence and lead to failures. Every now and then, on rare occasions, our suggested alternatives feel right on the first run-through.

There is considerable agreement that one should try on new ways of seeing oneself and new ways of acting even before it seems entirely comfortable or real to do so. Norman Vincent Peale's positive thinking approach suggests mentally visualizing one's objectives and believing you can accomplish them, and Maxwell Maltz's psychocybernetics suggests that seeing yourself as you wish to be guides your actions toward those objectives. Rehearsing alternative actions, often termed "behavioral rehearsal" and "role playing," is an integral part of behavioral and other active approaches. Adlerians suggest acting "as if" one agreed with a new position, and in a similar vein, Kelly's fixed role therapy suggests trying on new roles to form whole new identities. The "fake it until you can make it" slogan used in Alcoholics Anonymous has this same idea. Some use hypnotic trance states to encourage clients to become more and more comfortable with proposed changes. The rationale in all of these is that viewing and conducting oneself in a more constructive way help one to identify with and take over the better characteristics. Evidence that one who states a new position tends to change to agreement with that position is found in the social psychological research under "counterattitudinal acts." Trying on and practicing new views and new actions encourage comfortableness and identification with them, and make them one's own.

Cover It as Much as Is Needed

Commitments to existing views may be strong, and our new replacements must become familiar and practiced in order to overcome the old patterns and themselves become enduring. The amount of repetition required to establish and maintain new understandings can boggle the imagination. To really establish an idea, we present it, then often we need to go on to reiterate, answer objections, reiterate again, come at it from another angle, answer other objections or answer the same ones again, legitimize the problems the client is having in grasping it, introduce further supporting considerations, invite the client to make his own observations, restate the idea again, and so on. Considerable time and energy are often required to establish and maintain key understandings. The amount of repetition required is understandable when we consider how many years clients have held the old views and used them to structure their lives. The amount of repetition is justified when we recognize that key understandings can reorganize and alter for the better whole ways of life, and that in many cases easier shortcuts are simply not available.

Going over and over information requires of us as therapists considerable patience and comfort with the learning process others must go through to grasp something that is obvious to us, as well as some confidence that what we are suggesting is indeed important enough to be worth the trouble it takes to really get it across.

Behavioral orientations, because they grew up on the repetitiveness of the familiar conditioning paradigms, are notably strong on the use of repetition. Systematic desensitization alternates between imagining a stressful situation and relaxation, and several hours of repetition may be used to pair the situation to relaxation and calmness. Repetition is problably used in most active orientations much more than available writings suggest, for the repetitiveness of practice is not particularly fascinating and writings on the repetitiveness of practice are not particularly fascinating either. Case analyses giving the impression that a single therapeutic statement carries the day make more interesting literature, although single interventions seldom get us all that far in actual practice. So repetition remains a necessary, if not a necessarily intriguing, aspect of good psychotherapy practice. There is enough that is truly intriguing so that we should be genuinely thankful, and make the best of the repetition which is required of us.

The marked improvements in outlook from improved understandings may be quite transient: the new understandings must be maintained initially through continual vigilance; without continuing attention, they will give way to the older and more established patterns which they had replaced. One who learns to make stands may do so initially and have marked improvement in outlook, and then let the assertiveness issues slide as he goes on to other things and find himself with many of the same problems he had previously. One who is encouraged to grieve over a recent loss may feel markedly better—only to forget the lessons, stifle the grief process, and find himself with his previous confusions and fears. Solutions—even obvious and important ones—are not necessarily enduring, and issues that are solved once reemerge in the same forms requiring solution again. Issues once solved do not stay solved, and the note of caution here is to keep an eye out for those problems which we seem to have solved already. As a general principle: when problems reemerge, look first at the solutions which you put in place already and see that they remain in place; go on to other issues when you are satisfied that the previous basic solutions are still being used. The note of encouragement here is that the issues are much easier to clarify the second time, and we can point to the previous success to encourage the client for another go at it. The initial improvement indicates that we were on the right trail, and the relapse means only that we have not figured how to make it last. Some measures can be taken to promote carry-over of session gains and thus reduce the problems of relapses.

8. STRUCTURE CARRY-OVER

Psychotherapy is often a special place—understanding, supportive, and insulated by four walls from the stresses of ongoing daily activities. It is in such an atmosphere that important advances are made: situations are safely explored, better understandings are acquired, and new directions are attained. Such gains, however, are initially tenuous, and may be easily forgotten as the client leaves the session and again becomes involved in the old patterns of his everyday life. Some special measures may be needed then to structure carry-over of acquired understandings into the client's day-to-day activities and relationships.

Make Notes

One obvious means of promoting carry-over is to write down important information covered in the session and give the notes to the client. Suggest that he review them on occasion in the intervening week or that he consider further some of the implications. The notes are generally appreciated, as they help the client to focus on the important points of the session. The notes give him something to hold on to. Many clients are concerned anyway about failing to remember the important issues, and having a record of the session allays these concerns.

Notes should be simple and should contain the major points agreed upon in the session. For example, a note might read: "I expect the worst from people, so I reject them before they can reject me." Considerable time might have been spent exploring that issue, and the note summarizes what has been agreed upon already. Notes may include something to ponder, as in the following variation: "I feel that if I stay away from other people, then I won't get hurt so much. So after all the time I've been avoiding others, why aren't I safe by now? Is my strategy going to work?" We may invite the client to keep his own journal of therapy insights and refer to it as he finds himself slipping back into old patterns.

Keeping notes for ourselves is a good learning aid for therapist trainees but seems less useful for experienced practitioners. Maintaining adequate records has been until recently an ethical responsibility, but various freedom of information rulings may jeopardize the confidentiality of such records. Many agencies require conscientious record keeping, while professionals with the freedoms of independent practice may rebel against note taking altogether, seeing it as uninteresting and an infringement on their time. The policy here of taking notes and giving them to our clients avoids the confidentiality problems, and introduces some new meaning into an old chore.

Include Family and Friends

Changes may be better maintained when family or friends are involved in the sessions. The companions may come to understand and accept our therapeutic interpretations and recommendations, help the client recognize unconstructive patterns when they occur, and encourage more constructive alternatives.

Standard crisis intervention for one who has lost a loved one and is suppressing the grief process is to encourage the client to allow himself to grieve freely. But such clients generally have the fears that if they start grieving, they will be unable to stop, and others who see them grieving will be upset by it or feel that they are coming unglued. Such fears are answered by reassurance that the grief process is not indefinite, and that others can and do understand bereavement. Perhaps we can enable the client to grieve more freely during the session, but on the outside there is less support, the old fears return, and the grief is again suppressed. We might instruct such a client to talk to his family or friends about the grief process and its importance, so that they can understand and be supportive of it. The alternative is to have family or friends in the actual sessions, so that communication is opened on these issues. Either way, the inclusion of significant others may be an essential support for the continuation of the grief process outside the actual sessions. When others are grieving the same losses, sharing can be especially helpful for everyone concerned.

Assign Activities

Understanding may be maintained through activities which force awareness of the important themes: with the mother who has as her premise that being upset should cause better conduct, we clarify and challenge her premise during the session. Nonetheless, the old pattern is an embedded one and should be expected to reassert itself outside the therapy session. How then would one promote the continuation of the insights into the family's everyday activities? The therapist involves mother and daughter in an activity—a game here—which incorporates the attained insights into a reconstructed version of the old pattern: "You see how the pattern is working so far. What we need is some means to continue this understanding into your day-to-day activities. Let's try a sort of game, which goes like this. Your task, Ms. Jones, is to try to control your daughter's misbehavior without becoming upset yourself. So, whenever you are able to exercise authority and maintain control, then you score one point for your side. And you, Julie, you need to provide your mother with some worthy competition. So, you try to get her upset, and whenever you manage to get her upset before she gets you to behave, then you score a point. You both keep track, and we'll see who has scored the most points by next week. Okay?''

The assigned game thus rearranges the significance of the existing pattern. Until now the mother has counted being upset as an asset, since it should make the daughter behave. Now it counts openly as a loss. Now too the daughter's misbehavior counts openly as a fair and square tactic, which is exactly what it was for this youngster anyway. So the mother can hardly fail now to see it for what it is. In addition, since the daughter is generally oppositional, she may find it not so tempting or so satisfying to misbehave, because misbehavior now counts as compliance with agreed-upon instructions and not as straightforward opposition to parental authority. The scorecard is placed conspicuously on the refrigerator. On a day-to-day basis these two cannot continue to replay the old pattern without this continual reminder of what it is they are doing. The game thus structures the necessary insights into the family's everyday activities.

Review

In each session, we should follow up the major issues which were covered in the previous session and inquire about whether the client has thought about them further, whether or not they still make sense in the same way, and how he has done in applying them throughout the week. It is important for the client to expect to be asked about his progress with the material covered so that he has at least this incentive to do something with it now, rather than putting it off until that more convenient time which never comes.

When problems have been corrected and we are terminating therapy, it is often best to terminate gradually by spacing the sessions to every other week or to longer intervals. These intervals allow us to gauge how the clients do without the sessions and to monitor problems. In the initial phases of therapy, clients feel better during and after the sessions, but relapse later in the week as they lose sight of the new views and patterns which made things improve. We know that the new patterns we introduced have really taken hold and that therapy is nearly finished when clients make use of the new views and patterns during the week, and come to the next session feeling better for what they have accomplished on their own.

Various tasks and activities are assigned to structure carry-over in active approaches including behavioral, cognitive, rational-emotive, and reality therapies. Activities with a paradoxical twist, such as the game just discussed, are typical of communcations and family systems interventions.

9
Motivations and Summary

The guidelines presented here are suggestions for making use of whatever interests and values the client already has, rather than ignoring or trying to oppose them.

1. Appeal to what matters.
2. Avoid generating resistance.

These guidelines are followed by a synthesis and summary outline of the 25 guidelines for pragmatic psychotherapy.

1. APPEAL TO WHAT MATTERS

Any interpretation or suggestion should appeal to something which matters to the client, so that he has motivation to accept and utilize the intervention rather than to ignore or resist it. Motivations for specific actions arise from the individual's more general interests and values as applied to the immediate situation. We need to appeal to those existing interests and values to motivate changes, so that the person sees the suggested action as a way of getting something which matters to him.

General interests and values do change, but quite slowly, so that rapid motivational changes are best made by appealing to those values which already exist. We should present what the client needs to see and do in ways that make use of, rather than challenge, what already matters to him.

The guidelines in the previous chapters all involved implicit appeals to what matters to the clients. As we clarify operating premises, we show that the means the client is using cannot get for him what he is motivated to attain. When he becomes convinced that particular actions do not get him what he is after, he loses his reasons to continue. As we generate alternatives, we must show that they are appropriate and effective means to obtain what the client wants, so that he has reason to use them to get what matters to him. Note that we do not try to legislate what should or ought to matter, but we clarify the practical means for getting what actually does matter to the individual client.

Clients seize eagerly upon suggestions which they see as practical ways to get what genuinely does matter to them. Suggestions which appeal to what ethically or normatively should matter, but not to what really does matter, are ignored or resisted, and fail to promote changes. Indeed, an excellent means to see what does matter is to appeal to an expected motivational priority and see whether the client responds positively on the basis of those motivations, or whether he ignores or resists the appeal. When a client remains unenthusiastic about a practical means to do something we expected would matter to him, we should reevaluate whether his priorities are as we had expected.

To a mother who values her children's spontaneity but cares little for propriety and social conventions, we might suggest that structuring things more would improve the children's relationships with others and so leave them freer to be themselves. With one who values propriety and cares little about the inner lives of her children, we might take the opposite tack and suggest that giving them some freedom and accepting more playfulness would make the children calmer and better adjusted, so that they would fit in better and cause fewer social problems. Each program has its validity, and each is an attempt to appeal to the concerns of the parent. Were we to argue the importance of a program to increase children's freedom and spontaneity to the mother who values propriety above all, it would come to naught. She would be too worried about how these free and spontaneous children would fit in, and what sorts of embarrassments they would cause her by their inappropriate actions.

We may occasionally succeed by merely instructing a client to do something, for our authority and status as therapists do provide some reason to comply with our instructions. But reliance merely on authority wears thin, because many clients have other priorities and are not particularly interested in following instructions which they do not see as clear solutions. It is better to give the rationale and have a client see the objectives he might gain by taking the suggestion. Our clients, like everyone else, are better motivated when they see how the programs are going to gain them something they care about.

Our task is to show the clients that by making changes, they attain what matters to them and do not lose something else in the process. When they see sufficient reasons to change their actions, they change —and not merely because we have suggested, instructed, or ordered them to: they change because they see more clearly the reasons for and against an action, and see it as a way of getting what genuinely matters to them. So it is not a matter of making suggestions and then struggling to get our clients to comply with them. We clarify the reasons for a change, show how it might be done, and must rely on their existing interests and values to provide the motivation.

Formal written contracts may be used to make things explicit and to structure carry-over of the agreements into daily activities, but they do not really increase the clients' motivations to comply with the program. Those who are not sufficiently motivated before contracting remain insufficiently motivated after signing the contract, and fail to comply with the program. Such failures to comply can be extremely frustrating for therapists who are too strongly committed to the agreed-upon contracts: after all, they agreed to do it, it is here in black and white, and then they reneged on their agreements. It is too tempting, but notoriously unproductive, to hold the clients solely responsible and to require them to uphold their agreements before therapy can proceed. Contract or no contract, the same considerations hold: when the clients see sufficient reason, they comply; when they do not see sufficient reason, they do not comply. When contracts are broken, it is because the clients do not see sufficient reasons for compliance or have stronger reasons against it. Our task as therapists is to reevaluate the issues. If the contracted program does not appeal sufficiently to existing interests and values, it needs to be rewritten.

Consider emancipation issues so often encountered by young adults in their attempts to reconcile steps toward independence with parents who expect to maintain things as they have been. One university student is troubled by his relationship with his mother, who presents herself as generally miserable, complains that he does not telephone or visit her enough, and argues that he is ungrateful and does not love her. The young man feels obligated, inadequate, and trapped by the seemingly endless problems. He encourages his mother to find other friends and other interests, but she offers "yes but" excuses and continues to complain. His mother expects her children to stay with her, and through her misery and accusation she compels compliance with her expectations.

The young man seeks independence, but he also feels very responsible, wants to do what is right for his mother, and is wary of being the cause of even more unhappiness. He is being adversely affected by the essentially manipulative tactics his mother is using, and one important step is to clarify the manipulativeness. Perhaps that can yield some progress, although his concern for his mother runs deep and impedes his attempts toward independence.

One might suggest that he should look out for himself more and let his mother take care of herself, but that would run counter to something that matters considerably to him: acting responsibly matters a great deal, and ignoring mother seems quite irresponsible. A better strategy is one which attempts to incorporate, rather than to challenge or bypass, his sense of responsibility. An example of this follows.

We mention that compliance with emotional manipulation impedes any genuine solution, for compliance only satisfies and encourages further manipulation: "You are extremely concerned about your mother, but is your compliance with her emotional coercion the right thing to do? She has learned that by being miserable enough and blaming you she will force you to come to the rescue. If she solved her problems herself, she would ruin her case, so she has no incentive to do that and she is not trying to make the best of things for herself. Instead, she indulges in her miseries, for that has the desired effect of obligating and binding you to her. Whenever you comply, you strengthen the pattern because you confirm for your mother that unhappiness is the way to obligate you.

"Your intention through your compliance has been to make your mom feel better, but has it actually achieved your aims?" The conclusion here must be that, no, the mother is not getting better and may be actually getting worse. "Compliance may be the easiest thing at the moment, but if you really do want to help your mother with her emotional problems, then you will need to attempt something which has some real chance of working. Is it worth a try?'' We get an agreement by the client to consider an alternative.

"You will need to avoid complying with your mother's upsetness and emotional intimidation, for only when emotional manipulation is no longer working will she be free to seek some more constructive alternatives. Let's look at some alternate responses you might make, rehearse and practice them, and see how they would feel.''

Compliance with the manipulation is presented here as the too easy quick fix, while resisting the manipulation is the only really responsible course of action. If the student continues to worry that he should be taking more responsibility for mother's unhappiness, then the groundwork has been laid: "You may *feel* guilty in your conversations with your mother, but that does not mean that you *are* guilty. Your mom uses unhappiness to manipulate and obligate, and in opposing that tactic you already are acting responsibly and doing the right thing. In the long run, this will actually help your mother.'' It is no longer an issue of independence versus responsibility, but rather of integrating independence and responsibility into a viable way of life. Responsibility matters to this individual, and appeals to responsibility are used here to justify and to encourage his independence.

Poisoning the Well

Some actions involve motivations which are incompatible with other more general values, but the actions occur nonetheless because the actor remains unaware of his own motivations and fails to see the implicit contradiction. By pointing out these motivations, we appeal to his more important values and show the person that he has reasons to not continue the action.

A person who abhors the competetive pursuit of status may nonetheless stay aloof from others as a way of showing himself to be superior to them; one who fears harming others may sulk as a camouflaged way of getting even; one who genuinely loves her child may be too harsh on him in public to show other parents that she is not playing favorites. Such motivations continue unrecognized in contradiction to the individual's stronger and more general values. Interpreting such motivations calls attention to them and allows the client to see the contradiction. With one who values cooperation, we might comment: "By staying aloof from others, you present yourself as someone who is so superior that you are not even concerned with social recognition. When you consider it, that is quite some status claim in itself." If the person really does value cooperation and abhor competetiveness, then he has reason to give up his aloofness.

Motives which are in contradiction to more general values are hard for clients to acknowledge and accept. Our interpretations of these may involve some struggle and conflict, although in the context of a sufficiently strong therapeutic alliance we can get clients to accept them. Once the interpretation has been accepted, the previous satisfactions are ruined, and the clients have reason to not continue the action and are forced to look in other directions for alternative satisfactions. Such interpretations are termed "poisoning the well" by Ossorio and "spitting in the soup" by Adler. In both images it takes only a small dose of this to ruin what had been a reservoir of satisfaction.

For such interpretations to work, it is essential that the more general values really do matter. Sometimes we can be fooled, for most people want to appear to be loving and committed even when they are really not that way. A young woman who cares about propriety, status, and security would want to appear to be good and loving to her sweetheart, even if she has little interest in those things which would genuinely benefit him. Pointing out that she is angry and acting to obligate and subordinate him would annoy and embarrass her, and perhaps invite her to feel guilty, but it would not cause her to be more generous toward him. Interpreting improper intentions evokes changes only when it genuinely matters more to be individual to be another sort of way. With this woman it would be better to focus on and legitimize the anger and insecurity, and to avoid mentioning her professed commitment to being a loving companion.

"Games" interpretations in transactional analysis seek leverage by showing the manipulative aspects of the actions. If it matters sufficiently to the client to avoid those manipulations, then such interpretations spoil the satisfactions and give reasons to stop the manipulative actions. If it does not matter enough to change, then such interpretations may be mildy annoying or entirely unacceptable, and they are too soon forgotten.

Mining the Gold

Everyone is familiar with denial and rationalization, in which improper motives go unrecognized. As surprising as it might seem, many persons have good motives and fail to recognize the altruistic or noble aspects of their actions. Afraid of rationalizing, these persons deceive themselves instead by failing to see that which is genuinely good about themselves. They cheat themselves out of the confidence and satisfactions they should have earned by their actions, and weaken their reasons to continue those actions. By interpreting the good motives which do exist, we accredit the person as one of good character and also bring those positive values to bear to maintain or increase the beneficial actions. One might be genuinely concerned about a friend and act to protect him, but not want to be conspicuous and so shrug it off as merely meddlesomeness or idle curiosity. By interpreting for the clients their correct motives, we accredit and also strengthen the reasons they have to continue with those sorts of actions.

There is a popular misconception in our field that it is the clients' responsibility to be already motivated to make particular changes and that until they are so motivated they cannot progress in therapy. A recent joke asks, "How many psychiatrists does it take to change a light bulb?" The answer is "Only one, but it takes a long time and the light bulb has to really *want* to change." Motivation is certainly essential to therapeutic change, but it is not essential that clients come already motivated to undertake whatever programs a therapist is prone to suggest. Clients come with their own motivations, and it should be our responsibility as therapists to present programs for change which appeal to whatever motivations they already have. Clients are motivated to change as they become convinced that such changes are ways to gain what matters to them without losing in the process; they are not motivated to change when they see losses rather than advantages in such changes.

Behavior modification suggests explicit appeals to what matters: it assesses what matters to the client under the cover term "reinforcers" and then uses those things as incentives for behavior changes. Behavior consultants structure situational contingencies so that the person must follow the program in order to get something he values. Other orientations are more implicit in their appeals to what matters, but all effective intervention must appeal to what matters. *Logo* (meaning) therapist Victor Frankl (1963) appeals to what matters in the following sensitive comments:

> Once, an elderly general practitioner consulted me because of his severe depression. He could not overcome the loss of his wife, who had died two years before, and whom he had loved above all else. Now how could I help him? What should I tell him? I ... confronted him with the question, "What would have happened, Doctor, if you had died first, and your wife would have had to survive you?" "Oh," he said, "for her this would have been terrible; how she would have suffered!" Whereupon I replied, "You see, Doctor, such suffering has been spared her, and it is you who have spared her this suffering; but now you have to pay for it by surviving and mourning her." (pp. 178–179)

The comments clarify the possible significance of the suffering. The intervention appeals to the physician's love for his wife, so that his continuance of an otherwise empty life may attain a completeness now as a final expression of endearment and commitment to his beloved. "Suffering," comments Frankl, "ceases to be [merely] suffering ... at the moment it finds a meaning, such as the meaning of a sacrifice" (p. 179). The intervention has the effect it does because it appeals to an important and already existing commitment: it would be lost on an individual who was less altruistic.

2. AVOID GENERATING RESISTANCE

Perceptions, motivations, and performance in resistance

[Psychotherapy involves] a series of therapeutic thrusts and parries, ... in an effort to dissolve, to avoid, or to take advantage of, rather than to break down, resistance. Consequently, therapy ... follows the rule of least resistance in an effort to bring about therapeutic changes. . . .

Dimond et al (1978, p. 245)

An "old saying" has it that resistance is the second oldest form of human interaction ever conducted: when the first person suggested doing something, somebody else said no. While this is perhaps an overstatement, it suggests an important warning: resistance is an integral aspect of human nature which, unless carefully monitored, can attain an exaggerated importance, frustrating therapist and client alike by undermining the therapeutic alliance, overshadowing cooperative motivations, and so interfering with attempts to deal with anything more constructive.

Not every therapeutic failure should be taken as an indication of resistance, however. A client who does not accept an interpretation may be limited by his idiosyncratic concepts, misunderstandings, or insecurities, and not merely resisting the interpretation. One who does not comply because he is not capable of following the suggestion need not be resisting the suggestion; nor is one resisting who does not comply because he fails to see sufficient reasons to do so. A client who fails to understand an interpretation may be merely unable to understand and not necessarily resisting, just as one who fails to make a suggested stand with his boss may be genuinely fearful of the consequences and not merely resisting the therapist. Every failure to comply is not the result of resistance.

It is especially important to carefully delineate our concept of resistance, so that problems resulting from authentic resistance can be identified and distinguished from other problems, and treated accordingly. *Resistance,* as the term is used here, is active or passive opposition to something, and not merely confusion, lethargy, or inertia. It is a purposive action which is conducted for intelligible reasons and not merely an inadvertent failure to act. What is it that one perceives which gives him intelligible reason to resist? The situation as perceived has two aspects: it is seen as a force—an authority, power, or pressure to comply—and as unfair—as callous, intrusive, threatening, or otherwise unwarranted and unjust. These two together provide reason to resist: that which is resisted must be seen as force or pressure, for otherwise there would be nothing to resist; the force must be seen as unfair or unwarranted, for otherwise there would be no reason to resist and one would comply instead. The term "coercion" ordinarily refers to a force which is unjust; and is used in this sense here. Therefore, the occurrence of resistance indicates that the client perceives something as coercive.

Some obvious and unambiguous cases might help represent the concept. Resistance may be active opposition, as in the French resistance to German occupation, or passive opposition, as in Gandhi's "passive" resistance to British rule in India. Either way, it is something seen as coercion which gives one reason to resist, and the resistance is actual opposition and not merely inertia. The concept of resistance outlined here includes one major ordinary language meaning of the term but is more tightly restrictive than familiar psychiatric usage. Our use of the term specifically excludes merely withstanding something and is used only to indicate opposition.

The clarification is important, for it enables us to distinguish between quite separate varieties of noncompliance too often grouped together indiscriminately under the same cover term. Therapeutic failures resulting from various confusions and inadequacies, or to happenstance are not to be considered resistance. The client who is merely afraid of making a suggested assertive stance or who gets caught in unexpected traffic and arrives late for his appointment is not seen as resisting therapy.

A therapist who encounters instances of noncompliance such as these and routinely interprets them as resistance is going to have a peculiar effect on the client. Most clients would feel misunderstood, and perhaps mistreated and manipulated, and would oppose and resist the interpretations. Inappropriate interpretations of resistance are seen as coercive, evoke resistance, and so become self-fulfilling prophecies. To avoid generating resistance, a first principle is to avoid interpreting and thus creating resistance when it does not occur naturally on its own.

The distinction between opposition and confusion, incompetence, or mere inertia is important in choosing a course of action. When a client merely fails to understand or to accept an interpretation, we are free to pursue our case—to mention supporting information, to reiterate or rephrase the point, to use illustrations, and so on. Considerable support for an interpretation and reiteration may be necessary to familiarize the client with the information and enable him to use it himself, as suggested by earlier guidelines. But when a client is actually resisting an interpretation, further support generally evokes only further resistance, so we are advised to troubleshoot the resistance rather than to press the argument. Being able to tell the difference is essential to our course of interventions.

The occurrence of resistance is minimized by conscientious adherence to many of the earlier guidelines: maintaining a collaborative alliance, legitimizing and making acceptable the client's actions, appealing to what genuinely matters to the client, and so on. Nonetheless, some client resistance seems unavoidable, for in a course of interventions there is generally something objectionable, and there are of course those clients who feel oppressed by life itself and so are predisposed to resist anything that might be suggested.

When resistance does occur, we troubleshoot the problem using the concept that something perceived as coercion is giving the client reason to resist. Our initial task is to find out what aspect of the relationship the client sees as coercive, and why. Such troubleshooting often yields readily apparent solutions: one woman feels slighted by a friend whom she then undermines and subtly antagonizes. An interpretation to this client of her hostility meets with resistance, and attempts to show her the indications of her anger only generate further resistance. As sometimes occurs with anger interpretations, the focus on the hostility exposes the woman's own participation in the antagonism, which she sees not as assistance but rather as an indictment of her own position. She sees the interpretation of her anger as coercive. Continuation of the interpretation should be avoided, to avoid generating further resistance, and alternate means should be sought for dealing with the issue.

Resistance to an interpretation may be minimized by omitting that aspect of the interpretation which is objectionable. When the intentions are unacceptable, a client might nonetheless accept an interpretation of his behavior in the form of a behavior outcome description, in which intentions are specifically omitted. With the woman who undermines and subtly antagonizes a friend, we are well advised to begin with an outcome description, such as: "Your comments might seem to be ignoring or contradicting your friend quite a bit, and she is being antagonized by them." If she objects to the interpretation and argues that this is not what she is doing, or is not what she means to do, then there is room to more explicitly limit the thrust: "I'm not saying that you necessarily mean to antagonize her, but only that when you say those sorts of things, it has that sort of effect." The outcome, that the friend is antagonized, is obvious anyway. Since the interpretation omits the intention, it is not seen as an indictment and there is no reason to resist.

Although intentions are not here in play, a behavior outcome description does carry with it its own force and leverage. When one acknowledges that an action causes an outcome, whether intentionally or inadvertently, he thereby attains some reason to change the action if he wants to change the outcome: "Even though you may not mean to antagonize her, it has that effect. You have reason to make some changes if it matters enough to you to avoid further problems there."

Sometimes peculiar or unusual factors are involved. A young man has progressed from a mental breakdown to a level of at least minimal functioning, and the therapist comments that he might expect further progress and might even come to enjoy himself sometimes. Although the comment appears promising and supportive, the client resists, and any attempts to further support the good prognosis generate further resistance. The fellow argues that he is as well as he is ever going to be and, to further his point, suggests terminating therapy. In the absence yet of sufficient understanding, we should retract the prognosis to alleviate the resistance and reestablish an alliance, and should seek to understand the cause of the puzzling client reaction. Further inquiry reveals that the young man is closely involved with his mother, that each claims various infirmities and disabilities, and that by convention, the healthier one is morally obligated to care for and cater to the needs and complaints of the "sicker" one. To this individual, the significance of the positive prognosis is that he is again to be responsible for his mother, and the suggestion that he work for that is understandably seen as coercive.

The additional information provides the basis for a more acceptable intervention: "If you do get better, then you will feel obligated to take care of your mother and to struggle with her continual unhappiness, complaints, and accusations. Is she really all that ill, though, or is she merely appearing so miserable to manipulate you into feeling obligated and doing what she directs? Let's look into it, shall we? For now, though, there is no point in becoming healthy just yet if by doing so you have to give up your freedom and your happiness."

Clients' resistance does impede progress in therapy, but one should not conclude therefore that anyone values sickness. In the case just discussed, resisting therapy was the means used, and maintaining freedom from filial obligations was the significance of the client's action. Clients do not resist therapy merely to stay sick, but rather for some further and more understandable aims. Consideration of those more sensible reasons is a source of more appropriate and effective therapeutic interventions.

Resistance may be interpreted directly, although the approach is extremely important. "You are being resistive" would be an ineffective comment, for if the client is feeling mistreated already he would tend to see that as further accusation. Embellishments on the theme, such as "You are resisting seeing things as they really are" or "You are resisting getting well," would only make matters worse, for they offer the same accusation but with additional punch. They tend to engender further resistance. Legitimizing the resistance can offer the needed entrée, for example: "It may feel as though I'm trying to push you into seeing it my way and I'm not listening enough to what you have to say." This could be expressed in a slightly different form: "You're not the sort of person who is going to let someone else tell him what to do. You don't like it when others tell you what to do, and you don't like it when I tell you what to do. I realize that, and I see now that you need more room to make you own choices." We thus accept the client's position and agree to alter somewhat the directiveness which the client finds objectionable.

Clients may have vested interests which we should be well aware of before we begin a crusade. Mistaken attitudes and ideologies need to be challenged, but we should be aware of where our clients stand and of the extensiveness of their commitments. As a reminder: When you go out to slay a dragon, make sure it is not somebody's pet. When resistance does occur, look at the commitments the client has and tread lightly on favored icons.

The present ordinary language concept of resistance was clarified by Ossorio in his formal descriptive psychology concepts. A social psychological approach uses a concept of resistance similar to the present one but labels it "reactance" (cf. Brehm, 1976). The present formulation contrasts of course with the classical analytic formulations which focus exclusively on intrapsychic mechanisms and overlook the contributions of situations and relationship factors. As a general principle: When resistance occurs, assess what you are doing which is seen by the client as coercive, and then alter or avoid it, in order to maintain a cooperative relationship in which issues can be dealt with productively.

Exceptions

In some situations, we may choose to take advantage of resistance rather than try to avoid generating it. We might suggest that the client continue or even accelerate a troublesome pattern, but now with an awareness of his actions and of his reasons for the actions. The rationale may be that he needs to become consciously familiar with the troublesome tendency in order to gain fuller understanding and conscious control in the matter. But if the action is something which is already annoying, the suggestion to continue or even accelerate the pace will be especially obnoxious. Notice here it is the suggestion which is to be resisted, not the therapist or the relationship. The client should know full well that the therapist wants him to overcome his futile tendencies and is only instructing that he continue with them for his own best interest. The technique involves "paradoxical intention," since the apparent intention is to continue the troublesome action and the effect is that the client stops.

One who pressures himself continually to force himself to improve may instead frustrate and exhaust himself. His operating premise is that more pressure should cause improvement; our objective after clarifying his premise is to help him convince himself that it is invalid and so lessen his use of pressure for self-improvement. When the client is firmly committed to his approach, we may invite him to continue pressuring himself as long as he wishes and thus to invalidate the approach for himself: "Perhaps being tough on yourself is the golden road to improvement, and you just haven't yet given it a fair chance. You might want to try it for a few more days or a few more weeks or months, or you might try being even tougher on yourself. In any case, when you are being tough on yourself, say to yourself, 'I'm going to really force myself to really improve.' Then go at it with a vengeance." The pressure the client puts on himself has always been uncomfortable, and the conscious execution of even greater pressure should become exceptionally coercive. The client comes to resent the whole approach to self-improvement, but to actually resist the directive he must discontinue the pressure he puts on himself, which is of course the point of the exercise. As he follows the program he is learning a valuable lesson, and as he sees the good reasons to resist the program he is cured.

We may instruct the client who is generally resistive and oppositional to continue a troublesome activity, so that continuing the activity counts as compliance with the instructions. It is an appeal to what already matters, and if it matters enough to resist our instructions, then to do so one must discontinue the problem activity. This principle was applied in an earlier illustration in which a resistive teenager was instructed to challenge her mother's authority. Should she continue to challenge as she had been doing, she would be cooperating with our therapeutic program, but she must stop challenging her mother to resist the instruction.

A second illustration involves a mother's catering to her youngest son Tommy, now a young adult, to the detriment of both. The arrangement provides Tommy's necessities and finances alcohol, narcotics, and stagnation. The mother stays an emotional wreck. The family prevails on her over and over to put Tommy on his own, but she will have none of it. She had been forced too many times to comply with her husband's orders, and with him now deceased, she is unwilling to give in anymore. What matters to this woman is independence and control over her activities, and she is willing to resist anyone and everyone to maintain it.

The family naturally assumes that their mother should value her son's welfare and her own peace of mind as well, but in appealing to these considerations they merely frustrate themselves. The impasse is best solved by appealing not to what *should* matter, but rather to what actually *does* matter. We advise an older brother who consults us to send a notice to all the family members, and a copy to mother as well, that they should stop interfering in their mother's affairs. He argues in the letter that mother and Tommy are ideally suited for each other: Mom is growing older, she will need companionship and someone to look after her as advancing age diminishes her spirit and capacities, and dims her judgment. And Tommy, despite his shortcomings, is the only one in the family with the patience and temperament for the difficult task ahead.

Everyone is appalled by the uninvited intrusion, and the mother responds by reversing her course and forcing Tommy out on his own, where he falters initially but might grab hold when faced with the stark necessities. Why does the intrusive intervention have this paradoxical effect? Mother is not about to take orders from anybody, and she is not about to accept her suggested status as a deteriorating geriatric. What matters most dearly to her is maintaining control, and to resist the intrusion and maintain her independence, she is even willing to move out her younger son who is, after all, less competent than she. By seeming to force mother and by presenting her as a potential incompetent, the letter appeals in a backward way to what actually does matter. Paradoxical interventions such as these are a main staple in several family systems approaches.

The critical problem with a paradoxical intervention such as this is that it is altogether too appealing. The tactic is manipulative, for it involves fooling people to cause them to act in their own best interests. Also, it is a risky gambit, for the tactician is inviting the subject to tell him to go to hell and, in so doing, to change what that person needs to change. If it fails, the damage has been done, and there are fewer options for further interventions. Note that in the case just discussed, the paradoxical appeal to resistance was used by the brother to intervene in a family where cooperation mattered little and the other family members had no interest in changing. The manipulative tactic can be justified here since the family was stubborn and intransigent, there was no therapeutic relationship to rely on or jeopardize between the man writing the letter and his mother or younger brother, and straightforward nonmanipulative appeals had proved to be failures.

In this case, the therapist acted as a collaborator in explaining the intervention and advising the brother to try it out. Manipulative interventions such as this might be used directly on the clients themselves, but such tactics have limited utility and carry with them strong cautions. The use of manipulative tactics on clients can sacrifice an already fragile alliance, undermine our credibility and, when they fail, further restrict our options for more cooperative interventions. Clients generally have some interest in changing, and a wide range of more cooperative means is available to promote those changes. The recommendation here is that we avoid treating clients with tactics which are manipulative and which appeal solely to resistance, except when no therapeutic relationship can be established and when opposition is the only available motivation we can use for change. In general, we do considerably better by maintaining a cooperative alliance with our clients, maintaining credibility in ourselves and our programs, clarifying for the clients how the programs will get for them what they want, and appealing to interests and values other than opposition and resistance.

SYNTHESIS OF GUIDELINES

The guidelines cover the range of major therapeutic objectives, and we must select the ones which are important in any specific situation. Some are critical across sessions, while others pertain to circumscribed issues. Relationship guidelines are implemented across sessions, but in the pursuit of other objectives and with minimum precautions unless problems occur, and then they receive our full attention. Accreditation guidelines find their way into every issue. Assessment occurs throughout the sessions, and things are reassessed when expected progress fails to materialize. The clarification guidelines are used when there may be ambiguities and confusions about things—which means they are included in almost every issue imaginable. Clarifying what is so and how to change things is at the heart of therapy, and the other guidelines set the stage for these objectives. The motivation guidelines find their way into any attempt to promote changes.

Many of the guidelines are interrelated, so that by going after one objective we usually attain several more as well. Really good interventions may accomplish several related objectives. A statement which legitimizes may thereby make things more acceptable, maintain the alliance, maintain our credibility, appeal to what matters, confirm the client's control, and when the client agrees, it may help confirm our initial assessment of the problem.

In some cases, one guideline objective must be balanced against other objectives so that nothing is sacrificed. When we confirm his control with the client invested in being the victim, we risk antagonizing, so we must ease the thrust with other components which legitimize and make the interpretation more acceptable. When we clarify things and push alternatives too strongly, we risk leaving the client behind, so we must balance these moves by understanding any reluctance the client has and by accepting and legitimizing it. The guidelines overlap and complement each other. Covering the spectrum of critical objectives and techniques, they work together in a single integrated approach to psychotherapy.

Considerable sensitivity and clinical judgment may be involved in weighing which of the guidelines pertain in any specific situation and in figuring out what to say to accomplish those objectives. The application of the guidelines becomes easier as one becomes more familiar with them and gains experience using them in clinical practice. There is always room to improve, by figuring out better and faster ways of attaining various therapeutic objectives and by finding better ways to coordinate the objectives with each other. The guidelines serve to guide and assist us in constructing appropriate and sometimes innovative interventions well suited to the particular situations we encounter, but they cannot tell us what will be appropriate in every particular situation. The guidelines should augment and assist our sensitivity and clinical judgment, but not replace it.

The guidelines contain both broad therapeutic objectives and some techniques which are suggested as ways to attain the objectives. The objectives should be recognized by most eclectic psychotherapists as sensible and important aspects of therapeutic practice. The guidelines are used to organize and make sense of the wide variety of familiar therapeutic techniques, which are seen as ways of attaining one or more of the guideline objectives. In many cases, techniques from one orientation may be more appropriate in some situations and those from another orientation more appropriate in other situations. In some cases, techniques from one orientation are seen as preferred ways of attaining an objective, and techniques from other orientations are judged poor by comparison. Other practitioners may have slightly different impressions, and there are undoubtedly some techniques favored by some which were considered here as poor or simply omitted. Considerable personal judgment has been involved in selecting and integrating the techniques to the guideline objectives, and there is room here for questions, alterations, and improvements. The set of guidelines is suggested as an initial framework for a comprehensive eclecticism, but not as a final or complete coverage of all aspects of eclectic practice.

The guidelines can be used to look at any intervention, for any specific intervention or general technique can be rated by independent practitioners as to what it would tend to accomplish in which sorts of situations. Similarly, these guidelines can be used to judge other orientations, for they can be rated on how well they tend to accomplish each of the guideline objectives. The guidelines provide a grid for understanding, organizing, and evaluating the vast array of therapeutic techniques.

The use of physiological agents, when appropriate, must be coordinated with the psychological interventions suggested by the guidelines. As psychotherapists, it is our job to be alert to indications for physiological treatments and to refer for medication, nutritional advice, and so on. It also usually falls on us to address objections and convince the clients that an appropriate regimen of medication is indeed good for them, or that fewer calories or more exercise is really possible. The actions of medications or nutritional changes are physiological, but getting the clients to comply belongs in our realm of psychological interventions.

OUTLINE OF GUIDELINES
FOR PRAGMATIC PSYCHOTHERAPY

Guidelines are prescriptions for action based on considerations of our objectives, and of the principles and ways by which we might best achieve those objectives. The guidelines are general enough to apply across cases and to a wide range of problems. Proper application of these guidelines yields immediate tactical advantage and over the long run should markedly improve our effectiveness as therapists.

I. The Therapeutic Relationship

1. Be on the Client's Side.   Act in the best interest of the client. Be committed, and avoid or resolve attitudes and feelings which interfere.

2. Maintain an Alliance.   Act to enable the client to see you as an ally. Begin where you are welcome. Be personable and active, correct misunderstandings, and counter transference.

3. Maintain Credibility.   Show the sense of what you are doing, and relate improvements to the contributing therapeutic procedures. Avoid statements which are untrue, and be careful with those which appear naive or false to the client.

4. Communicate an Understanding of the Client's Position.   Share your impressions of the client's feelings and concerns.

5. Share Responsibility for Improvement.   Take responsibility in ways which enable the client to better take responsibility. Provide what the client is unable himself to provide, and encourage him to do what he is able to do. Tailor interventions to the client's capacities to learn.

II. Affirmation and Accreditation

Accredit existing strengths. Treat the client as one who already makes sense, is acceptable, and is in control. Clients underestimate themselves, and acknowledging existing strengths is an essential step to using those strengths to better advantage.

1. Legitimize (Show the Client the Sense He Makes).   Any of the everyday explanatory concepts can make sense of existing experiences and actions. Misunderstandings or unusual reasons may make sense of puzzling actions; unusual situations or individual characteristics make of those reasons; and personal learning experiences may make sense of confusing individual characteristics.

2. Make It Acceptable.   Decriminalize. Interpret your client's characteristics in ways he can accept. Create a comfortable atmosphere. Use humor. Select acceptable phrasings. Emphasize positives; underplay negatives. Introduce norms.

3. Confirm the Client's Control.   See the client as someone who is already in control of his actions. Show the reasons he has for the ways he controls. Show the ways he is successful.

4. Don't Buy Victim Acts.   A client may present himself as a victim in order to avoid responsibility or to gain sympathy. Interpret and legitimize the reasons for the act. Challenge the ideology which affords special sympathy and privileges to the sufferer.

5. If It Works, Don't Fix It.   See strengths as strengths. Avoid introducing uncertainties into areas which are already appropriate and functional.

III. Assessment

1. Assess What Matters. Assess what is needed for effective intervention, including problematic characteristics and also strengths. Most important are those factors which contribute significantly to the overall problems and which can be altered most readily by intervention. Stay with specifics. Omit extraneous information.

2. Use Ordinary Language Concepts. Use norms for points of reference, and avoid explanations which are too general. Recognize what the client means by the words he uses.

3. Collaborate. Ask for particulars. Outline plausible interpretations, and collaborate on which ones apply. Monitor judgment. Recreate key episodes; invite interactions with family or friends.

4. Learn As You Go. Interweave assessment and intervention. Intervene, and learn from the clients' reactions. Successes may confirm initial assessments; use failures to further understand the problems. Begin with the simplest adequate interpretations, and elaborate as additional leverage is needed.

5. Don't Expect the Client to Be Somebody Else. Realize that problems are often entrenched and may survive your initial or most obvious solutions. Avoid holding the client responsible for that which he is unable to do.

IV. Clarifications

Address inabilities to understand what is happening and how to change things to one's advantage.

1. Clarify Situations. Address errors, and suggest clearer views of the real world. Weigh alternatives with the client, and encourage the client to observe for himself. Legitimize misunderstandings. Emphasize understandings over misunderstandings.

2. Clarify Concepts. Introduce and apply distinctions which the client can use himself. Build upon existing ordinary language concepts. Elaborate impoverished concepts. Untangle confounded concepts.

3. Use Illustrations and Images.   These may be used to introduce or clarify critical distinctions, and to maintain interest and avoid resistance.

4. Deal with the Reality Basis of Emotions.   Fear and anxiety are related to perceived threat or danger; anger, to provocation; guilt, to wrongdoing. Deal constructively with the circumstances generating the emotion and not merely with the experience or feeling.

5. Clarify Operating Premises.   Look at the means by which the client is trying to get what he wants. Analyze operating premises which are the basis of impractical attempts, and show that they are invalid.

6. Clarify Alternatives.   Clarify how the client can more effectively get what he is after. Deal with objections, and clarify the risks involved.

7. Familiarize (Bring It Home).   Support, restate, and deal with objections, so that the client may truly assimilate the information rather than merely hear it. Involve the client: have him try on more positive statements and practice new approaches.

8. Structure Carry-over.   Promote the continuation of session gains into the client's everyday life. Make notes for the client to review. Have the client talk to family or friends about key insights, or include them in the sessions. Assign homework activities which maintain awareness of the suggested changes.

V. Motivations

1. Appeal to What Matters.   Values change slowly, and motivational changes in particular circumstances are made by appealing to what already matters to the client. Assess the client's motivations and values, and present what he needs to see or do in ways that make use of, rather than contradict, what counts. Show the client how what you are suggesting is a way to get what he really wants.

2. Avoid Generating Resistance.   Resistance undermines cooperative collaboration. Coercion elicits resistance, and the occurrence of
resistance means that the client sees the therapist as coercive. When
resistance appears, look at what you are saying which the client sees as
coercive. Redescribe information to make it acceptable, bypass objections, or leave the issue until later. When intentions are unacceptable,
use outcome descriptions which specifically omit intentions.

Exceptions: Minimize resistance, unless using it paradoxically to
motivate a constructive reaction.

SECTION III
APPLICATION AND SYNTHESIS

10
Varieties of Self-Criticism

> We has met the enemy, and it is us.
> Walt Kelly, "Pogo"

"I'm no good" statements have a variety of forms: "I'm stupid," "I'm ugly," "I'm awful," "I'll never amount to anything," "What a fool I've been!" "I never do anything right," and "It's all my fault." The list is familiar to everyone and seemingly endless. The phenomenon is known as self-criticism, self-condemnation, self-depreciation, or self-contempt; as being too tough on oneself, giving oneself a hard time, punishing oneself, or putting oneself down. Being overly tough on oneself squashes the spontaneity and enjoyment one might otherwise experience, and qualifies in that way as an obvious source of psychopathology. Being overly tough on oneself is readily seen as a significant contributing factor in a range of psychological problems including anxiety, embarrassment, insecurity, passivity, obsessiveness, moodiness, depression, social withdrawal, and a general ill opinion of oneself. Not surprisingly, the issue is addressed in some way by most major systems of psychotherapy.

Because it contributes so strongly to personal maladjustment and is prevalent, richly complex, and of concern in various psychotherapies, the phenomenon offers an excellent arena in which to apply and further illustrate our pragmatic approach to psychotherapy. In this and the following chapter, our concepts and guidelines are used to analyze the sometimes sticky issues in self-critical tendencies and to suggest therapeutic interventions.

Self-criticism varies in severity: it is sometimes mildly and appropriately critical, and other times ruthlessly and unfairly harsh. Some self-criticism is normal and can be quite adaptive. It is self-criticism which is frequent, inappropriate, and ruthlessly harsh that contributes so heavily to psychological problems.

Two positions are apparent in any critical act: the actor, or person making the criticism; and the recipient, or person being criticized. The same person is in both of these positions in self-criticism: the person as actor is making the criticism, and the same person as recipient is the one criticized. Self-criticism may be restated as "he" (subject) criticizes "himself" (object), which again shows the two positions. When self-criticism is unfairly severe, these may be stated as perpetrator-victim positions: the person as perpetrator is inflicting harsh and unjustified criticism on himself, the victim. This distinction is crucial to an analysis of the phenomenon. Clearly, to understand something that is being done, we must view the one doing it, not merely the one to whom it is done. It is the person as actor who has the reasons for the action, and we should look at him and expect to find answers there. The reminder is "Keep your eye on the actor."

Some self-critical persons have little awareness of the complementary perpetrator-victim positions, seeing themselves mainly as victims of the harsh treatment but not as the perpetrators. They experience the condemnation, humiliation, and pain as if it were caused by something other than their own actions. Certainly, one might assume, the infliction of such suffering is merely irrational or merely a conditioned pattern, rather than an understandable attempt to deal with one's world. But by failing to understand the legitimacy and sensibleness of his self-criticism, a person leaves himself in a weak position to do much about it. How can one redirect what he claims he is not in charge of in the first place? The current analysis accredits the self-critic, for it shows him to be acting on legitimate, understandable reasons, and thus in charge of his actions, and it confirms that he is the perpetrator rather than merely the victim of the actions.

Words are also deeds, and one says something not merely because it seems so but always *in order to* have an effect. Any self-critical statement is itself a purposive action. One says "I'm no good" not merely because it seems so or because he thinks or feels or sincerely believes it is so: one says it in order to accomplish something which he wants or has some reason to accomplish. It is this pragmatic or "in order to" aspect of the "I'm no good" statements which is the basis here of the analysis and categorization of self-criticism. The person's understanding or misunderstanding of his inadequacies is included in the analysis as one of several contributing factors, but the initial and fundamental focus is on the pragmatics of the self-critical statements.

Many self-critics are unaware of the pragmatic aspects of their self-critical statements. They see themselves as inadequate, and they fail to consider that any apparent inadequacy is not itself sufficient reason to condemn and criticize. The inadequacy is only the ammunition, and the ammunition is not itself a reason to shoot the cannon at oneself. A major objective in altering self-critical patterns is to show the clients the reasons they do have for criticizing themselves, so that they can reassess and alter those reasons.

In analyzing this phenomenon, it is imperative therefore to look at what the person is actually doing: what he is after, the reasons he has, and the satisfactions which may be gained. One who says "I'm no good" might be doing so in order to attain any of a number of objectives, so we must survey the range of possible objectives and reasons one might have for making such statements. As an assemblage of possible reasons, a survey so constructed gives a broad overview of the phenomenon and can assist us in assessing which of the possible reasons is involved in any particular self-critical remark. The following survey identifies and illustrates 12 major categories of objectives and issues which may be involved in any specific instance of self-criticism.

The presentation is organized so that suggested intervention tactics follow and are integrated into each section of the analysis. The suggested interventions are constructed to deal with, and give proper weight to, the major reasons and objectives involved, and to alter the reasons the client has for perpetrating the criticism. The analysis uses common language concepts, and the interventions use and illustrate the guidelines for pragmatic psychotherapy.

1. UNDERSTANDING LIMITATIONS

Self-criticism may be a good-faith appraisal made in order to clarify and better *understand one's inadequacies*. Someone concerned with his action might reasonably ask, "Was it unethical or unsafe, or was it ineffective in getting what I wanted?" It is important to size things up after an action, in order to be better prepared for future actions. An action appraised as poor, bad, or wrong need not be considered again in making future choices—it has already been found lacking.

Given reasonable standards, the appraisals should include a balanced combination of both positive and negative opinions. A preponderance of negative appraisals indicates standards which are high in comparison to what one could be reasonably expected to achieve.

One might look to clarify his inclinations, capabilities, or social status. One who recognizes that he is poor at algebra might avoid such a course or plan to study more in order to compensate. One might invite assistance from others. One who says he did something badly may be asking friends to confirm his judgment or to suggest an alternative. The high school student who suggests she is not popular enough to date the captain of the football team may be asking her companions a legitimate question: Is she right?

These are the simplest forms of self-criticism to manage. The client is merely mistaken about himself, but is inviting our input and seeking to clarify things. Our task is to correct the mistake by providing additional information or by clarifying and challenging standards which are inappropriately high. A mother whose child falls and hurts himself may see herself at fault for not watching him closely enough. She might be reassured to hear that falling is natural for children, that most parents expect a certain number of falls, and that falls are not as harmful as she expects them to be. Her standard for being a good mother is that you never allow your child to hurt himself, and we might clarify her standard and challenge its practicality. We ask her to consider what life would be like if she expected herself to prevent all hurts. Could anyone tolerate that sort of anxiety?

If the client is generally too critical of himself, we may point to this and suggest that he give himself the benefit of the doubt: "You are generally too hard on yourself. When there is a possible mistake or failing, you rush to judgment and condemn. You might try giving yourself the benefit of the doubt. When you start to wonder, consider that you have done well enough unless there is glaring evidence to the contrary."

If the client is negative, but appropriately or accurately so, we avoid challenging. Reassurance here would be false and unhelpful. We might compliment the client on his willingness to face difficult things about himself, mentioning the personal honesty that is required to do that. It is only frequent and overly severe self-criticism which is so troublesome and which needs to be addressed and challenged in therapy.

2. SELF-IMPROVEMENT

Self-criticism may be pressure in order to *force oneself to improve*. It is a painful reminder of inadequacies and a challenge to get moving. The aim is to mobilize pressure toward renewed and more energetic efforts to succeed. The person takes it for granted that being tough on himself will lead to improvement. The following *Putting the Screws to Yourself* image can be used to illustrate the issue: "When required to do something you are uninterested in, you can generally buckle down, get tough with yourself, and get the job done. Being really tough on yourself does increase motivation, at least temporarily, and hopefully long enough to do what you have to do. But while being tough on yourself for a short time produces temporary improvements, being extremely harsh on a continual basis usually results not in improvement but in discouragement, loss of confidence, exhaustion, and resistance. Thus, the connection you see between being tough on yourself and improvement is incomplete; improvement may occur, but too much pressure makes things worse."

The operating premise is that being tough on oneself should lead to improvement. The premise is implicit, for the client is not conscious that it guides his actions. Because it goes unrecognized, the premise is particularly immune to invalidation by observation and experience. The person sees his continual failure and concludes only that he has not been tough enough on himself. Exhaustion, resistance, and failure are misread as laziness; so he applies even more pressure. Further pressure leads to further exhaustion and resistance, and that leads to further failure, which in turn provokes further pressure, and so on. The individual misunderstands how one goes about generating improvements.

Criticizing oneself to force improvement is similar to criticizing someone else to force that person to do better. A parent might criticize and punish a child in order to increase the pressure and make the child improve his conduct. If used judiciously, such criticism may produce compliance and improvement. Harsh or continual criticism is more likely to result in loss of confidence, exhaustion, defiance, and failure. Unfortunately, the failure does not necessarily lead the parent to try better methods, for the operating premise is an implicit one and not readily invalidated by failure. When the child fails to improve, the parent may easily conclude that he has been too lenient and so increase the criticism. The approach may even get unjustified validation. Children will often straighten up and comply immediately following criticism, keeping quiet for a moment and doing what they are supposed to do, but returning a few minutes later to their previous misbehavior, often even noisier and less compliant for having received what they see as unjust criticism. A youngster growing up with this treatment may assimilate the implicit premise and come to see continual criticism as the way to generate improvement. One who is criticized to force him to improve learns to criticize himself to force himself to improve.

We begin by interpreting the aim of the self-criticism and by clarifying the implicit operating premise. Most clients will readily agree that being tough on yourself does, will, or should make you improve. We legitimize the misunderstanding, by using the Putting the Screws to Yourself image to show that the premise is sometimes correct and that it has apparently been validated by observation. When the client has grown up being criticized, the prevalent premise—that criticism should lead to improvement—can be used directly to account for the client's approach: he simply assimilated that way of doing things. Legitimizing affirms the client as one who is rational and makes sense, and thus makes it easier for him to accept the ways in which he is mistaken.

Our objective is that the client become convinced that harsh self-criticism is not a good means of self-improvement. Our task is to challenge and invalidate the operating premise, without generating resistance in the process. Some clients see the mistake as soon as the premise is mentioned. With those who do not, a good step is to ask, "Is it working?" The client comes to his own conclusion that, no, it does not work for him. For emphasis, we might add playfully: "If it does make you improve, you ought to be just about perfect by now, because you sure do enough of it."

With clients who are strongly committed to the premise, we might suggest that they must figure it out for themselves because they are not going to take our word for it. We might even add, again playfully: "Perhaps being tough on yourself *is* the golden road to improvement, and you just haven't given it a fair chance. You might want to try it for a few more days or a few more weeks or months. Perhaps you need to be even tougher on yourself, but everytime you do it, say to yourself,

'I am condemning myself in order to pressure myself to improve.'
Then add, 'And I figure it is going to work.' Then see if it does.'' We
thus invite the client to make the observations needed to invalidate his
own premise.

Most clients see the mistake and stop the self-criticism for the time
being, but it reappears nonetheless a short while later. Reminders are
necessary until the client becomes able to catch himself. ''Ah, there
you go with your self-improvement program again'' may become an
in joke with these clients.

To bring it home, we may involve the client more actively by having
him state his premise aloud: ''If I punish myself enough, I will force
myself to do better.'' It is important for the client to be able to catch
himself in his self-critical attitudes, for such patterns are hard to
break, and reappear again and again when one is not looking. We
might ask the client to keep a list and to catch himself at least six times
a day being too tough on himself. We can instruct the client to repeat
his premise to himself whenever he is being too self-critical, and to ask
himself each time if it really is the royal path to self-improvement. In
this way, we structure carry-over into everyday activities.

These clients may see harsh pressure not as the preferred means of
self-improvement, but as the only means. They see themselves as incompetent or lazy, so that only by constant pressure could they possibly accomplish anything. ''If I were not putting the screws to myself,''
they ask, ''then what would make me ever do anything?'' It is an
honest question. These people have been pressuring themselves for so
long that they have failed to develop any intrinsic interests or any
sense of what they genuinely want to do, and see only what they
should do or have to do. Since personal interests are squelched
through overwhelming pressures, it is only through lessening those
pressures that such interests are understood. The prescription is to
lessen the pressure long enough to see what one is genuinely interested
in, for one will not find out otherwise.

We take seriously the clients' interest in self-improvement and attempt to convince them that self-condemnation is a poor means to
that quite legitimate objective. The approach appeals to what matters,
for we show the clients that they would improve more and get what
they want by being easier on themselves. Some other approaches try
instead to convince the clients that their ambitions are too high, that
they do not really have to be perfect, and that they should care less

about trying to improve. But to suggest that improvement is not so important is to fight against what matters, since clients who pressure themselves to improve obviously want and value what they are striving for. So this sort of suggestion fails to generate real interest and does not make a lasting impression.

Self-criticism in order to improve is presented in the Gestaltist's *Top Dog–Under Dog* contest, in which the person as Top Dog condemns himself to force himself to improve, and the same person as Under Dog resists the pressure. The Putting the Screws to Yourself image was introduced by Ossorio.

3. HIGH OPINION OF ONESELF

Self-criticism may be used to maintain a *high opinion of oneself*. The person sees himself as special—somebody with high standards and excellent potential. From the vantage of such high standards, his actions fall short and compromise his sense of himself. So he criticizes the actions, to renounce them, so that they do not reflect on who he is. He claims that the actions are not worthy of him and that he is still a person of high standards despite the appearance to the contrary. Although it may seem paradoxical, the person actually affirms himself by renouncing his own behavior.

The unfavorable appraisal is an expression of a vision which is restricted and directed downward by unreasonably high standards for oneself. But in a more important sense, it is more than merely a comment: renouncing the action serves to protect, maintain, and enhance the high standards and superior opinion the person has of himself. The satisfactions are in the implicit claims to high standards and superior characteristics. The following three images illustrate these subtle workings.

The *Kissinger Joke* conveys the grandiosity involved in holding yourself accountable for that which is outside your control: "A man stops by a bar after work and has a couple of drinks. The television commentator announces that Henry Kissinger is going to Peking—top secret negotiations and such, and possible opening of diplomatic relations. 'How could I have been such a fool?' the man moans. 'It's a mistake; I shouldn't have let him go. Now I've ruined everything.' While he is ostensibly bemoaning his stupidity, one gets the sense that there is something funny going on." At this point, we ask the client what it is that is fishy. Usually the client gets the point, and if not, we provide it. "In criticizing himself for allowing Kissinger to go to Peking, the man is making an implicit claim that he was someone in a position to do something about it. In this case, he was claiming to be the president, and that's high status indeed."

As with other images, we present the image to the client and then make the connections to the relevant issues. We explore what he was claiming to be in a position to have accomplished and how realistic the claim is. The grandiosity of holding oneself accountable for things one is in no position to do anything about is conveyed in a light and humorous manner, but conveyed nonetheless. An inability to see oneself in more modest and humble ways is also involved, and it is worthwhile to explore why it is uncomfortable for the client to accept more modest views of himself.

The client has been able to maintain a sense of superiority by condemning himself, but he sees in the image that self-condemnation does not enhance himself but only maintains his pretense of superiority and status. While he can continue his self-condemnation, he no longer finds it satisfying in the same way. The Kissinger Joke is a "poisoning the well" move because it ruins the client's satisfactions.

There is a risk of offending a client by calling him grandiose. The Kissinger Joke takes the initial focus off the client and presents the grandiosity issue in a light and humorous manner, allowing the client to enjoy the presentation. One who enjoys the image and sees the rationale is usually a good enough sport to accept its application to his own actions.

The *Art Critic* image conveys the status claims in excessively high standards. The status an art critic has with the public is maintained by his reviews, and some critics write a preponderance of adversely critical appraisals in order to present themselves as persons with superior standards. The critic who conveys that a movie looks just fine to him is leaving himself wide open to be one-upped by another with a less favorable review. The one who gives an unfavorable review says in effect that it may be good enough for the competition, but it certainly does not meet his (higher) standards. So to stay one-up as a critic, you need to have high standards, and it helps to look down a bit and condemn. The art critic image fits the client who criticizes himself to stay ahead.

The *Supercritic* image is used to illustrate ultimate superiority and absolute perfection. The ordinary things that are good enough for ordinary people are not good enough for the Supercritic. He conveys that nothing is good enough, in order to show that his standards are just that high. He is in a position so far above everyone that he can judge it all and find it lacking.

The Supercritic is readily recognized in academia. The dissertation student who cannot get underway with his thesis is often a Supercritic. Each topic seems too limited for him, and each methodology seems inadequate. The Supercritical student expects that his is going to be a major contribution, and he is rejecting available options in order to maintain his sense of importance. Any thesis he actually completes may fall quite short of his ambitions. By rejecting each of his initial attempts, he maintains his great expectations and protects his sense of himself as someone with something of real importance to contribute.

Each of these images illustrates the issue in an easily recognized and nonthreatening way, and is then applied to the client's situation. Should the client be suspicious or overly sensitive, we might suggest rather than force the analogy: "That sort of issue might apply to what you're doing here. Can you see any connection?" Once the connections have been made, key words can evoke the entire issue and familiarize the client with the applications: "Ah, remember the Supercritic."

These images outline the satisfactions involved in doing the criticizing and confirm the client as the perpetrator, rather than merely the victim, of the harsh treatment. He is already in control, and the issue then becomes one of exercising the control in a more beneficial manner.

The client may still ask helplessly how he can stop the self-criticism, thus countering our affirmation and maintaining himself as the helpless victim. We refer to the satisfactions involved: "Given the satisfactions involved, the issue is not that you are unable to stop criticizing yourself but whether you are willing to give up the satisfactions." When the client is unwilling, we respond that it is understandable, that maybe he does not see anything to replace the satisfactions, or that it is difficult to give up something so familiar. We cast the client as an active participant and reaffirm his control of his self-criticism. The three images above and their applications were suggested by Ossorio.

4. PENANCE AND RESTITUTION

Self-criticism may be to *make amends* for wrongdoing. One who has done wrong has reason to make amends and may do so by acknowledging his wrongs, and by penance and restitution. All are ways of showing good faith—of renouncing the transgression, claiming that decent standards do count, and reaffirming moral character.

In everyday conflicts, it is often unclear who is doing wrong and who is being wronged. The issue is negotiated by information, insinuation, ploys and counterploys, argument, and social alliances. When one acknowledges that he is in the wrong, he thereby resolves the conflict. He accepts whatever loss of face is his as the wrongdoer, and by clearing the others of fault, he takes a step toward making amends. One may thus criticize himself to acknowledge wrongdoing and to make some restitution. Familiar forms of this are "It was my fault," "I was mistaken," and "I feel awful about how much trouble I have caused you." When others accept the acknowledgment and see it as a good faith commitment to do better, the person regains his standing in those relationships. By acknowledging his wrongdoing one also sets a precedent which invites others to acknowledge their own parts in the conflict, and may thus move things toward an amicable settlement. When others fail to accept the apology, the problems continue. Acknowledging wrongdoing may be a step in regaining moral integrity, by reconciling oneself with others and with the community that one has wronged. Acknowledging wrongdoing is emphasized by O. H. Mowrer (1968) in an approach he terms integrity therapy.

However, one does well to weigh and evaluate whether an action was genuinely wrong. Any appraisal of wrongdoing is by some standards of conduct, and we look at what standards are involved. What are the client's standards, what might we consider reasonably appropriate standards, and in what ways does the behavior fall short? Do the standards truly fit the client, or are they the standards of others which he unquestioningly accepts and applies to himself? Does he himself judge that he did wrong, or does he merely accept the opinions of others which may reflect their own narrow interests?

If the standards are too strict, inconsistent, or otherwise inappropriate, clarifying and reevaluating them with the client may alleviate much of the guilt. When the client is setting the standards himself, direct discussion of moral and ethical issues is usually helpful. When the client is submitting to the unreasonable dictates of family or friends, such dictates need to be examined and challenged, and therapy may involve rearranging relationships with family and friends.

If the client has violated standards which appear to be appropriate and just, the guilt is real and we should deal with it as real. Some benefit can be attained by acknowledging the wrongdoing, but a personal or public acknowledgment can carry only so much benefit. So how else might one go about regaining moral standing? Consider closely the distinction between penance and restitution. Both are seen as ways of reaffirming oneself in the face of wrongdoing, but only penance emphasizes self-condemnation and suffering to atone for wrongs. Restitution emphasizes the correction of the wrongs rather than loss to the wrongdoer. While it may involve some sacrifice, it is the benefit to the wronged party which is paramount and not the suffering of the wrongdoer.

The overriding theme in current ethics and morality is to affirm and benefit others, to avoid harming them—and to treat oneself in the same way. We clarify the operating premise that by suffering one affirms his morality, and we question its validity: "You are willing to suffer for your wrongs. You are punishing yourself—doing penance, if you will—as a reaffirmation of your good moral character. But can you really accomplish it that way? Can you become more moral merely by making yourself suffer? Maybe not." We can also challenge penance on the grounds that it does absolutely nothing to affirm or benefit others, and may even annoy or disturb them instead: "Note that your penance does absolutely nothing to benefit anyone else, and may even make them uncomfortable. While penance may make you *feel* more moral, it cannot make you *be* more moral. In its own way, it is even self-serving. It allows you to get without giving—to feel moral without doing anything for anyone else." Our task may be to encourage the client to use restitution rather than penance. We steer the client away from self-punishment and toward making real amends.

Some religious practices suggest that the willing infliction of suffering atones for sins and restores moral soundness. Yet voluntary suffering is not the sole property of those with formal religious training and may be a component of any culture, or perhaps of human nature. Formal religion too may be turning from penance to restitution: one who confesses may be told to do something good for the individual or community he has sinned against, rather than merely to contemplate his misdeeds. Penance may be a leftover from medieval times when there was little hope of bettering existence on earth, the church supported the status quo, and morality was insulated from issues of everyday social relationships.

In many cases the client feels guilty, but does not feel that he *is* guilty. He feels that others are manipulating him to make him feel guilty and that those who are manipulating him are the ones who are doing wrong. So he feels resentful and angry, as well as guilty. Suggestions for restitution go nowhere, for the client would resent having to do anything to benefit those who have manipulated him into feeling guilty. The person is willing to suffer for his alleged wrongs, but he is too angry to make amends to those he feels are also at fault. Restitution has no appeal here. It is best in these cases to focus on the ways the client himself is being mistreated and to channel his anger into assertive stands toward those he feels are manipulating him into feeling guilty.

With those strongly committed to penance, we might use a paradoxical affirmation, encouraging the penance: "Your guilt feeling is penance. You are willing to punish yourself for your wrongdoings, to show that you really do care. So you may wish to continue punishing yourself, or perhaps to punish yourself more harshly, to show that you *really* care." The tactic accomplishes two objectives. It affirms the client's good moral character, thus lessening the pressure—with the aim of the penance already accomplished, why continue it? If he does continue, then, under this description, he is attempting to be moral. He thus finds himself in the familiar therapeutic double bind: if he continues the self-criticism, he is affirming his good character; if he stops it, he is cured.

We may invite the client to gauge how much more self-punishment is needed to complete his penance, thus pushing his premise to its necessary conclusions and generating resistance; "Your premise is that punishing yourself is the right thing to do to make up for your wrongs, but you've been punishing yourself for quite a while now and you still feel awful. Are you sure it is going to work?" We allow time for reflection and then continue: "It hasn't worked so far, but perhaps you have not been tough enough. You might try doubling your self-punishment, and see if that works. I question whether it will, but you may have to try it to see for yourself."

We might suggest that there is no real reason to string out the penance over the whole day. A single concentrated self-condemnation session should suffice, perhaps 20 minutes before bedtime, leaving the client free of the guilt most of the day but assured of a full measure of self-punishment nonetheless. We may have the client imagine actually freeing himself of the "guilties," relegating them to a concentrated time period and being assured they will be experienced then. The absurdity of a commitment to punishing oneself becomes clearer when the self-punishment is given in a concentrated dose.

Sometimes it is not merely good faith or moral soundness which the person wishes to convey, but rather moral superiority and ethical infallibility. The *Hanging Judge* image illustrates self-righteousness and vindictiveness toward the wrongdoer. The hanging judge metes out maximum penalties, seeking not merely justice but the angry and vindictive destruction of the criminal. He attains a reputation for toughness which suggests that he is ultramoral and certainly beyond suspicion of criminal acts himself. Nonetheless, one wonders why he invests in being so ultramoral. One obvious interpretation is that he himself has been sorely tempted by sinful acts, so he appears ultramoral to renounce such activities, to regain moral status, and to maintain the necessary self-control over his evil urges. Vengeful punishment toward oneself may be used similarly to convey ultramorality. We use the Hanging Judge image to illustrate the issue, and we question why the client is impelled to appear so ultramoral. What has gone on that could possibly require such stern reaffirmation of moral standing? The Hanging Judge image was suggested by Ossorio.

One who does penance may be also seeking restraint against temptations, safety from condemnation by others, and the avoidance of accountability.

5. SELF-RESTRAINT

Self-criticism may be to *restrain* oneself in the face of temptations or other possible errors. One who wants something unsafe or unethical has reason to do it and reason not to do it, and therein lies the conflict. When safety or ethics provides compelling reasons against an action, good judgment is to avoid it. One who is inclined to do it anyway obviously needs better means to restrain himself.

The most straightforward means of self-restraint is to convince oneself of the reasons against the action, maintain awareness of these reasons, and act on them. But this is not always possible, particularly when one is unable to personally accept the reason against the action. So alternate means of self-restraint are needed. One means is to be in no position to get involved, or to convince yourself that you are in no position.

Self-critical statements may serve to remind oneself that one is in no position to undertake tempting but unsafe activities. Saying this brings it home, makes it real, lowers confidence, and thus serves to restrain oneself. An unattractive person is in no position to pursue a love affair with someone who is attractive; an incapable person is in no position to attempt difficult activities; an unworthy person should not expect the support of others for his actions. More generally, a nobody is in no position to act as a somebody with any real chance of success. The doors of opportunity are shut.

The common and almost obsessive concern among teenagers over flaws in appearance may serve as self-restraint. The social expectation among teenagers is not only that they socialize with the opposite sex, but that they be good at such relationships and enjoy them. Opposite-sex relationships are obviously desirable, but most teenagers are new at assessing their standing with potential partners and cannot navigate anything close to a safe course in such relationships. Fears of appearing publicly inappropriate, inadequate, out of place, and rejected are worsened by poor communications among friends and lack of support. There are also concerns about the ethics of sexual intimacies. Being unattractive is but one way a teenager would not fit in, but it is an obvious and tangible one, and often serves as a focus for the more complex and unfamiliar issues of social standing. It may be better to remind oneself of one's place, however modest, than to overstep it and be socially humiliated.

An attractive married woman held an inner sense that having an affair would be immoral and that she could get caught, but she would not accept these reasons as sufficient restraints. She felt her husband mistreated her and did her dirty, that he deserved infidelity, and that she was going to be sure he got what he deserved. What did she do? She became obsessed with what she considered unattractive or flawed features, and that obsession ate up her time, ruined her confidence, and restrained her from having an affair. Her obsessions with unattractive features ensured that she lacked the necessary confidence, so no action was possible.

There are parallels between a person criticizing another person and criticizing himself. The Grier and Cobbs (1968) analysis of Negro families before the black equality movement suggested that mothers who were usually loving and nurturant were nonetheless at times harshly critical and demeaning toward their children—especially the boys—in effect undermining their confidence and thwarting their masculinity. While such messages appear hostile, the authors saw that the real aim was to teach the boys their place in order to promote their safety. A Negro man who did not know his place might become enraged, challenge white authority, and perhaps end up being lynched. The mothers' criticism was based on a good sense of culture and status, and the intention was to protect the boys against their own masculine self-assertive impulses.

Our task in therapy is to find better ways to remain ethical or safe. The initial step is to clarify those issues: clients must understand their legitimate concerns for ethics or safety before being able to reevaluate their means of attaining it.

With a teenager who is self-critical about appearances, we might comment on the difficulties of teenage dating, the pervasiveness of anxieties, and the need to have somebody to talk to. The possibilities of acceptance or rejection should be explored, and the youngster questioned on how one could know if a guy or gal is really interested. With the issues spelled out, the youngster may accept an interpretation of his self-criticism, such as: "I think that your standing with fellows is what you're really concerned about. Being so upset about your looks is one way of asking, 'Will I fit in? Will they like me?' And looks are certainly one thing that matters a lot to fellows, though not the only thing. Perhaps we would do better talking about how you do fit in. At least, that is something you can do something about."

With the married woman mentioned above, the safety and morality of having an affair should be discussed. We might make an outcome interpretation of the self-criticism, suggesting but not forcing the issue of intentionality: "Your obsession with your flawed features destroys your confidence, and you end up staying home anyway. I wonder if you're trying to tell yourself something like 'Watch out, I'm not ready for that affair'?" An initial objective in therapy might be to help her better evaluate her interest in the affair, and from there either increase her confidence to act on her inclinations or help her accept her legitimate reasons for refraining from such actions. Larger issues such as the unfairness of the marriage remain, and ways to improve it must be addressed.

If the self-restraint seems overly conservative, we should encourage more confidence, for the risks are not as great as they appear. If the restraint reflects good judgment, we might expect the self-criticism to remain until the client has alternate ways of managing his impulses. Self-management strategy may be appropriate. We might persuade the client to delay the desired experience until better able to handle the situation, with the expectation that he can have it then and enjoy it more. The ideal is not merely to restrain desires, but somehow to reconcile what one wants with what is practical and safe, and we work toward this overall goal.

Self-criticism might also be used to restrain oneself from making ordinary mistakes, which are not tempting but occur nonetheless in any reasonably complex human activity. Condemning oneself and being obsessed with one's mistakes are ways of keeping them continually in mind in order to force oneself to avoid making those mistakes in the future. The approach is to avoid what is wrong rather than to strive for what is right, and the obvious issue is whether one can alleviate mistakes by concentrating on them and having them continually in mind. The following *Wrong Keys* image shows the obvious pitfalls: "Suppose a piano player is trying to improve his performance by studying the wrong keys, in order to avoid hitting them at the wrong times. He keeps track of all the mistakes he makes and keeps them always in mind, so that he will remember not to make them anymore. He concentrates on all the wrong keys and finds his performance is becoming continually poorer. So what is the problem?" Most clients find it easy enough to fill in the answer: "You have to have your mind on what you are doing and not on everything else which you should not do instead. There are any number of wrong keys, so that you cannot avoid them all merely by thinking about them. To hit the right keys, you have to focus your concentration on the right keys." The image is then applied to the client: "You focus on your mistakes, but that does not help you to figure out what you should be doing instead. To do something well, you have to concentrate on doing it well and not on avoiding doing it badly."

We encourage clients to catch themselves in their self-critical tendencies, to become conscious of them, and to begin to control them. But many clients who catch themselves being self-critical address their mistake by condemning themselves further. As obviously contradictory as it seems, the person applies his favored method—self-condemnation—to try to obliterate his worst problem, which is also self-condemnation. Each time he catches himself, he perpetuates the problem. He makes catching himself extremely painful, and the most obvious way out is to forget about the program altogether. To counter this, we remind the client to count the reaction as well: "I suggest you tally six times each day when you are too tough on yourself. When you catch yourself condemning yourself and then condemn yourself for your mistake, then you get to count it as a doubleheader. Count it once for being tough on yourself and again for punishing yourself for the mistake. That should make it easy for you to score at least six instances." The point is to enable the client to catch the self-criticism, and to react not with further self-condemnation but with an easy smile of recognition.

6. AVOIDANCE OF DISAPPOINTMENT

Self-criticism may be used to *avoid potential disappointments*. Persons with high expectations may be shocked, startled, stunned, disappointed, and hurt when things go wrong. Persons with low expectations take no such chances, for while they may be surprised by good news they cannot be shocked by failure—that they expect. So there is the advantage of safety in maintaining low expectations for oneself. Those who maintain low expectations stay in control of their emotional states: they generate their own opinions of themselves—albeit unfavorable ones—and do not allow the capriciousness of circumstances to do it to them. It may not feel good, but at least they are in charge of their own views and feelings.

A familiar example is the student who does well in his courses but is obsessively concerned nonetheless about failing every exam. As he sees it, he is too stupid or too unprepared, or the test is too difficult for him. Such impoverished expectations generate anxiety and pain, and waste energy, but there is an advantage: if he were to expect to do well, he could be shocked or embarrassed by a poor showing. By committing himself to low expectations, he is prepared for the worst and cannot be shocked by any outcome. Even real failure could not be all that bad in comparison with his anticipations and with the suffering he has already acclimated himself to. He maintains control of his own emotional state and does not allow the results of the examination to do it to him.

To intervene, we outline the protective function of low self-assessments: "Were you to expect to do well, you could be shocked and unsettled by the outcome. By seeing yourself as stupid and expecting the worst, you take no such chances because you are already prepared for the worst. The advantage is that you cannot be caught by surprise by something going wrong." Most clients sense the safety issue already and thus readily agree.

The comment shows the client the legitimate reasons he has for clinging to his low self-expectations. From there it is an easy step to ask, "Is it worth it?" Most clients have the good sense to see that it is not. Change occurs through showing the client the reasons he has for his poor self-expectations; being conscious of the reasons places him in a position to reevaluate them and conclude that they are not worth it. Should he feel them to be worth it, there is some gain nonetheless for he now sees himself as someone who is in charge of his self-critical tendency.

Where it appears worth the price, we might find ways to tip the balance the other way. We question, "How much shock and pain need accompany life's disappointments?" Some persons see disappointments as embarrassing indications that they have been foolish and immodest in expecting too much. Their concept of disappointment includes the extraneous meanings of foolish and immodest, and we clarify the concept: "When you look forward to something and fail at it, you feel you have been foolish and out of place to have ever expected it. Is there any way to see yourself as more than just merely foolish? Is it wrong to expect things even if you do not always get them?" "Might you still see yourself as somebody who accepts challenges and takes risks, and does his best when things are not guaranteed? Could you see yourself as something more than just a loser when things go badly?"

Some feel they should not have to endure disappointments and assume that their more optimistic acquaintances do not face failures. We convey that disappointments are part of the human condition and challenge the client on his claimed privilege: "You feel you are somebody who should not have to endure disappointments. Everybody else has to, but you are above all that. You have the special privilege of never having to be disappointed." The client sees his pessimism as a break-even strategy; we suggest instead that it is a claim to special privilege. There is some comfort in realizing that disappointments are a part of our shared humanity.

To address these safety issues, some humanistic and group orientations suggest to their clients that they take more risks. Here we clarify the advantages clients seek by playing it so safe, mention the price they pay, and ask them if it is worth it. We mention that there is some safety in taking what may appear to be risks and that what they are doing instead is settling for the certain loss. Is it not safer to risk succeeding, rather than settling for the false safety of sure failure? These clients trade uncertain advantages for certain losses, and we give them credit for being able to figure out for themselves whether it is worthwhile to continue.

Like other sections, this is an outline of treatment issues. In practice, these issues are presented with greater elaboration and complexity, and tailored to the individual client. The issues may be dealt with several more times in a similar but abbreviated manner before the self-critical tactic is relinquished.

7. SAFETY FROM ATTACK

Presenting oneself to others as humble or troubled may secure a position *safe from challenge* or attack. Statements about oneself are implicit claims to a corresponding social standing, which others accept by treating the person as who he says he is or fail to accept by overt challenge, by subtle insinuation and undermining, or by simply not going along with his claim. Claims to being someone of importance may be subject to considerable challenge, reaffirmation, and negotiation.

The social safety in self-critical statements is that they are claims to lower or less preferred status. One who claims to be an incapable and unworthy nobody is extremely difficult to attack—he is already too low. Only the truly callous would accuse and attack someone suffering already from his own self-condemnation; most people would avoid attacking and would support instead. Others who disagree may argue with him that he is really more than he says he is, but in so doing they merely frustrate themselves.

A claim to higher status is more vulnerable. A person presenting himself as somebody worthy and capable may have his views of himself challenged and rejected, and find himself seen and treated as less than he has implied he is. Having one's self-presentation undermined by others is a blow—an insult, a slap in the face, an embarrassment, a wound to one's pride. One who is unprepared to deal with status challenges and rejections would find the needed safety in sticking with lower and less preferred positions. The person riding high may be shot down out of the saddle, while the person who is already on the ground takes no such chances. There is a certain safety in being down low, especially if one is in hostile territory and is not particularly good at fending off attackers. It is especially dangerous when attack is to be expected from important others. Not surprisingly, self-critical persons are often closely involved with family or friends who are critical and undermining.

There are norms and conventions against saying positive things about yourself since this may be seen as boastful and conceited. The person who says he has done well may make others uncomfortable, for he invites unfavorable comparisons and can evoke envy and jealousy. He may invite challenge and negation from others who try to "put him in his place." Convention holds that modesty is a virtue, for it allays unfavorable comparisons and puts others at ease. Modesty may be considered a virtue, but the harsh self-critic is carrying it a bit too far.

The mother who says she is doing well as a parent may generate an unfavorable comparison between herself and others who are having troubles with their children. The other parents, rather than seeking to learn from her, may attempt instead to challenge and undermine: "Ah, just wait until the kid gets to be a teenager—then you'll be in for a big shock," or "That's what I thought, too, before I learned better." As a consequence, parents can talk to each other about the difficulties they are having, but seldom do they say much about the exceptional jobs they are doing as parents.

We begin by clarifying these issues for the client. Clients often assume that any attacks they receive are somehow deserved. Understanding that others' attacks may be motivated by competitiveness and jealousy helps put the issue into perspective. Such undermining is still unpleasant, but clients need not see it as an indication that they have been immoral, improper, or wrong. Those people who characteristically undermine should be distinguished from those who are more accepting. The client may need to watch himself carefully with some people, but be more open and trusting with others. We clarify the situations and relationships the client is in.

Being challenged on one's self-presentation does not mean that the game is lost. It is a contest, and the initial self-presentation may be maintained by an appropriate comeback. But the client may be unable to fend off the challenge, or more commonly, he does not even consider doing so. We attempt to improve his combat abilities. A good beginning is to sketch possible counterstrategies. We show the client that there are workable comebacks to challenges and that he himself might be able to do this. Through portraying his comeback, we affirm the legitimacy of his position and we credit him with a possible winning position.

One good comeback for an adverse insinuation is simply to clarify it. The client asks innocently: "You don't think I should have so much confidence?" or "You feel I think too highly of myself?" Such comments hold the adversary responsible for his challenge and put the client on an equal footing. We introduce and support counterchallenges to critical and unfair attacks through the familiar range of assertiveness training techniques. The point of appropriate assertiveness is to maintain one's own rights and status in social relationships, and to prevent unfair subjugation.

We may ask the client to make positive statements about himself and then show our approval. The client sees that someone can accept and affirm his positive self-presentation. In sessions with a family member or friend present, trying out positive self-presentation may have additional benefit. The questions and problems become apparent, and can be dealt with there in the sessions. When a spouse supports the client's optimistic statements, a new pattern may be established. When the spouse reacts adversely to the positive statements, there is grist for the mill.

8. SYMPATHY

Self-criticism may be used to enlist *sympathetic involvement*. Being overly tough on oneself invites others to be sympathetic and reassuring, and to try to cheer one up. Someone who is isolated, lonely, and unloved has reason to seek sympathetic involvement, and condemning oneself is an easy way of attaining it. The sympathy shows that he is not alone in his miseries, for others are joining with him in taking them on. But too often the person counters the reassurance with continuing "I'm no good" statements, for there is reason not to really accept the reassurance. If others do succeed in reassuring him, the job would be done and his friends would feel free to go on to other things. That would mean abandonment and renewed isolation.

Reassuring friends often share in the misery, saddened by what they hear and frustrated by their inability to do anything about it. If misery loves company, as it is said, the self-critic finds good company indeed. There is added advantage when sympathetic friends join in the sorrow, for an unfavorable comparison is avoided between the person's own situation and what might have otherwise been happier and better-adjusted friends.

However, continual self-criticism is hard on one's friends. Others weary of hearing the same sob story, of giving so much reassurance, and of seeing no improvement. Eventually they may try to avoid the sympathy-seeking self-critic. This in turn evokes fears of abandonment, anger at being neglected, and feelings of worthlessness. The person's implicit premise is that being tough on himself should bring sympathetic involvement, and the premise is not necessarily challenged by occasional failures. Indeed, withdrawal by others may lead to further and more excessive self-criticism, out of loneliness and anger, in an attempt to reinvolve others and show them that he really does need their support.

We ask the client how others react to his frequent self-criticism. Are others straightforwardly sympathetic and supportive, or do they get annoyed and weary? The client may already recognize that others reassure him out of obligation, but are frustrated and would not wish to continue were they not feeling so guilty. So it seems that they do not really mean it, and the client feels he is a burden and his friends are untrue. We give others the benefit of the doubt here and place the responsibility on the way the client is going about things. Obligating others does indeed elicit obligatory support, but what else could one expect? The client forces others to support him, so how can he believe their support to be genuine? There is no way of knowing. The obvious conclusion here is that to be able to see others as genuine, one has to give them the freedom to be genuine. Is the client willing to take such a chance on another's good faith?

These clients usually lack any good idea of how to talk about themselves other than by dwelling on their problems. So we may account for the negativity by suggesting to the client that he is simply unable to talk about himself in any other more positive way. These clients need to learn to talk about attitudes, interests, ambitions, achievements, feelings, opinions, or almost anything other than their own problems. We generate alternatives. They may find to their astonishment that friends are interested in something other than their problems. If their restrictions are embedded, we may have to suggest particular statements as illustrations and have the clients practice them aloud. If a family member or friend is in the session, the client can try out being optimistic, and see if the other responds with encouragement and support. This type of interchange has quite an impact when the client's optimism gains him support, and we can troubleshoot any difficulties which may occur.

9. AVOIDANCE OF RESPONSIBILITY

Self-criticism may be used to *avoid responsibility*. One is responsible only for what one is in a position to do something about. Fair standards of accountability follow similar lines, for a person should be held accountable only for what he is in a position to do something about. There are two parts here—holding oneself accountable and being held accountable by others—and the same argument applies to both. One should hold himself accountable, and be held accountable, only when he is in a position to do something to make a difference.

Self-criticism may be a statement that one is less than it otherwise appears. "I'm no good at anything," "I always mess everything up," or "I can't control my nerves" are statements that the person is incapable, and one who really is incapable is in no position to influence the matter and so should not be held responsible. The message is "Don't expect too much from me because, you see, I've got this 'wooden leg.'" Self-criticism is thus a claim to the status "incapable," which carries with it the advantage of being not accountable.

We may see friends or family members actually competing for standing as the most miserable of the group. The "winner" of the contest is out from under the burdens and has a claim to being cared for by the others. The loser is saddled with the obligation to take care of the needy ones and is accountable for whatever goes wrong.

Those who reassure are taking implicit responsibility for making the self-critic feel better. They are the ones concerned about his feelings and well-being, and not the person himself. They either raise his spirits or fail at it, and either way everyone agrees that it is their responsibility. A person with the general miseries surely finds relief, and perhaps even some satisfaction, when others take responsibility for his feelings and take the pressure off him.

Seeing and presenting oneself as incapable carry with them the obvious price: one acts accordingly, and misses the satisfactions and joys open to competent people. This choice becomes intelligible when we consider that responsibility can be a weighty burden indeed. These persons may feel absolutely overburdened and overwhelmed by responsibilities. Managing responsibility is not always easy even for the most thoughtful and capable. It may indeed be unmanageable for confused persons in chaotic relationships.

These persons usually misestimate just what they are and are not responsible for. One who feels accountable for everything finds it understandably overwhelming. If the choice is between being always to blame for everything and being a nobody who cannot be blamed, it is easy to choose the latter. These persons have had inadequate or incorrect training in setting reasonable standards for personal accountability, and others may be holding the person accountable for far more than anyone should be expected to manage.

The main therapeutic task is to enable the client to see responsibility as fair, understandable, and manageable. We might begin by interpreting and legitimizing the client's position: "You are arguing that you are incapacitated, which is a tough state to be in, but it does have one quite apparent advantage. While so incapacitated, you are incapable of meeting the sorts of responsibilities that are weighing so heavily on you, so you are not to blame for things. Also, the way you talk about those responsibilities, they do indeed sound overwhelming. It's not surprising at all that you want to get out of them, and you're doing just that. But let's look further, and see if responsibility has to be so terrible."

If the client holds himself overly accountable, we should introduce and advocate more reasonable standards. Perhaps the client evaluates himself only by his results, and disregards his intentions and efforts in the matter. We might make responsibility more acceptable by mentioning the good intentions: "Even when you've done your best, you still condemn yourself if everything doesn't turn out well. You're missing the intentions in what you're doing—you're missing the part that you contribute. Seems like you're blind to the better part of who you are and what you're about."

Others may be using manipulative tactics to make the person feel so accountable. We clarify such influences, emphasizing their unfairness. We encourage the client to challenge those expectations and to seek to establish fairer relationships.

Avoidance of responsibility tends to run in families. The client may have assimilated the "wooden leg" strategy from a parent who used it to control and obligate him. He is only trying to break even, to out-manipulate using the same tools. Challenging the parent's manipulativeness first allows us to maintain an alliance, for we come across as supportive. It is then easier to interpret that the client himself has adopted the strategy because it may have been the only way he had of breaking even.

10. HOSTILITY

Self-criticism may be camouflaged *hostility*. One who sees himself as wronged has reason to strike back; yet retaliation is often seen as wrong itself and invites counterretaliation and further problems. By being hard on oneself, one may have an uncomfortable or painful effect on family and friends who care, but remain almost immune from the obvious countermeasures.

A person using self-criticism to express hostility is angry and often appears angry. The angry "I'm such an awful person" or "I'm no good at anything" statements appear to be anger directed at himself, but this is a tactic which camouflages hostility toward others, making it hard to see or challenge—and thus particularly tormenting. This person is to be admired for the ruggedness of the camouflage. Failing to see his aims, others do not hold the person accountable for the hurt he is causing, and should they suspect, the person already appears so miserable that challenge and accusation would seem intolerably callous.

These persons may use the immediate circumstances to make the case that someone else is responsible for their awful feelings about themselves. In one incident, the wife has spent several hours making a gourmet meal. The husband comes home late, eats in silence, but comments that the duck is dry, perhaps overcooked. The wife states angrily that she is an awful cook and nothing she does is ever right. She dumps the dry duck in the garbage, platter and all, and runs from the table, sobbing. In doing so, she conveys that it was the husband who caused her such suffering and that he was responsible. He caused her problems, and he should feel awful about how much he made her suffer. The husband's comment was the provocation, and she gave it back to him in spades.

Our initial move is to clarify the issue in a way which is acceptable to the client. Ordinarily, we avoid straightforward interpretations which would make the client feel accused, exposed, and vulnerable. These persons go to considerable expense to camouflage their retaliation as anger toward themselves, and they may need the cover. Unless there is an exceptionally trusting relationship, interpreting the hostility would be seen as pejorative and coercive, and would elicit client resistance. We gain entry through legitimizing the anger. Mentioning the provocation serves to make sense of and justify the anger. Without forcing the person to admit that she was angry, we can invite her to accept that she or anyone else might have been legitimately angry in that situation.

In the case of the hapless duck's journey to the garbage, we legitimize: "That must have been really annoying, to invest so much in cooking a really special meal and get nothing but the silent treatment. His comment about your cooking must have been the last straw. That sort of thing is enough to make anybody angry." Sometimes legitimizing allows clients to accept their anger, but in other cases, they maintain their cover: "I wasn't angry—I was just hurt/upset." We sidestep the resistance here and continue legitimizing: "I'm not necessarily saying that you were angry. I'm just saying that it was extremely thoughtless of your husband and was the sort of thing that would make most people angry." Most clients will not argue with this, for they agree that they were mistreated, and do not feel accused or vulnerable because of our intervention.

These self-critics are lashing back through self-derogatory rather than self-affirming positions. They fully embrace the worst that might be said about them, exaggerate it, and then turn it back to torment their adversaries. Our task is to enable these clients to channel their anger so as to affirm themselves and improve their situations, thus redressing the unfairness and lessening the provocations which evoke anger. Instead of condemning themselves to strike back, we encourage them to deal constructively with the reality basis of the anger. Most of these clients have definite reservations about self-affirmation. They feel it is selfish and wrong to assert themselves, and are afraid to put their own interests ahead of others. The expression of hostility through self-criticism is thus a next best solution, because it has the appearance of being unselfish.

When the client is able to see and accept his legitimate anger, it may be used as a rationale for self-affirmation. The actual choice is no longer between selfishness and unselfish modesty, but between legitimate self-affirmation and continued harm to oneself and others. There is no innocence, and we emphasize that failing to make a stand causes its own problems. Self-affirmation must be seen as the lesser of the evils.

Standard methods may be used to teach assertiveness, including illustrating assertive moves and practicing role-play situations. Hostile self-criticism lessens as these clients become able to deal affirmatively with everyday social provocations.

11. LOYALTY AND BELONGING

Self-criticism may express *loyalty and belonging*. One who lives with severe criticism is a member of a social order in which he must find a place, and one way to fit in is to accept and carry on the critical messages.

A youngster whose parents criticize him harshly while he is growing up finds that accepting the authority and force of that criticism is one obvious way of fitting in with the family. Opposing or ignoring his parents' criticism would appear disrespectful, cause argument, upset everybody, and leave the child isolated and on his own. While he might feel wronged by the harsh treatment, he considers it disloyal to oppose the authority and set an independent direction. So the child is socialized to see accepting the criticism as a way of accepting the family and being a member in good standing. Later on, if loyalty and belonging are still important, he may repeat the criticism to himself as an affirmation of his place in his family. Through criticizing himself, he carries on the family tradition: he is upholding the order of things he grew up with, and he clings to the security of that order.

We may begin by outlining these loyalty and membership issues. Our task is to counter the critical messages his parents have given, without running afoul and generating resistance by challenging his loyalty and respect toward his parents. One good way to do this is to agree initially that offspring should love and respect their parents, and further to credit him already with such feelings as seen in the loyalty and commitments he has shown toward his parents. We then mention that real people are fallible and do indeed make mistakes, and we raise the question of whether the client loves an ideal—a fantasy of his parents—or whether he loves the parents as they really are, failings and mistakes included. We ask: "Is not more compassion and real loyalty required to see another's mistakes and still love him, than merely to love him as an ideal?" Appealing to what matters to the client, we make acceptance of the parents' failings count as a sign of real love and so open the door to overturning the acid of the parents' criticism. Seeing the parents as overly harsh, mistaken, and even perhaps mean, becomes itself an indication of real loyalty for it means seeing and loving them as they actually are and not merely as a fantasy. We use the client's loyalty to move him toward independence.

As an adult, the client might be in a better position to alter his relationships with his parents. We might suggest tactics to improve his status in the family, so that he fits in as an equal rather than as a misbehaving subordinate. In some cases, the parents change easily; but in other cases they remain intransigent, and the client must adapt by learning to separate himself and ignore their attitudes. Some clients overvalue their relationships with their parents, perhaps because of insufficient personal involvement in their present relationships. Improvement of present relationships should be a main task of any treatment and can balance the residual force of earlier critical relationships.

One may criticize oneself to affirm his loyalty and membership in other groups and communities. One who proclaims "I am a sinner" over and over may be a member of a church which expects that sort of statement, so that it is a way of affirming faith and commitment to a Christian way of life. Such statements may be relatively innocuous in most cases, but troublesome if taken too seriously and not countered with other more positive messages.

12. ARGUMENT

Finally, self-criticism may be to *argue*. The self-critic finds his remarks challenged by friends, family, or even by casual acquaintances. His "I'm no good at anything" statements are met with "But you do a lot of things really well"; his "I'm afraid I'll fail" statements with "Don't worry, it'll turn out OK." Such counterstatements, while meant to be reassuring, are in effect directly contradictory, conveying the message that the original statement is merely mistaken and of no real consequence.

Recall again the two-position heuristic in self-criticism: there is the person as actor making the criticism, and the person as recipient being criticized. Friends are trying to give support to the person as recipient of the criticism, but their reassurance is just as surely opposition to the person as actor making the criticism, although it is not intended that way. Their reassurance is a challenge to the person who is criticizing himself and a contradiction of what he is saying. It is an attempt to undermine and subdue the person as perpetrator of the criticism, so that their own more positive messages will carry the day. The reminder is "Keep your eye on the actor." In most cases, the actor-critic does not simply vanish when challenged. On the contrary, the challenge gives him reason to respond by reaffirming his position. He may do so by repeating his self-critical statement, by arguing it stronger and louder, and by marshaling more evidence to support his contention that he is no good.

The argument, even though self-critical, is nonetheless an affirmation of oneself. The person who sees himself as worthless contends that he is someone at least capable of seeing who he is and of stating freely his miserable position. The contradiction he gets is a challenge to this last vestige of his ego and status, and he fights tenaciously to hold on. He maintains his right to state his own opinions of himself.

The issues may be personally sensitive and important, so that being contradicted leaves the person feeling badly ignored, misunderstood, or even betrayed when others fail to take his important message seriously. Such feelings may lead to further isolation, to further urgency in expressing his message, and thus to further self-criticism.

In medicine, the term "iatrogenic effects" covers those side effects and additional sickness caused by the physician's attempts to cure the patient. The concept applies equally well here, for it is the friends' good-faith attempts to alleviate the self-criticism through reassurance which provide the person with additional reasons to continue the self-criticism. We should avoid trying to force an argumentative client into a more optimistic outlook. The most obvious first step to alleviate iatrogenic self-criticism is to avoid causing it.

Nonetheless, we usually need to convey that the client is misstating things and that he is not really as badly off as he is presenting himself to be. Our task is to convey that information without opposing or contradicting the client's critical statements about himself and thus provoking him to argument. We might focus on what the client is doing, without stating directly that he is wrong. We might say: "You're really tough on yourself," or "You seem to be ready to stomp yourself for any failing." The client may agree or disagree, but the issue is whether he is too tough on himself, and he cannot argue against us by simply continuing to criticize himself. If he does attempt that, saying, "But I really am that awful," we can counter "See what I mean? You are at it again." The only effective counter open to the client would be to argue that he is gentle with himself, and to give evidence to support that he must lessen the self-criticism.

Clients who call on us to agree or disagree with their critical statements may put us in something of a bind. If we disagree, we evoke further argument; if we agree, we could be offensive and untherapeutic, as well as untruthful. We might express our opinion but minimize its importance, and it is best to focus instead on the objectives of the self-criticism.

Suppose a moderately attractive woman argues emphatically that she is ugly. We might respond: "I'm not sure I see it that way, but if you were ugly, then that would be a difficult thing to have to deal with. Is there a place in this world for people who are not so attractive?" The above comment avoids argument and provides an additional benefit as well. In claiming to be ugly, the woman is saying something about herself which ordinarily would hurt. Others who reassure her and argue that she is attractive thereby protect her from the pain that her argument should carry with it. When allowed to experience it freely, the pain itself may lessen further self-criticisms: hearing such awful things about oneself hurts too much, and that is its own reason to stop saying them.

SUMMARY

This chapter has outlined 12 categories of objectives, issues, and reasons that may be involved in any particular instance of self-criticism. In summary, self-criticism may be:

1. A self-appraisal, to better understand one's limitations
2. Pressure, to force oneself to improve
3. A renunciation of one's failings, to maintain a high opinion of oneself

4. Acknowledgment and amends for wrongdoing, to affirm moral standing
5. A reminder of limitations, to restrain oneself against temptation or error
6. A low expectation for oneself, to avoid the shock of disappointment
7. A downtrodden self-presentation, to prevent others from attacking
8. A pitiful self-presentation, to evoke sympathetic involvement from others
9. An appearance of being incapable, to avoid responsibility
10. Camouflaged hostility, to frustrate others and get even
11. An acceptance of limited status, to affirm loyalty and belonging
12. An argument, to reaffirm one's opinion against challenge

11
Integrative Treatment

One major reason or several reasons in combination may be involved in any instance of self-criticism. When a person has but one reason, assessment is simpler and treatment more straightforward. When he has several reasons in combination then each must be addressed, and treatment involves complex sequences of assessments and interventions. If a person has a second reason to do something, he has a stronger reason to do it than if he had just one of the reasons. Unfortunately, multiple reasons are involved in many of the harsher and more stubborn cases. It is often those second, third, and fourth reasons which account for the frequency and harshness of the self-criticism, and for its resistance to treatment.

MANAGING MULTIPLE REASONS

Some reasons for self-criticism commonly occur in combination with other reasons. When a person criticizes himself to argue with those who are contradicting him, he generally has another reason as well since he has criticized himself initially for that other reason, been contradicted, and then responded by arguing. When someone criticizes himself as a hostile act, he always has a second reason: to camouflage the hostility and so avoid retaliation from others. It is the two reasons in combination which account for the use of self-criticism rather than some other more straightforward means of striking back. If the person feels that hostility is wrong as well as unsafe, then his self-criticism may be penance as well: he criticizes himself to lash back, to camouflage the attack and thus remain safe from retaliation, and to do penance for the harm he is doing. Another combination of reasons may occur when one has done poorly: one may criticize oneself as

235

pressure to make oneself improve, to restrain oneself from making further mistakes, and to do penance for the failings or wrongs which one has committed. Again, if someone is concerned about his position, he may criticize himself to make himself safe from challenge by others and to lower his expectations in order to avoid the shock of disappointment.

Illustration

Reasons may also combine in configurations specific to a given person. With a client who is extremely self-critical, perhaps half a dozen reasons may be identified and challenged in the course of therapy. We try to address each of the reasons as we identify them, and we continue to work on them as we identify and address others. To illustrate, consider a schoolteacher, married, with several good friends and a competitive, overinvolved mother. The woman claims that she is inadequate, stupid, and a poor mother to her children. Her husband and friends argue otherwise, but to no avail, while her mother criticizes and undermines her to her face but is quite complimentary about her to other acquaintances. The woman seeks therapy for help with a shaky marriage and recurring moodiness and depression.

The husband is present in many of the sessions. The woman is continually annoyed at her husband, and as she criticizes herself, he seems to take responsibility for her upsetness and responds with continual reassurance and growing frustration. The interaction suggests a pattern: she may be criticizing herself to make her husband take responsibility for her inadequacies, and to make him support and reassure her; to frustrate and annoy him for his insufficient responses; and to argue with him and resist his unconvincing reassurances. We might intervene as follows: "You, Bob, expend considerable energy trying to reassure your wife, and you, Bonnie, are trying without much success to talk about something that is sensitive and important to you. The pattern is entrapping both of you, and with your permission, I want to try something different." They agree that an alternative is needed, and we invite the wife to discuss her inadequacies with us and ask the husband to merely listen.

As she talks of feelings of being stupid and inadequate, we convey our understanding and legitimize: "You are concerned that your social gaffes are more than little mistakes—that they mean you are awkward and out of place, and that you don't belong,'' or ''You are afraid that no matter how much you do as a parent, you will never be able to do enough and someone may find fault.'' The woman finds it easier to talk about herself and criticizes herself less. We then invite both of them to see what has just occurred: ''When you reassure her, Bob, you see that the self-criticism merely continues. What I did was to try to understand the feeling and to convey that I understood. As I did that, you, Bonnie, became more relaxed and less self-critical. Perhaps you felt understood and supported, and most surely you did not feel contradicted and challenged.''

We suggest a change in their interaction: ''You have seen that responding in a new way does make a difference. Would you, Bob, be willing to try reflecting the sentiment, rather than reassuring?'' The husband feels he should reassure, and we deal with his objections to the new program. To gain reasonable assurance of success, we should have them practice in the sessions. The wife is invited to criticize herself again, and the husband is taught to respond by conveying that he understands the sentiment. Since the pattern has been persistent, it may be difficult for the husband to avoid reassuring, and having something else to say helps. We give support and encouragement to each during the practice.

This initial intervention addresses several of the wife's reasons for criticizing herself. Since the husband is no longer contradicting, she loses argument as a reason. When the husband no longer becomes frustrated and upset by her comments, she loses the opportunity to upset him through criticizing herself. When he no longer reassures her, she loses the attention and also the opportunity to make him take responsibility in that way for her problems.

Additional reasons are seen in later sessions. Her mother continually criticizes and undermines her for the way she raises her children. She argues her own inadequacies as a means of allaying her mother's criticism, of accepting and becoming comfortable with that criticism in order to avoid being so shocked and upset by it, and of maintaining the peace rather than fighting and hurting her mother. Our objective is to enable her to establish a more viable status with her mother. We encourage her to see herself as someone who should be respected rather than interrogated and undermined, and we train her to make the assertive stands needed to change the relationship. She might begin by clarifying to her mother the messages implicit in the criticism: ''It sounds like you feel it is up to you to tell me how to raise my children. That must be quite a burden on you." She might try the following: "Perhaps you feel that I need your criticism to punish me for my mistakes or to make me a better parent." The mother may be startled by the comeback, but it exposes a slice of truth, and because of its clarity and unconventionality it is difficult to counter. Several other responses might be explored, and the most acceptable agreed upon and practiced. As the woman practices each new response, she implicitly tries on the new status it conveys: she presents herself as someone who has the right to challenge the criticism and be respected as a parent, and we support her. There is benefit in practicing the new response, and further benefit as she challenges the intimidation and secures for herself a stronger position with her mother.

As her reasons for criticizing herself become weaker, she criticizes herself less frequently and is free to accept better and more stable ways of seeing herself. While presented here in abbreviated form, such issues may require a range of interventions and ongoing attention over a number of sessions.

Assessment

Assessment and intervention must be closely interwoven. As we begin to interpret the excessive self-criticism, the client provides additional information by reacting to our interpretations and by saying more about his experiences and concerns. He might state the grounds he uses for seeing himself as such a failure. Where faulty information is involved, we may challenge there, offer a more supportive viewpoint, and make some progress if the client is receptive. If the client adamantly rejects the new information, then that may indicate argument, and we must cautiously avoid further reassurance. Perhaps the client states that he feels he should do better, or that he makes too many mistakes and must always watch himself. The former suggests he is pressuring himself to do better; the latter, that he is being obsessive about his failings to avoid making further mistakes. Perhaps we get the sense that the client expects us to continue to reassure, and we ask how spouse, parents, or friends react when he is down on himself. Is he lonely and insecure, and thus seeking reassurance—and does he usually get it? Perhaps the client indicates that others intimidate him or that we intimidate him, and we mention that attacking yourself prevents others from doing it to you. Has he found that others back off when he is down on himself? Our interpretations try to legitimize and show the sense of the self-criticism, and are usually accepted by the client when they are accurate. When an interpretation is rejected, if we have confidence in it we may look for more acceptable ways to phrase it; otherwise, we go on to an alternative interpretation. Clients give information by their responses, and we follow the clues. When an initial assessment appears weak or does not offer sufficient leverage, we go on to other possibilities. A working familiarity with the survey of possibilities encourages flexibility in therapeutic tactics.

When the client does not indicate on his own the important issues, we may present some reasons that people commonly have for such actions and see how he reacts to each of them. We present the possibilities and invite him to sort through them to see what looks plausible: ''I'm not sure what is going on with this, but let me suggest some common reasons that people frequently do have for being overly tough on themselves. See which of them look familiar and might apply to you.'' This is a no-risk move, for we are merely stating the possibilities and not committing ourselves to them. The client is being invited to look and appraise for himself, and does not feel that he is being pushed into anything he does not wish to accept. Most clients can identify one or more reasons which seem to pertain, and we can go on from there.

The assessment is absolutely crucial to choosing appropriate interventions. Would anyone want to treat one client who is tough on himself to pressure himself to improve in the same way as another who is tough on himself to gain sympathy from others, or in the same way as one who is tough on himself to stonewall accusations from others? It is not sufficient to merely note that the client is too critical of himself and to run a course of intervention from there. The interventions must be closely aligned to the significant reasons and objectives in the self-critical statements. The focus here on the ''in order to'' aspect of self-criticism meets the standard for pragmatic assessment: assessment to be clinically meaningful must have practical implications for the course of treatment. Any practice which does not distinguish between the varieties of this phenomenon but suggests the same treatment for any instance of self-criticism must be seen as grossly inadequate in comparison to the assessment and corresponding treatment tactics outlined here.

When we see the ''in order to'' aspect of the self-criticism, we can explain it by various situational factors and individual characteristics, and explain those by the ways they were acquired. But unless we see what the person is attempting to do, we are in no position to give further explanation of the behavior, for we would not really understand the behavior we are trying to explain. Explanations of why one pressures himself to improve are not of the same genre as explanations of why one seeks sympathy, although being tough on oneself may be the means used in both actions. Adequate descriptions of the behavior itself are first order explanations which anchor the phenomenon: from there, we can go on to give second and third order explanations.

One who is familiar with the varieties of self-criticism is in a better position to identify them when they occur, and to legitimize and clarify them to clients. One familiar with the corresponding treatment suggestions is better prepared to apply and adapt them to the problems at hand. The pragmatic survey organizes and familiarizes, and thus serves as training material for therapists.

RELATED ASPECTS

Unspoken Statements

Our analysis has focused on self-critical statements which are spoken aloud, but the same analysis and interventions are equally appropriate to other statements and opinions which are not spoken overtly but are made to oneself. There is a continuum from actual spoken statements, to thoughts (which are statements one makes to oneself), to feelings about oneself (which have the force of unspoken statements but which do not have actual words to them). The varieties of self-criticism which are made in order to affect others usually occur in actual spoken statements, although one can say them to oneself in preparation to familiarize oneself with them before saying them to others. The varieties of self-criticism which are made in order to influence oneself are usually made to oneself as observations, obsessions, thoughts, or feelings, but they may be stated aloud for emphasis. Thus, to get attention or allay attack, one would usually say something aloud, while to pressure oneself to improve or to restrain oneself from making mistakes, one would usually say it to oneself or merely feel or experience it.

Actual statements anchor the analysis, because as observable purposive actions they are the complete and most understandable instances of the phenomenon. But the analysis is easily expanded to also include thoughts and statements to oneself and also the feeling or experience of being no good. Self-criticism which is actually spoken is the easiest to identify clinically. Thoughts, feelings, experiences, and statements made to oneself are more readily overlooked, and we must watch for them. When a client seems to be stressing or punishing himself—even though he is not stating aloud that he is down on himself—we should inquire: "Do you ever find yourself feeling that you are wrong or stupid, even though you do not say anything about it?" Clients will usually acknowledge such feelings. We see these as unspoken self-criticism, look for the aims and objectives, and proceed from there.

Benefits

Self-criticism in its milder and more appropriate forms may be adaptive and beneficial. Many of the same issues observed in pathological self-criticism are seen in tamer versions in the ordinary garden-variety forms of the phenomenon. In the midst of the otherwise unfavorable press it receives, some acknowledgment of the constructive aspects of self-criticism should be noted.

Adaptation in complex and changing circumstances requires that one act as best he can, observe his actions and appraise their adequacy and appropriateness, and use such appraisals to alter or regulate further actions. Actions which fit should be appreciated and continued. When an action is poor, one should note the inadequacy and attempt to understand and to correct the personal limitations which led to the mistake.

An ideological rejection of any criticism of oneself is seen in apparently opposite manifestations. One person feels that he should never make a mistake, for he is conscientious and competent, and should always do well. Another feels that nothing he does is ever a mistake because he is spontaneous, expresses his real feelings, and so is doing as he should. Although poles apart, both philosophies indicate the same failing: in each, the person fails to accept that there is merit in regulating oneself.

An analogy to a self-regulating mechanism may be useful. Consider a thermostat-controlled heating system, in which the furnace acts to provide the output; the thermometer "observes" and "describes" the resulting temperature; and an executor device "appraises" by its set standard whether the output is too much or too little, and regulates the furnace accordingly. Imagine a furnace acting without observation, appraisal, and regulation of itself, and realize how readily it would go amiss. The analogy may be used with the client who expects himself to act without mistake and not to have to observe, appraise, and reassess his behaviors. Were one to attempt to set a furnace to function properly without observing and regulating itself, one would be continually dissatisfied with the results, or one might fail to set it at all. This is appropriate as well for the client who allows himself any action he feels is genuine and spontaneous: if one allowed the furnace to do anything it did spontaneously, it would cause more problems than others could remedy.

Each of the varieties of self-criticism is a way to gain something, and most can be constructive when used appropriately and in moderation. Being tough on oneself may actually increase motivation in the short run, and aid in stressful situations; renouncing a failing may help one maintain appropriately high standards; recognizing mistakes, but not being obsessive about them, may help one avoid them the next time; acknowledging wrongdoing helps settle conflicts when others are willing to compromise; recognizing potential catastrophies may help one prepare and adapt to them; appearing modest allays competitiveness in others, wards off attacks, and may help one get along more smoothly in social relationships; some of the support one might gain by acknowledging weaknesses may be appropriate and beneficial; some responsibilities are indeed overwhelming, and getting out of them may be adaptive; appearing to accept the limited views others have of you is sometimes easier on everybody than fighting them; and argument when others do not understand or accept is a way to affirm oneself.

The major problem with self-criticism is not that it does not work, but rather that it works too well in moderation, and one gets addicted to large and lethal doses of it. By showing the benefits of appropriate self-criticism, we legitimize and cast the client as one who makes sense. We go from there to clarify the problems of the same actions in harsher and overextended versions. Even in its harsher versions, self-criticism may have some benefit, but not enough to outweigh the considerable problems it causes. It is helpful to clients to see their own uses of self-criticism in comparison to more moderate and appropriate uses. Many feel that their self-criticism is essential to their survival, and it is more practical to steer them toward moderate and appropriate uses than to push them to give up self-criticism altogether.

COMPARISONS TO OTHER ORIENTATIONS

A Pragmatic Survey

The survey analysis presented here is intended to cover the range of common reasons for self-criticism. As far as I know, it is the first attempt to survey the range of reasons for criticizing oneself. Ordinary language categorization necessarily involves individual judgment, and another categorization might distinguish reasons somewhat differently. Also, there can be no guarantee that no reason has been overlooked and inadvertently omitted. The survey was constructed from the concept of behavior as purposive action, from review of actual cases, from analysis of logical possibilities, and with the assistance of other therapists. Thus, despite the cautions, it may be taken as a fairly thorough and complete survey of the major reasons for criticizing oneself.

This survey should be distinguished, on several grounds, from what would ordinarily be considered a general theory of self-criticism. Whereas a theory usually purports to formulate the fundamentals that generate the phenomenon, the survey attempts to describe the phenomenon itself. Whereas a theory often uses special concepts and terminology, the survey attempts to stay within ordinary language. Whereas a theory attempts to provide a general explanation for the entire phenomenon, the survey portrays instead a range of possibilities: the aim here is not to give an overall explanation, but to facilitate our abilities as therapists to make and act on the appropriate distinctions. Finally, whereas theories compete with each other, or claim to, the dozen accounts given here complement rather than compete: written from the same orientation, each provides an essential aspect of the whole picture.

Correspondences

The present survey of the varieties of self-criticism provides an excellent vantage point for viewing the already existing accounts of this phenomenon. Each of the various theoretical orientations seems to have one or more accounts of self-criticism, and for each such account, a correspondence may be constructed with the survey categories presented here. We can compare and contrast our analysis with the views of various familiar systems and use this to show how common language pragmatism provides an adequate framework for eclectic psychotherapy.

1. When a person criticizes himself to understand his limitations, but uses standards which are too high, the rational-emotive approach sees the conclusions as irrational and attempts to correct the problematic standards and beliefs.

2. When one criticizes oneself to pressure oneself to improve, the Gestalt approach involves Top Dog–Under Dog controversy, with Top Dog attempting to force and correct, and Under Dog resisting.

3. When one renounces failings to affirm his standards, Top Dog and Under Dog are again appropriate, with Top Dog enjoying the status of being superior.

4. When one criticizes oneself as amends for wrongdoing, analytic parlance considers it the dynamics of a strict superego.

5. When one criticizes oneself as a means of self-restraint, in analytic terminology this is a superego reaction against breakthrough id impulses.

6. When one criticizes oneself to maintain low expectations so as to avoid disappointment, humanists prescribe that one should take risks; personal construct theory focuses on the importance of anticipating possible problems; and fixed role therapy has the client try on new roles to break out of the old expectations.

7. When a person criticizes himself to be safe from attacks from others, rational-emotive therapy challenges the client's assumption that he needs approval from everyone, and behavioral approaches encourage assertiveness to combat the anxiety and improve relationships.

8. When one criticizes oneself to evoke sympathy and involvement, behaviorists hold that the attention of others reinforces and thus maintains the self-criticism.

9. When one criticizes oneself to claim inadequacy and avoid responsibility, existentialists are quite at home and offer much the same

explanation; transactional analysis calls it playing the game Wooden Leg.

10. When a person criticizes himself to camouflage hostility, here again transactional analysis might note the switch between the appearance and the resulting satisfaction, and call it playing a game.

11. When one criticizes oneself as an affirmation of loyalty and belonging, family systems approaches hold that the symptom takes on the family pain and thus maintains family stability.

12. Finally, when one criticizes oneself to argue, a communications orientation implicates resistance and suggests paradoxical solutions; reality therapy minimizes therapist intrusiveness so that the client may see and profit from the consequences of his own actions; client-centered counseling reflects back the feeling but does not challenge it.

Many of the familiar orientations have their own favorite slants on the aims and objectives of human action. Rational-emotive does not mention the motivations, leaving the impression that one who says critical things about himself does so merely because he believes they are so. Analytic and Gestalt emphasize the conflicts and inner jostle of acting in order to control oneself, whereas transactional analysis in contrast focuses on a variety of social influence objectives. Behaviorists are more comfortable with measurables, such as getting attention, than with other objectives which are observable but not readily measurable, such as avoiding responsibility or getting even.

Accounts from each of the theory-based orientations correspond to one or more of the common language possibilities, and so can be spliced together to cover the phenomenon of self-criticism. But no single theory deals adequately with *all* the possibilities contained in the present descriptive survey. Accounts from the various theoretical orientations each contribute, but do not stand up as sufficiently adequate and complete when compared to a pragmatic survey of the varieties of this phenomenon.

Attempts by eclectics to use aspects of various theories can be a catch-as-catch-can practice, for the lack of consistency among the theory-based terminologies introduces troublesome ambiguities and confusions. It is difficult to tell when theoretical accounts with special terminologies are competing with each other or when they are unknowingly complementing each other. While the analyses and interventions in the present survey may be similar to those of various existing orientations, the common language used here encourages an integration which would be difficult to attain by merely splicing together aspects of various theories. Common language pragmatism is seen here to be quite adequate to deal with the whole range of issues encountered in analyzing and treating the clinical problems of self-critical tendencies.

Content versus Pragmatics

Some aspects of various orientations are not easily included in the present survey because they wander astray and overlook key concepts and guidelines. The pragmatic or ''in order to'' aspect of statements is used to anchor the entire survey analysis and the corresponding treatment suggestions. One who does not attend to the pragmatics of statements might analyze a self-critical statement strictly from the content or information in the statement, and explain why the client thinks, feels, or really believes that he is no good. An orientation seeing only the content of ''I'm no good'' statements may postulate that the person has a poor self-concept or inferiority complex, or that he is insecure and that is why he is running himself down. Such accounts are not entirely wrong, for self-critical persons may indeed have poor self-concepts, inferiority complexes, and insecurities. But the accounts are impoverished indeed in comparison to a pragmatic survey analysis and leave one with too few tactics for strong interventions. An account that one is trying to pressure himself in order to improve or to get attention gives us clearer directions for interventions than does an explanation that one is criticizing himself because he has a poor self-concept or an inferiority complex.

The specifics of self-critical action can be used to understand and account for the more general poor views of oneself, for there is causality opposite to that which is so familiar in much of the literature. By being too tough on themselves, persons thereby convince themselves that they are inferior—they come to believe their own propaganda. Poor self-concepts and inferiority complexes may contribute to self-criticism, but excessive self-criticism contributes obviously, quite strongly, and in many ways to poor self-concepts, inferiority complexes, and generally unfavorable views of oneself. We go after the excessive self-criticism since that is an obvious and most readily altered contributing factor. Self-criticism is a key factor for therapeutic intervention, for it contributes considerably to further problems, and can be assessed and altered through a range of practical therapeutic interventions. As persons become easier on themselves, their views of themselves become less unfavorable—their self-concepts improve, their inferiority complexes lessen, and they become more confident in themselves.

12
Conclusions

The concepts and guidelines presented here provide the basis for a comprehensive approach to counseling and psychotherapy. The concepts are ordinary language concepts familiar enough to be understood by everyone, and clarified and tightened up to make them suitable for use as a technical and scientific language. They are seen to map the range of interests of the social sciences, and they provide a way of integrating and organizing concepts and terminologies from familiar theories.

The guidelines are objectives and principles which are important in session after session and with a wide variety of clients. Each is a prescription to attain particular objectives and includes suggested ways to reach those objectives. The guidelines are crafted as far as possible to cover the essential objectives of psychotherapy: while complete coverage cannot be guaranteed, every effort has been made to include the major practical objectives from a wide variety of therapeutic techniques. The guidelines cover the therapeutic relationship, accrediting existing strengths, assessment, clarifying the way things are and how to change things, and motivating clients. The guidelines provide a way of organizing and integrating techniques from familiar therapeutic orientations, for such techniques are alternate ways to attain the guideline objectives.

TRAINING

The concepts and guidelines of pragmatic psychotherapy have been presented here with enough elaboration and illustration to allow one to grasp some sense of their application and to use them on one's own. Many of the guidelines will be familiar already, while others may be new. Many will feel natural and obvious, while others may require special attention and supervised practice. The concepts and guidelines are basic and essential, and thus provide for trainees a good introduction to solid therapeutic practice. They also organize and elaborate on the basics, and thereby provide something for experienced practitioners as well. Puzzling through the rationale and applications should yield some benefit for trainees and experienced therapists as well.

Various aspects of the book make better sense in the light of other aspects, and it all seems easier and more obvious when you see it applied to cases. There is real benefit to rereading the material after some personal experiences in trying to apply it. We see an essential interplay between the reading material and related experiences including practice and case consultation. Practical experience gives you a chance to try out aspects of the system, and to see how they fit with what you are familiar with and can actually accomplish. Case consultation is important in ironing out individual questions, confusions, and misunderstandings. To become sufficiently familiar with how the approach works, you must combine the readings with practice and consultation. You can improve most rapidly through clinical practice accompanied by consultation with someone familiar with the pragmatic system.

Training in this orientation has several noteworthy features. Even beginning trainees do many things well already, and we have here a way to explain why some of these initial moves are the right things to do. Ordinary language concepts and common sense may provide a basis for some of your assessments, and initial interventions may be ways of attaining one or another of the guideline objectives. We can explain to a trainee which guideline objectives he or she might be seeking through any intervention and why that particular intervention might fit in the given situation. By identifying initial strengths, we affirm already existing competencies and can use these as a solid basis for further training. Trainees thus gain a better grasp of the principles they are already using and are in a better position to repeat them, to build upon them, and to teach them to others.

Experienced practitioners may have the sense that particular interventions are especially good, but be unable sometimes to identify or explain exactly why they are good. We can use the present system to better understand these interventions, for they can be identified as original or especially appropriate ways of attaining one or more of the guideline objectives. An advantage of the present system is that it shows the sense that we make already on a sometimes intuitive basis, and so accredits and affirms our existing competencies. Those who become familiar enough with the principles can readily go beyond their instructors in constructing beautifully appropriate on-the-spot interventions. The approach uses set concepts and prescriptive guidelines, but appeals to the ingenuity of the practitioner to utilize them in original and ever more adaptive ways.

Slow or stagnant sessions and failures to progress occur when we miss the important aspects of the case or fail to apply the appropriate guidelines and make them work. We gain a more adequate understanding as we come to see the information which is apparent, act to uncover the missing pieces, weigh all the information, and splice it together properly to arrive at practical conclusions. Failures to understand may indicate inadequacies in any of these facets. Supervision and consultation can clarify the case by making use of information already available to the trainee but focusing on the essentials and putting them together into a more coherent picture. The common language concepts and assessment guidelines clarify some of the aspects, but seeing it work with actual cases is essential to becoming really familiar with the assessment process.

Effective interventions are statements which are appropriate in a given situation to attain one or more of the guideline objectives. Failures to intervene effectively indicate an inadequate understanding of the case, or an inability to see which guideline objectives are important in the situation or how to accomplish those objectives. As consultants, we point out what one should try to accomplish and give specific suggestions on how to go about it. It is important for the consultant to give both the relevant guidelines and the specifics of what one might say to attain those objectives, so that the trainee understands the rationale and sees how it actually might work in practice. The task is to familiarize the trainee with which objectives are critical to particular types of problems, and with the wordings of specific statements that might accomplish those objectives in those types of situations. Understanding and application must work together. Consultants who suggest specific things to say on an apparently intuitive basis can use the guidelines to make the specifics more understandable, for they can explain these interventions as appropriate ways of accomplishing one or more of the guideline objectives. As trainees become more familiar with applications, they improve in their ability to see what needs to be accomplished, and to construct better and more appropriate intervention strategies.

Slow cases become more interesting, and frequently therapeutic progress can be seen to increase following case consultation. The concepts and guidelines are easily understood as they are applied to actual cases, so trainees see readily the point of the case analysis and why the particular suggestions might be effective. The credibility of the approach improves most readily when trainees see that the suggestions can make marked improvements in the course of a case and that the same principles can be applied with considerable benefit to other cases.

MAJOR FEATURES

Our orientation has several features which are especially noteworthy because they are tailor-made for an eclectic approach but in contrast to single theory orientations. Many of these have been explained already, but others have remained implicit so far.

1. Ordinary Language.   Ordinary language provides a language system immediately familiar to everyone, and so builds upon our already existing language competencies and provides a single system which all can use relatively easily regardless of prior theoretical training. Analysis of key ordinary language concepts provides the rigor and security associated with a formal system.

The concepts apply as easily and as well to ourselves as therapists as to those we talk to as clients. Our clients act for reasons and in order to accomplish things, and we as therapists act for reasons and in order to accomplish things. Our clients change as their reasons for doing things change; we too change as we see reasons for doing things another way. The adequacy of the common language system is shown both in principle and through its application to psychotherapy.

2. Common Sense.   Everyday understanding and common sense provide the beginnings, and we clarify and build upon these to further our understanding. Issues are clarified and controversies resolved through appeals to common sense, rather than through bold speculations which violate common sense. We take things as they appear unless we have reason to believe otherwise, thus placing the burden of proof not on our ordinary understandings but on those who seek to challenge them.

Some aspects of the orientation have the puzzling quality of being both too readily overlooked and at the same time quite obvious once they are mentioned. We call attention and show how to apply that which seems familiar enough but might be otherwise missed.

The focus on ordinary language and common sense does not point the approach toward the mundane. Rather, ordinary language and common sense promote a clarity and sensibleness which allow us to organize and manage quite well an extraordinarily wide range of issues and concerns.

3. Comprehensiveness. An attempt is made in each area studied to give an overview of the range of that area. The common language concepts of behavior are intended to include all the parameters of behavior, so that any aspect of behavior might be adequately described using these concepts. The scheme for behavioral explanations is intended to classify all psychological explanations, so that we need not go outside these concepts to look for psychological explanations. The major objectives of psychotherapy—or as many of them as possible—are packaged into the various guidelines. In the analysis and treatment of self-criticism, every attempt is made to include the entire range of reasons and objectives that might be involved.

The breadth of the coverage provides a single system in which we can organize a comprehensive eclectic practice. The common language concepts organize their theory-based counterparts, and the guideline objectives classify and make more understandable techniques from various orientations. We may need to make better observations or to construct more appropriate interventions, but there is no need to go outside of our common language pragmatic system.

4. Varieties. All concepts are distinctions, and the point of our concepts is to separate and distinguish the various forms that a phenomenon might take. Instead of an arbitrary definition of behavior, we explore the varieties of forms that behavior might take—complete actions, failures, accidents, and so on. Instead of a general explanation of behavior, we outline the variety of factors that ordinarily qualify as psychological explanations. Instead of a general theory of psychopathology, we mention various factors and give the criteria by which such things qualify as psychopathology. Because of their numbers, the guidelines too are not general prescriptions of what to do, but statements of the variety of objectives that are to be accomplished in psychotherapy. Time and again, the system surveys the varieties of forms that things might take and does not settle on simple generalizations which are to apply across cases.

This focus on varieties contrasts with the focus of those familiar theoretical paradigms which have been expected to provide broad generalizations that explain an entire phenomenon. The varieties approach was used at the turn of the century by William James in his classic *The Varieties of Religious Experience,* but it was ignored—as were James and his pragmatic philosophy—by the succeeding generations of theorists who sought broad speculative generalizations. A working familiarity with the varieties of forms that things may take improves our abilities to observe and describe the particulars of each case at hand.

5. Observation and Description of Specifics. Our objective is to understand the specifics of each case at hand, and for this we rely on on-site observation and straightforward description. Observation of specifics is seen to be quite adequate as a basis for therapeutic interventions. Broad generalizations and widely respected theories cannot substitute for on-site observation and analysis, for generalizations may be so in general but need not apply that closely to any particular case in front of us. The focus here on specifics contrasts with the emphasis on broad general theoretical explanations seen again and again in familiar theories.

6. Personal Judgment. Discrimination and judgment are involved in observation and intervention. Our formal concepts outline the possibilities, but force us to rely heavily on personal judgment to figure which of these possibilities is involved in any specific case. The guidelines outline interventions, but ask us to use our judgment to determine which guideline objectives are most pertinent in any specific situation and to construct techniques to accomplish those objectives. The principles and case illustrations are meant to familiarize the reader with some of the considerations for particular judgments. The concepts and guidelines are meant to clarify the basis for personal judgment, and to assist and augment good judgment. But we cannot replace personal judgment, nor can we go that far beyond it. We try here to understand it, to improve on it when possible, and to learn to live with it.

The methods of the familiar experimental sciences give the impression of trying to supersede personal judgment—to give us a virtuoso performance unflawed by human fallibilities. We seek here an empirical approach which includes the judgment of the observer as an integral aspect.

7. Personal Experience. In every way possible, the orientation makes use of and supports the personal experiences of the practitioner. In its focus on ordinary language and commonsense it respects, clarifies, and encourages the personal competencies gained from years of experiences in everyday situations. By organizing aspects of familiar approaches, it encourages each of us to carry over those training experiences we have had in other approaches and use them to enrich a comprehensive pragmatic practice.

The value of our writing in pragmatic psychotherapy is that *it assists us to see things for ourselves*. The aim of this book is not merely to state and reference information, but to interest, familiarize, and enable us to see and use things for ourselves. This book is offered as a learning experience, and its significance is in the difference it makes in our actual practice.

The concepts and guidelines point us in the right directions and improve our sensitivities to key issues, but are best seen as tools we must use to gain personal experience with how things actually do work in our own sessions. The point of these tools is to broaden and enrich the experiences we have as practicing therapists. As practitioners we are most certainly empirical investigators as well as activists, for we observe continually, try interventions, observe further, question our observations, puzzle through things, observe further, and so on. The common language system helps us organize and critique these observations. Through practice and consultation, we become familiar with patterns of how things fit together and how they work out, and we learn to identify and recognize these patterns.

Any aspect of the approach can be broadened and enriched by personal experience; thus, the approach is open-ended and well adapted to the improving competencies of its practitioners. Individual characteristics and current experiences contribute to the ways persons use and expand upon the system, so that there may evolve any number of ways of practicing suited to individual capacities and inclinations, and yet completely consistent with the principles of pragmatic psychotherapy. A familiarity with the approach provides the organization; after that, the way in which you build upon it depends on your own circumstances and personal inclinations.

The emphasis on personal experience is preferred by most practitioners, but contrasts to a more formal research tradition which seeks first and foremost a methodological and theoretical purity and is interested secondarily if at all in how it can be assimilated into our personal experiences.

8. Practicality. Every aspect of the pragmatic system is geared toward practical application so that the too familiar chasms between theory and application do not appear here. The focus on the pragmatic or "in order to" aspect of things is maintained throughout. We use it in understanding our clients, and also in understanding and appraising each aspect of our pragmatic approach to psychotherapy. Each aspect of the system is expected to contribute somewhere to therapeutic practice, and we can evaluate any aspect to see whether it does make some practical difference in how we organize and conduct our practice. The common language concepts give a practical organization to the observations we make in our practice, and the guidelines organize our intervention objectives and suggest ways of attaining them. Each of the major features is included because of its practical relevance. Ordinary language gives us a familiar way of organizing things; common sense is a practical way of weighing alternatives and drawing conclusions; the comprehensiveness of the system provides the obvious benefits of allowing us to stay within the same system; seeing the varieties provides for flexibility in responses; and so on. Practical application is the standard for including and evaluating each of the other aspects of the system.

We use practical application as a standard to guide and organize investigation, and so improve the practical quality of our information. Basic and applied aspects complement each other, for that which is critical in application is considered most truly basic, and formulations which have no practical application are seen not as basic at all but as simply not relevant. A standard for pragmatic research is that it address practical problems and suggest solutions of benefit to us as practitioners. The primary focus here on practicalities is preferred by most practitioners, but contrasts with a tendency in academics to seek information for its own sake and to leave issues of practical application to others.

COMMON LANGUAGE PRAGMATISM: AN ALTERNATIVE PARADIGM

At the level of broad overviews, the term "paradigm" refers to patterns, conventions, standards, ideals, rules, and ways of proceeding characteristic of a particular orientation or practice. Thomas Kuhn (1970) contends in *The Structure of Scientific Revolutions* that science proceeds not always through the gradual accrual of small increments of information, but sometimes through the overthrow of an entire paradigm or way of proceeding and its replacement with an alternative order. Such major changes occur when the existing ways are seen to be inadequate to organize the available information and when a better alternative is available.

Electicism has all the earmarks of a scientific revolution in the making. There is the obvious failure of any single theoretical system to organize and manage the entire range of behavioral phenomena and a growing sense among practitioners that no single theory can be adequate, so that we must sort and choose from among the various orientations. Eclecticism is readily identifiable as a separate paradigm with a range of distinctive features in contrast to the earlier single theory approaches. One of its most obvious features is that it frees us from the ideological battle lines drawn between theoretical encampments and allows us to select from among various orientations to suit the needs of particular problems.

Common language pragmatism is a specific way of understanding and organizing eclectic practice, and should be seen as a distinctive paradigm for investigation and practice. The eight items discussed earlier are major features of this alternate paradigm, and each serves to distinguish it from the more familiar single theory orientations.

Because common language pragmatism involves so many contrasts to the more familiar paradigms, it may take a bit of getting used to. Some eclectics are doing something quite similar to ordinary language pragmatism already and should feel quite at home here. But others who are more committed to the tenets of the theoretical traditions may sense that the standards and rules of those familiar paradigms are being ignored, and may feel vaguely uncomfortable or justifiably annoyed. Some uneasiness and jostle is to be expected and is all part of the process in any paradigm shift.

Since it is a formal system, some might question whether common language pragmatism is really true eclecticism or simply another individual system. The approach is surely systematic, and there are choices made in the ways we include and organize various aspects, and in what we omit. Nevertheless, the present paradigm contrasts to single theory orientations in several critical ways, and is indeed more complete and more versatile than any of the particular theoretical systems which it is used to integrate. It is for this reason that it is presented not as simply another theory but as a paradigm for organizing theoretical systems and for managing the range of interests and concerns in the behavioral sciences.

Other eclectic systems are of course possible, based perhaps on similar premises, although none is yet available which is judged here to be entirely adequate, and none has caught the imagination of many practitioners. When other such systems are available, there will be ample room to compare and contrast. But for now, even a single system which claims to be adequate to a comprehensive eclectic practice should be ample to maintain considerable interest and strong practical application, and perhaps some lively controversy among supporters and critics.

References

Angell, R. *Reasoning and logic*. New York: Appleton-Century-Crofts, 1964.

Atkinson, D.R. and Carskaddon, G. A prestigious introduction, psychological jargon, and perceived counselor credibility. *Journal of Counseling Psychology*, 1975, *22*, 180–186.

Brehm, S.S. *The application of social psychology to clinical practice*. Washington, D.C.: Hemisphere, 1976.

Corsini, R. and Contributors. *Current psychotherapies* (2nd ed.). Itasca, Ill.: F.E. Peacock, 1979.

Davis, K.E. (Ed.). *Advances in Descriptive Psychology* (Vol. 1). Greenwich, Conn.: JAI Press, 1981.

Dimond, R., Havens, R., and Jones, A. A conceptual framework for the practice of prescriptive eclecticism in psychotherapy. *American Psychologist*, 1978, *33*, 239–248.

Driscoll, R. and Edwards, L. The misconception of Christian suffering. *Pastoral Psychology*, 1983 (in press).

Farber, A. Castaneda's Don Juan as psychotherapist. In K.E. Davis (Ed.), *Advances in Descriptive Psychology* (Vol. 1). Greenwich, Conn: JAI Press, 1981.

Frank, J.D. *Persuasion and healing*. Baltimore: Johns Hopkins, 1961.

Frankl, V. *Man's search for meaning: An introduction to logotherapy*. New York: Washington Square Press, 1963.

Garfield, S. and Bergin, A. (Eds.). *Handbook of psychotherapy and behavior change* (2nd ed.). New York: John Wiley and Sons, 1978.

Garfield, S. and Kurtz, R. Clinical psychologists in the 1970s. *American Psychologist*, 1976, *31*, 1–9.

Ginott, H. *Between parent and child*. New York: Macmillan, 1965.

Goldfried, M. Toward the delineation of therapeutic change principles. *American Psychologist*, 1980, *35*, 991–999.

Gordon, T. *Parent effectiveness training*. New York: Peter H. Wyden, 1970.

Grier, W. and Cobbs, P. *Black rage*. New York: Bantam Books, 1968.

Haley, J. *Strategies of psychotherapy*. New York: Grune & Stratton, 1963.

Haley, J. Approaches to family therapy. In J. Haley (Ed.), *Changing families: A family therapy reader*. New York: Grune & Stratton, 1971.

Haley, J. *Problem solving therapy*. San Francisco: Jossey-Bass, 1976.

Hall, C. and Lindzey, G. *Theories of personality* (2nd ed.). New York: John Wiley & Sons, 1970.

Hass, R.G. and Linder, D.E. Counterargument availability and the effects of message structure on persuasion. *Journal of Personality and Social Psychology,* 1972, *23,* 219–233.

Heider, F. *The psychology of interpersonal relations.* New York: John Wiley and Sons, 1958.

Holmes, J. *Psychotherapy: A means-ends study* (LRI Report No. 5). Boulder, Colo.: Linguistic Research Institute, 1970.

Homme, L.E. Perspectives in psychology: XXIV. Control of coverants, the operants of the mind. *Psychological Record,* 1965, *15,* 501–511.

James, W. *The varieties of religious experience* (Forward by J. Barzun). New York: New American Library, 1958.

Jones, R.A. and Brehm, J.W. Persuasiveness of one- and two-sided communications as a function of awareness there are two sides. *Journal of Experimental Social Psychology,* 1970, *6,* 47–56.

Kagan, J., Kearsley, R., and Zelazo, P. *Infancy: Its place in human development.* Cambridge, Mass.: Harvard University Press, 1978.

Kelly, E.L. Clinical psychology—1960. Report of survey findings. *Newsletter: Division of Clinical Psychology of the American Psychological Association,* 1961, *14* (1), 1–11.

Koch, S. (Ed.). *Psychology: A study of a science* (Vols. 1–6). New York: McGraw-Hill, 1959, 1962, 1963.

Kuhn, T.S. *The structure of scientific revolutions* (2nd ed.). Chicago: University of Chicago Press, 1970.

Landfield, A. and Leitner, L. (Eds.). *Personal construct psychology.* New York: John Wiley & Sons, 1980.

McWilliams, S.A. Eclecticism: Comprehension or jumble? A review of J. Palmer's *A primer of eclectic psychotherapy. Contemporary Psychology,* 1981, *26,* 301.

Morris, C. *Signs, language, and behavior.* New York: George Braziller, 1955.

Mowrer, O.H. Loss and recovery of community: A guide to the theory and practice of integrity therapy. In G.M. Gazda (Ed.), *Theories and method of group psychotherapy and counseling.* Springfield, Ill.: Charles C. Thomas, 1968.

Oppenheimer, J.R. Analogy in science. *American Psychologist,* 1956, *11,* 127–136.

Ossorio, P.G. *Persons* (LRI Report No. 3). Boulder, Colo.: Linguistic Research Institute, 1966.

Ossorio, P.G. *Clinical topics* (LRI Report No. 11). Boulder, Colo.: Linguistic Research Institute, 1976.

Ossorio, P.G. *Meaning and symbolism* (LRI Report No. 15). Boulder, Colo.: Linguistic Research Institute, 1978 (originally published in 1969).

Ossorio, P.G. Notes on behavior description. In K.E. Davis (Ed.), *Advances in Descriptive Psychology* (Vol. 1). Greenwich, Conn.: JAI Press, 1981 (originally published in 1969).

Ossorio, P.G. A multicultural psychology. In K.E. Davis and R. Bergner (Eds.), *Advances in Descriptive Psychology* (Vol. 3). Greenwich, Conn.: JAI Press, 1983 (in press).

Pepinsky, H.B. and Patton, M.J. Informative display and the psychological experiment. In H.B. Pepinsky and M.J. Patton (Eds.), *The psychological experiment: a practical accomplishment.* New York: Pergamon Press, 1971.

Pitkin, H. *Wittgenstein and justice.* Berkeley: University of California Press, 1972.

Plotkin, W. Consciousness. In K.E. Davis (Ed.), *Advances in Descriptive Psychology* (Vol. 1). Greenwich, Conn.: JAI Press, 1981.

Ryle, G. *The concept of mind.* New York: Barnes and Noble, 1949.

Shontz, F. *Research methods in personality.* New York: Appleton-Century-Crofts, 1965.

Skinner, B.F. *The behavior of organisms.* New York: Appleton-Century-Crofts, 1938.

Sloane, R.B., Staples, F.R., Cristol, A.H., Yorkston, N.J., and Whipple, K. *Psychotherapy versus behavior therapy.* Cambridge, Mass.: Harvard University Press, 1975.

Smith, D. Trends in counseling and psychotherapy. *American Psychologist,* 1982, *37,* 802–809.

Strong, S.R. Counseling: An interpersonal influence process. *Journal of Counseling Psychology,* 1968, *15,* 215–224.

Strong, S.R. Social psychological approach to psychotherapy research. In S. Garfield and A. Bergin (Eds.), *Handbook of psychotherapy and behavior change* (2nd ed.). New York: John Wiley & Sons, 1978.

Strupp, H.H. Psychotherapy research and practice: An overview. In S. Garfield and A. Bergin (Eds.), *Handbook of psychotherapy and behavior change* (2nd ed.). New York: John Wiley and Sons, 1978.

Wachtel, P.L. *Psychoanalysis and behavior therapy: Toward an integration.* New York: Basic Books, 1977.

Wachtel, P.L. What should we say to our patients?: On the wording of therapists comments. *Psychotherapy: Theory, Research, and Practice,* 1980, *17,* 183–188.

Watts, A. *Psychotherapy east and west.* New York: New American Library, 1961.

Wessler, R.A. and Wessler, R.L. *The principles and practice of rational-emotive therapy.* San Francisco: Jossey-Bass, 1980.

Whitehead, A.N. *The aims of education and other essays.* New York: New American Library, 1929.

Wilson, J. *Thinking with concepts.* Cambridge: Cambridge University Press, 1963.

Wittgenstein, L. *Philosophical investigations* (trans. by G.E.M. Anscombe; 3rd ed.). New York: Macmillan, 1968.

Index